The Making of African America

OTHER BOOKS BY IRA BERLIN

Generations of Captivity: A History of African American Slaves

*Many Thousands Gone: The First Two Centuries of
Slavery in Mainland North America*

Slaves Without Masters: The Free Negro in the Antebellum South

EDITED

Power and Culture: Essays on the American Working Class

CO-EDITED

*Culture and Cultivation: Labor and the Shaping of
Slave Life in the Americas*

*Families and Freedom: A Documentary History of African-American
Kinship in the Civil War Era*

*Free at Last: A Documentary History of Slavery, Freedom,
and the Civil War*

Freedom: A Documentary History of Emancipation (4 volumes)

Freedom's Soldiers: The Black Military Experience and the Civil War

A Guide to the History of Slavery in Maryland

*Remembering Slavery: African Americans Talk About Their
Personal Experiences of Slavery and Emancipation*

Slavery and Freedom in the Age of the American Revolution

Slavery in New York

*The Slaves' Economy: Independent Production by
Slaves in the New World*

Slaves No More: Three Essays on Emancipation and the Civil War

THE MAKING OF
AFRICAN
AMERICA

The Four Great Migrations

IRA BERLIN

VIKING

VIKING

Published by the Penguin Group

Penguin Group (USA) Inc., 375 Hudson Street, New York, New York 10014, U.S.A. • Penguin Group (Canada), 90 Eglinton Avenue East, Suite 700, Toronto, Ontario, Canada M4P 2Y3 (a division of Pearson Penguin Canada Inc.) • Penguin Books Ltd, 80 Strand, London WC2R 0RL, England • Penguin Ireland, 25 St. Stephen's Green, Dublin 2, Ireland (a division of Penguin Books Ltd) • Penguin Books Australia Ltd, 250 Camberwell Road, Camberwell, Victoria 3124, Australia (a division of Pearson Australia Group Pty Ltd) • Penguin Books India Pvt Ltd, 11 Community Centre, Panchsheel Park, New Delhi – 110 017, India • Penguin Group (NZ), 67 Apollo Drive, Rosedale, North Shore 0632, New Zealand (a division of Pearson New Zealand Ltd) • Penguin Books (South Africa) (Pty) Ltd, 24 Sturdee Avenue, Rosebank, Johannesburg 2196, South Africa

Penguin Books Ltd, Registered Offices: 80 Strand, London WC2R 0RL, England

First published in 2010 by Viking Penguin, a member of Penguin Group (USA) Inc.

10 9 8 7 6 5 4 3 2 1

LIBRARY OF CONGRESS CATALOGING IN PUBLICATION DATA
Berlin, Ira, 1941–
   The making of African America : the four great migrations / Ira Berlin.
   p.   cm.
   Includes bibliographical references and index.
   ISBN 978-0-670-02137-6
   1. African Americans—History. 2. African Americans—Migrations—History. 3. Slave trade—United States—History. 4. Slave trade—Atlantic Ocean—History. 5. Migration, Internal—United States—History. 6. United States—Emigration and immigration—History. I. Title.
   E185.B473 2010
   973'.0496073—dc22   2009028366

Printed in the United States of America
Set in Scala • Designed by Carla Bolte

JOHN HOPE FRANKLIN

Scholar, Teacher, Friend

Contents

Prologue 1

Chapter One
Movement and Place in the African American Past 14

Chapter Two
The Transatlantic Passage 49

Chapter Three
The Passage to the Interior 99

Chapter Four
The Passage to the North 152

Chapter Five
Global Passages 201

Epilogue 230

Acknowledgments 241
Notes 245
Index 289

[The preacher] says one thing and the congregation says it back, back forth, back forth, until we're rocking together in a rhythm that won't stop. His voice is low and rough and his guitar high and sweet; they seem to sing to each other, conversing in some heavenly language . . .

—B. B. King and David Ritz, *Blues All Around Me*

The Making of African America

Prologue

Some years ago, amid a dispute over "who freed the slaves?" in the Civil War South, I was interviewed on Washington's public radio station about the meaning of the Emancipation Proclamation. I addressed the familiar themes of the origins of the great document: the changing nature of the Civil War, the Union army's growing dependence on black labor, the intensifying opposition to slavery in the North, and the interplay of military necessity and abolitionist idealism. I rehearsed the long-standing debate over the role of Abraham Lincoln, the Radicals in Congress, abolitionists in the North, the Union army in the field, and slaves on the plantations of the South in the destruction of slavery and in the authorship of legal freedom. In the process, I restated my own position that slaves played a critical role in securing their own freedom. The controversy over what was sometimes mistakenly called "self-emancipation" had generated great heat among historians, and it still had life.[1] As I left the broadcast booth, a small knot of black men and women—most of them technicians at the station—debated the authorship of emancipation and its meaning. What surprised me was that no one in the group was descended from families who had been freed by the Proclamation or any other Civil War measure. Almost all had been born outside of the United States—two in Haiti, one in Jamaica, one in Britain, and three others in Africa, two in Ghana, and one, I believe, in Somalia. Others may have been children of immigrants. While they were impressed—but not surprised—that slaves had played a part in breaking their own chains and were deeply interested in the events that had brought Lincoln to his decision during the summer of 1862, they insisted it had nothing to do with them. Simply put, it was not their history.

The conversation weighed upon me as I left the studio and it has preoccupied me not a little since. Much of the collective consciousness of black people in mainland North America and then the United States—the belief of individual men and women that their own fate was linked to that of the group—has long been articulated through a common history, indeed a particular history: centuries of enslavement, freedom in the course of Civil War, a great promise made amid the political turmoil of Reconstruction and a promise broken, followed by disfranchisement, segregation, and finally the long struggle for equality capped by a speech on the steps of the Lincoln Memorial, a celebration in the Oval Office, a heart-stopping moment on the balcony of a Memphis motel, and the euphoria of the elevation of a black man to the American presidency.

History—that particular history—was so important that long before the latest triumphant event, Carter G. Woodson, an extraordinarily prescient black educator, established a week that would annually be devoted to its contemplation and celebration. Black politicos have since expanded and transformed Woodson's "Negro History Week" into "Black History Month," and have helped elevate the commemoration of Martin Luther King, Jr.'s birthday into a national holiday. These commemorations have become an occasion to bewail old oppressions, rehearse the struggle, honor achievements, and reassert the need to do more.[2] In the process, celebrants have rightly laid claim to a unique identity.

Such commemorations, their memorialization of the past, are no different than those attached to the rituals of Eastern Orthodox Christmas, Tet, or Passover, or the celebration of the birthdays of Christopher Columbus, José Martí, or Casmir Pulaski, for social identity is ever rooted in history. But for African Americans, their history has always been especially important because they were long denied a past.[3] For most of their stay in mainland North America, people of African descent have seen their homeland portrayed as a primitive society in an arrested state of development, and themselves as a congenitally backward people. In 1835, the governor of South Carolina asserted what would become conventional wisdom for most white Americans during the century that followed. "The African negro is destined by Providence to occupy a condition of servile dependency. . . . It is marked on the face, stamped on the skin, and evinced by the intellectual inferiority and natural improvidence of the race. . . . They are in all respects—physical, moral, and political—inferior to millions of the human race . . . [and] are doomed to this hopeless condition by the very qualities which unfit them for a better life."[4]

In inventing Negro History Week, Woodson—like Phyllis Wheatley, Benjamin Banneker, and George Washington Williams before him and John Hope Franklin, Benjamin Quarles, and numerous other African American scholars after him—challenged this skewed perspective. Each insisted African American history had as much integrity as any, and few would gainsay their conclusion.

The significance of history in African American life gave the disclaimer "not my history" by people of African descent particular poignancy, especially in light of the transformation of black life in the last third of the twentieth century and the first years of the twenty-first.

In 1965, the United States Congress enacted two landmark pieces of legislation, the Voting Rights Act and the Immigration and Nationality Act. The passage of the Voting Rights Act proved to be a critical marker in the second emancipation. Given the opportunity, black Americans voted and stood for office in numbers not seen since the collapse of Reconstruction almost a hundred years earlier. They soon occupied positions that had been the exclusive preserve of white men for more than a half century. By the beginning of the twenty-first century, black men and women had taken seats in the United States Senate and House of Representatives, as well as various state houses and municipalities throughout the nation. In 2009, a black man assumed the presidency. African American life was transformed.

Within months of passing the Voting Rights Act, Congress enacted the Immigration and Nationality Act. The new law replaced the nativist policies put in place by the Johnson-Reed Act of 1924, which had favored the admission of northern Europeans by a peculiar accounting of origins of previous immigrants. The new law scrapped the rule of national origins and enshrined a first come, first served principle, giving preference to the recruitment of needed skills and the unification of divided families.

Although the Immigration and Nationality Act dramatically altered American immigration policy, few expected the reform to have much practical effect. Earlier, Senator Edward Kennedy, chair of the Senate's subcommittee on immigration and naturalization and one of the sponsors of the legislation, defended it by asserting, "Our cities will not be flooded with a million immigrants annually," and others nodded in unison.[5] Later, even as he embraced the new law, President Lyndon Johnson downplayed its significance. It "is not a revolutionary bill," Johnson intoned. "It does not affect the lives of millions. It will not reshape the structure of our daily lives. . . ."[6]

But the Immigration and Nationality Act had a profound impact on American life. At the time of its passage, the foreign-born proportion of the American population had fallen to historic lows, in large measure because of the old restrictions. Not since the 1830s, more than a century before, had the foreign-born composed such a tiny portion of the American people. Whatever the United States once was, in 1965 it no longer was a nation of immigrants. During the next four decades, the transformation set in motion by the Immigration and Nationality Act, its subsequent amendments, and the allied executive orders changed that. The number of immigrants legally entering the United States rose sharply, from some 3.3 million in the 1960s to 4.5 million in the 1970s. During the 1980s, a record 7.3 million people of foreign birth entered the United States. Those entering the United States in 1981 doubled that of 1965. In succeeding years, the admissions continued to swell, so that by the beginning of the twenty-first century, the United States accepted immigrants at rates higher than at any time since the 1850s. In the last third of the twentieth century, America's legally recognized foreign-born population tripled in size. The number of men and women who entered the United States but were not officially recognized added yet more to the total, as the United States was transformed again into an immigrant society.[7]

The Immigration and Nationality Act not only changed the number of new arrivals, but also their character. This too was something the authors of the new legislation had not expected, as they had promised, in Kennedy's words, that "the ethnic mix of this country will not be upset." But in the 1970s, the number of immigrants from Latin America and Asia began to increase. Before long, they were joined by Africans. Moreover, many new arrivals from the Americas also claimed African descent, as did black peoples from Europe and elsewhere. Although these immigrants represented a small portion of the total immigrant inflow, their arrival initiated a transformation of black America.[8]

Perhaps no one paid less attention to the passage of the Immigration and Nationality Act than the leaders of the Civil Rights movement, many of whom had witnessed President Johnson signing the new voting rights law. They had smiled broadly as the president distributed the ceremonial pens, and then celebrated a great victory for themselves and their people. Not one, however, joined Johnson several months later at the Statue of Liberty to witness the approval of the new immigration legislation. Preoccupied with the struggle for voting rights, which moved out of Congress and into the courthouses and then onto the streets, the black press hardly noted the occasion. Few African Americans imagined that the expansion of immigration might have as profound an impact on black society as the expansion of the suffrage.

They would soon learn differently.

Among the peoples entering the United States after 1965 were millions of men and women of African descent. Prior to that date, the number of black people of foreign birth residing in the United States was so tiny as to be nearly invisible. According to the 1960 census, the proportion was a fraction somewhere far to the right of the decimal point.[9] Demographers, noting the small number of African arrivals between the closing of the slave trade in 1808 and the immigration reform of 1965, declared black America a closed population, the product of a century and a half of natural increase.[10]

The same was not true at the beginning of the twenty-first century. While by then only 3 percent of the new arrivals derived from Africa itself, the changes set in motion by the Immigration and Nationality Act would transform black America as much as white America.[11]

The arrival of foreign-born black people began slowly in the 1960s, and it increased steadily in succeeding decades. During the 1990s, some 900,000 black immigrants entered the United States from the Caribbean and another 400,000 came from Africa, while Europe and Australasia supplied still others, profoundly altering the African American population. By the beginning of the twenty-first century, more Africans had arrived than during the centuries of the slave trade. Other peoples of African descent—particularly from the Caribbean—joined the influx. The number of black immigrants was increasing faster than the number of American-born blacks, and, between 1990 and 2000, black newcomers accounted for fully one-quarter of the growth of the African American population. Black America, like white America, was also becoming an immigrant society.[12]

In 2000, more than one in twenty black Americans was an immigrant; almost one in ten was an immigrant or the child of an immigrant. In many American cities, the proportion of black people of foreign birth was double that. In New York City, always an anomaly but often also a harbinger, immigrants comprised better than one-third of the black population and immigrants and their children well over half the city's black population.[13] Writing at the beginning of the twenty-first century and speaking only of the Afro-Caribbean migration, one scholar predicted that if the current rate of immigration persisted, first- and second-generation immigrants would soon outnumber native black New Yorkers.[14]

In many ways large and small, African American society has begun to reflect that transition. In New York, the Roman Catholic diocese has added masses in Ashanti and Fante, while black men and women from various Caribbean islands march in the West Indian Carnival and the Dominican Day Parade. In Chicago, Cameroonians celebrate their nation's independence day, while the DuSable Museum of African American History hosts the Nigerian Festival.[15] To many of these men and women, Juneteenth celebrations are at best an afterthought.

The new arrivals frequently echo the words of the men and women I met outside the radio broadcast booth. Some have struggled with established residents over the very name "African American," as many newcomers—declaring themselves, for instance, Jamaican Americans or Nigerian Americans—shun that title, while other immigrants have denied native black Americans' claim to the title "African American" since they had never been in Africa.[16] Black immigrants have joined groups such as the Organization for the Advancement of Nigerians, the Egbe Omo Yoruba (National Association of Yoruba Descendants in North America), the Association des Sénégalais aux USA, or the Fédération des Associations Régionales Haïtiennes à l'Étranger rather than the NAACP or the Urban League. Old-time residents often refuse to recognize the new arrivals as true African Americans. "I am African and I am an American citizen; am I not African American?" asked the dark-skinned, Ethiopian-born Abdulaziz Kamus at a community meeting in suburban Maryland in 2004. To his surprise and dismay, the overwhelmingly black audience responded, "No, no, no, not you."[17]

Behind this prickly matter of nomenclature stand more substantial issues involving experience and its meaning which emerge in matters as intimate as marriage partners or as public as electoral debates. "Barack Obama claims an African American heritage," asserted Alan Keyes, the black Republican candidate for an Illinois Senate seat in 2004, about his equally dark-skinned Democratic opponent. But, he continued, "we are not from the same heritage. My ancestors toiled in slavery in this country. My consciousness, who I am as a person, has been shaped by my struggle, deeply emotional and deeply painful, with the reality of that heritage."[18] Eventually African Americans embraced Obama, especially when it was discovered that he was too black for some white Americans. The differences that sparked the momentary hesitation created similar controversies. In a like, if less publicized, conflict in the District of Columbia, one longtime African American leader dismissed aggressive foreign-born challengers, noting that "They look like me, but they don't think like me."[19]

While important matters of access to resources—jobs, housing, and college scholarships—underlie such contests, the past also looms large in these struggles. Consensus-minded black leaders try to find common ground between those who are historically African American and others who are literally African American, but the differences that continue to emerge and manifest themselves point to how historical circumstances give new meaning to familiar circumstances. When Ethiopian American businessmen proposed to rename the historically African American Ninth Street in the District of Columbia "Ethiopian Boulevard," longtime black residents responded that "Ethiopian businesses have the money to afford the $45 per square foot that it costs to have business here, but that doesn't mean it's their history."[20]

This controversy over who owns African American history and, by extension, what is the meaning of the African American experience and who is (and was) black—although particularly intense at the beginning of the twenty-first century—is certainly not new. The entire African American experience can best be read as a series of great migrations or *passages*, during which immigrants—at first forced and then free—transformed an alien place into a home, becoming deeply rooted in a land that once was foreign, unwanted, and even despised. In the process, they created new understandings of the meaning of the African American experience and new definitions of blackness.

The reemergence of the old struggle over history within the black community suggests how understanding past migrations can lead to a greater appreciation of the changes that are remaking African American life at the beginning of the twenty-first century. More significantly, these migrations provide a glimpse of the future, for the new history has not one story line but many and has not one direction but several. Exploring this complex struggle does not create a single culture, produce an established political goal, or culminate in a pre-established outcome. Rather it raises questions about the character of the master narrative of African American history.

Viewing the history of African Americans as a series of migrations offers an alternative to the linear story that has informed black society at least since the American Revolution. Brilliantly captured in the title of John Hope Franklin's classic text *From Slavery to Freedom*, this master narrative has been articulated in everything from spirituals to sermons, from folktales to TV docudramas.[21] Like Booker T. Washington's *Up from Slavery*, Alex Haley's *Roots*, and Martin Luther King, Jr.'s "I Have a Dream," it retells the nightmare of enslavement, the exhilaration of emancipation, the betrayal of Reconstruction, the ordeal of disfranchisement and segregation, and the pervasive, omnipresent discrimination, along with the heroic and ultimately triumphant struggle against enslavement, Jim Crow, and second-class citizenship. Its heroes—real and fictive, from Frederick Douglass to Kunta Kinte, W. E. B. DuBois to John Henry, and Monroe Trotter to Oprah Winfrey—personified the master narrative.[22]

Such narratives articulate a sense of collectivity and what has been called, in another context, "imagined communities."[23] They affirm social unity by reminding men and women how a shared past binds them together, even when distance and radically different material circumstances and experiences create diverse interests. The insoluble bond of history infuses otherwise innocent events with a collective meaning, for—ultimately—"we are who we were."

For black people, the slavery-to-freedom narrative also integrates their history into an American story of seemingly inevitable progress. While recognizing the realities of black poverty and inequality, it nevertheless depicts the teleological trajectory of black life moving along what Martin Luther King, Jr., referred to as the "arc of justice" in which exploitation and coercion yields, reluctantly but inexorably, to fairness and freedom.[24] By its very name, the narrative of slavery to freedom suggests that, however slowly, liberty replaced slavery, and the coercive and exploitative system that followed it.

Yet, for a growing minority of African Americans—perhaps a prospective majority—the story of slavery to freedom has little direct relevance. Their forebears did not labor as slaves in the cotton fields of the South, follow the drinking gourd to freedom in the North, thrill at the words of the Emancipation Proclamation, or suffer the indignities of disfranchisement and the humiliation of segregation. Rather than being descended solely from those who were sold, some trace their ancestry to the sellers of slaves. Others interpret the slave experience differently than African Americans, perhaps because emancipation left them as an empowered majority rather an abused minority. Rather than condemn their forced removal from Africa, they celebrate their arrival in America, in the words of Barack Obama's father, as a "magical moment."[25]

Fleeing from poverty of the sort rarely experienced even by the poorest of contemporary black Americans and from tyranny unknown to even the most oppressed, many of the new arrivals have little sympathy for the narrative of the freedom struggle and some are quick to embrace a society that offers them far greater opportunity than any they had previously known in their homelands. Rather than dwell upon the grievances of the past, these new immigrants recognize their reality and then seize the opportunities of American life, going about the business of establishing their families, educating their children, and building their fortunes. While subjecting themselves to the grossest sort of exploitation and self-exploitation by working long hours and underconsuming to save for the future, they often ignore the connection between their own travail and that of generations of African Americans.

The long and ultimately successful struggle against Jim Crow might be admired and embraced by new arrivals, but it is not their story and it is perhaps only vicariously their victory. Richard Allen, Frederick Douglass, and Martin Luther King, Jr., might be heroic figures, but they are not their heroes or even their forebears. As in the past, new circumstances require a new history.

Such a history neither denies nor contradicts the old master narrative, whose value remains incalculable. Indeed, any new narrative must incorporate the familiar elements of the slavery-to-freedom story that gave it its lasting power: the long struggle against slavery; slavery's aftermath of poverty, disfranchisement, and segregation; and the ubiquity of the virulent racism that for centuries has color-coded the larger Atlantic world. In short, a new history reemphasizes the global reach of the slavery-to-freedom narrative in a globalized age.

Whether viewed from the reeking bottoms of seventeenth-century caravels or the antiseptic seats of twentieth-century jets, the great crossings cannot be understood apart from the ever-changing demands of global capitalism and its voracious appetite for labor which has reduced men and women—whether slave or free—into factors of production that can be extracted from one place and located elsewhere.[26] Between the sixteenth and the twenty-first centuries, peoples of African descent rarely moved as mere tourists or visitors, but in response to the constantly changing requirements of the plantation and then of the industrial order. The same demands for labor that forced Africans into the stifling holds of ships and propelled them across the Atlantic to mainland North America in the seventeenth and eighteenth centuries and then shipped these slaves across the North American continent in the nineteenth century uprooted still others once slavery ended. The movement of peoples in the twentieth and the beginning of the twenty-first century—whether it be open and legal immigration, the infamous surreptitious movement of undocumented peoples, or illegal trafficking of human beings—is part of the continued transformation of the global economy. Transnationalism, which tries to capture the contemporary movement of people, is just another name for massive movements of people set in motion by the joining of Africa, Europe, and the Americas centuries earlier.

Labor requirements established by the men who controlled production—be they masters or employers—determined, in considerable measure, who stayed and who left. Some migrations moved men while others demanded women; some required skilled workers and others strong backs. The brain—and muscle—drains created by these vast diasporas rest upon a yet larger process.[27]

Long after the shackles of slavery were broken, people of African descent entering the United States were quick to see the racial inequities of American life, if for no reason other than that those same painful restrictions were applied to them. Many saw the connections between the racial imperialism of American life with that of European colonizers in their homelands. They understood the common root of modern racism in slave societies that shaped relations between Africans, Europeans, and Native Americans for the last five centuries. For them, the connections between W. E. B. DuBois, a founder of the NAACP, and John Langalibalele Dube, a founder of the African National Congress, or between Martin Luther King, Jr., and Nelson Mandela were—and remain—manifest.

The old master narrative of slavery to freedom—which has framed the identity and informed the political consciousness of black people for so long—thus becomes a matter of some contention, sometimes gaining new adherents and sometimes becoming an ancient article of curiosity, much as it did for those who were earlier dragged across the Atlantic to an unknown land and for those who fled the rural South for the urban North. As the old narrative waxes and wanes, the themes derived from centuries of migration, both forced and free, grow in significance, and notions of the diaspora become central to the study of African American life. The multiple strands, nonlinear character, and unpredictable outcomes may better fit a history whose moral complexity has long militated against teleological certainty and Whiggish notions of progress.

A new narrative offers the opportunity not only to incorporate recent changes in African American life into the existing story but also to see the entirety of African American experience afresh, give old themes a new perspective, and in the process broaden the reach of the African American experience. Rethinking the history of black America not only places recent changes in the light of the long durée of the African American past, but also sharpens awareness of how African American history is, in the end, of one piece. As always, however, the story begins with the Middle Passage.

CHAPTER ONE

Movement and Place in the African American Past

More than any other single event, the Middle Passage—the transit from Africa to America—has come to epitomize the experience of people of African descent throughout the Atlantic world. The nightmarish weeks and sometimes months locked in the holds of stinking ships speak to the traumatic loss of freedom, the degradation of enslavement, and the long years of bondage that followed. But the Middle Passage also represents the will of black people to survive, the determination not to be dehumanized by dehumanizing circumstances, and the confidence that freedom would eventually be theirs and that they—or at least their posterity—would take their rightful place as a people among peoples.[1] In its largest meaning, the Middle Passage represents the burdens of the past and the hopes for the future.

The designation "Middle Passage," strictly speaking, refers to the transatlantic journey from Africa to the Americas that forcibly propelled some eleven million Africans across the Atlantic between the sixteenth and nineteenth centuries.[2] But for people of African descent in North America—what became the United States—it was only the first of many massive relocations. *The Making of African America* is a history of the three great migrations that made and remade African and African American life in the United States, as well as a glimpse of a fourth, which is presently transforming African American—and American—society. Over time, the great migrations swelled like some giant tsunami increasing in mass and velocity, engulfing larger and larger numbers of men and women and sweeping them, their loved ones, and their possessions into a vortex for which none could fully prepare.

The first of the great migrations, the forcible deportation from Africa to mainland North America during the seventeenth and eighteenth centuries, enslaved roughly 400,000 free men and women and transformed the many peoples of Africa—Angolans, Igbos, Kongos, Minas, Mandes, and others—into Africans and, in time, African Americans.

The second forced transfer—more than twice the size of the first—transported some one million men and women from the Atlantic seaboard to the Southern interior during the first half of the nineteenth century to create a new slave regime in the Deep South. It transformed tobacco and rice cultivators into growers of cotton and sugar, setting African American life on a new course.

That course changed in the middle decades of the twentieth century, when some six million black people—about thirty times the number of the original African transit—fled the South for the cities of the North, making urban wageworkers out of sharecroppers and once again reconstructing black life in the United States.

Finally, at the end of the twentieth and the beginning of the twenty-first centuries, people of African descent entered the United States from all over the world—Africa, the greater Caribbean, South America, and Europe—again changing the composition, character, and cultures of the black population of the United States. The pace of these massive movements increased with their size, as ever-greater numbers arrived during a shorter period of time.[3]

Each of these massive migrations incorporated, in varying proportions, unspeakable brutality, dispossession, and death. They also provided the occasion for extraordinary acts of kindness and generosity, generated astounding creativity, and gave birth to new life. While it is impossible to calculate fully losses and gains, happily the latter increased and former decreased over time. But none of these passages was entirely free of either tragedy or triumph, either moral degrada-tion or moral elevation. They changed the migrant's world and every-thing that surrounded it. Status was transformed, cultures remade, and politics reshaped. The great migrations dehumanized, but they were all too human. Although the movement from the South to the North and the late twentieth-century diaspora never equaled the vio-lent degradation that attended the transatlantic and transcontinental slave trades, they too pushed men and women to their limits.

Whether the transit was from Africa to America, Virginia to Ala-bama, Biloxi to Chicago, or Lagos to the Bronx, the upheavals that accompanied the physical uprooting would touch the lives of genera-tion after generation of black people. For many, perhaps the vast majority, it was the single most important event in their lives—a moment that would mark them and their descendents forever.

The forced march from the seaboard to Arkansas during the mid-dle years of the nineteenth century deeply affected Helen Odom's grandmother, much as the seventeenth- or eighteenth-century Atlan-tic transit had earlier burdened Odom's forebears. Years later, in the fourth decade of the twentieth century, grandmother Odom's pas-sage still gripped her granddaughter. "I heard this told over and over so many, many times before grandmother died," Helen Odom told an interviewer for the Works Project Administration in the 1930s. "Seemed it was the greatest event of her life," Odom reiterated. "She told other smaller things I can't remember," but grandmother Odom never forgot her long march to Arkansas. Neither did her grand-daughter.[4]

Others also remembered or learned through their memories, for the immigrant experience resonated across generational lines. Jacob Lawrence, whose great work visualized the epic journey of black peo-ple from the agricultural South to the industrial North, was raised in a household that knew nothing but movement. Lawrence was born in the North and did not travel south until he honeymooned with his

Southern-born bride. But he, like many children of immigrants, none-theless insisted that he "was part of the migration, as was my family: my mother, my sister, and my brother." He explained, "I grew up hearing tales about people 'coming up,' another family arriving." At age thirteen, living in Harlem with his Virginia-born mother and his South Carolina-born father, he himself had already experienced a move from Atlantic City, New Jersey, to Easton, Pennsylvania, and then to Philadelphia. Rapid-fire sequential migrations were so central to Lawrence's life that when asked to explain the origins of his picto-rial characterization of the northward migration, he reflectively replied: "This was such a part of my life."[5]

From Frederick Douglass's *Narrative* to Paul Dunbar's *Sport of the Gods*, from Richard Wright's *Native Son* to Ralph Ellison's *Invisible Man* and Toni Morrison's *Jazz*, migrants have been as much a part of African American literature as they have been part of African American life.[6] Much the same can be said for African American music, from the spirituals of the Jubilee Singers to the blues of Bes-sie Smith and Riley "B. B." King, not to mention other artistic accom-plishments such as Langston Hughes's poems, Gordon Parks's photographs, August Wilson's plays, and of course Lawrence's Migra-tion Series paintings. These extraordinary works and the symbols connected with the migratory theme—the slave ship, the auction block, the railroad pointed north—announce movement as a central theme of the African American experience. Langston Hughes was doubtless only one of many young black men and women in St. Louis who would periodically "walk down to the Santa Fe station and stare at the railroad tracks," just as Otis Redding was only one of many, who—while "sittin' on the dock of the bay"—calculated the benefit of a trip from Georgia to Frisco.[7]

The significance of movement elevated the importance of place in African American life. Between these massive movements of men and women stand periods of physical—although rarely social—stasis, during which black people developed deep attachments to place, be it the eerie beauty of the Sea Islands, the rich alluvial soils of the Delta, or the maze of streets and alleys of South Side Chicago—that "baddest part of town." In such places, men and women worked together, married and raised their families, worshipped, and socialized in ways that created trust and built solidarity, so that their attachments were ultimately about people. Such places were also celebrated in literature, song, and art. While Langston Hughes spoke of the "One-Way Ticket" from the South, Robert Johnson celebrated "Sweet Home Chicago."[8] Such attachments to place riveted black people to familiar ground; many could not conceive of life apart from their home.[9]

Because this contrapuntal narrative—movement and place; fluidity and fixity; or, in Paul Gilroy's phrase, "routes and roots"—ripped across some four centuries of black life in mainland North America, the alternating and often overlapping impact of massive movement and deep rootedness touched all aspects of the experience of black people, from language and theology to cuisine and music.[10] Over the course of four hundred years, through slavery and freedom, the contrapuntal narrative—perhaps more than any other—informed the development of a distinctive African American way of thinking and acting, as black society unraveled and then was reknit. It produced, on the one hand, a malleable, flexible cultural style that became a touchstone of African American life, recognizable in such different spheres as art and politics and in such different times as the post–Civil War jubilee and the interwar cultural renaissance. It created, on the other hand, a passionate attachment to place, reflected in the earthy idioms of the rural South and the smashmouth street jive of the modern "hood." Its drama was played out in the grand oratory of James Forten, Frederick Douglass, Booker T. Washington, and Martin Luther King, Jr., as well as the anonymous verbal duels of the hollers, toasts, dozens, and other forms of signifying. Taken together, movement and place informed the lives of peoples as different as enslaved tobacco hands and urban free people of color in the nineteenth century, the fastidious black bourgeoisie and the free-spirited zoot-suiters in the twentieth, and the hip-hop artists and buttoned-down buppies in the twenty-first.

Cultural malleability was and is reflected in all aspects of life. Commenting on people he had forced into the hold of his slave ship, one eighteenth-century slave captain noted the "facility with which they form new connexions," often reinforced—in the words of yet another slaver—by having "partaken of the same food, and to have slept on the same plank during the voyage."[11] The same process of transforming shipmates into kin would be repeated a century later in the coffles transporting slaves from Virginia to Mississippi, yet another century later in the boxcars carrying African Americans from Mississippi to Chicago, and most recently in airplanes carrying black people from Accra to New York. No aspect of black life in the United States has been untouched by the great migrations—by the contrapuntal interplay of movement and place.

Place—like movement—gained special meaning because of its unique relationship to the African American experience. For much of American history, place was not merely a geographic locale, but a social imperative—as in "stay in your place"—that black men and women violated at great risk. From the time black people were driven up the gangplank of that first slave ship, white authorities defined the "place" of black people as one of subordination, and they diligently patrolled the color line in the slave quarter, the back of the bus, the segregated schoolhouse, the urban housing project. Manifested at times in fugitive slave laws, racial covenants and redlines, or urban renewal policy that required "Negro removal," the struggle for place was an ongoing part of the African American experience. Place, in short, was more than a locale. It was an attitude, a condition, a policy that white people required to be reenacted again and again with a tip of the hat, a downward glance, a silent acceptance of subordination.[12] Yet these same places of subordination became sites of subversion and, ultimately, sources of liberation. In a similar fashion, movement also secured a larger meaning because it suggested the possibility of escape from place, be it a visit to a "broad wife," respite in a maroon colony, or the train or highway northward toward home.

Place gained particular significance because it had to be reconstituted again and again from the remembered fragments of a premigration past and the new circumstances of a postmigration world. The difficulties of preserving the sounds, tastes, and smells of the past bumped against the reality of new languages, food stocks, and landscapes. At times, men and women labored to preserve their cultural baggage, maintaining languages, cuisines, and rights of passage: the ways their parents brought children to the world, celebrated their coming of age, and buried their dead. At other times, these same men and women worked equally assiduously to lose their past— overbearing elders, rituals that confined, and attitudes that limited cherished aspirations. But whether remembered or forgotten, welcomed or denied, the old and the new came together in a form that gave place a special meaning.

As this process suggests, the very definition of movement and place were contested. Movement—forced and free—sometimes meant material loss, social dislocation, and spiritual fragmentation, yet sometimes signaled material gain, social improvement, and spiritual renewal. In slavery and in freedom, black people twisted the meaning of movement and place, transforming places of repression into places of liberation and places of confinement into routes of escape. What was generally true of these tropes was even truer for the great migrations or passages. The powerful combination of movement and place—the particular migrations and homelands they created— informed the making and remaking of African American life. The slave ship and Africa, the slave coffle and the black-belt plantation, and the northbound train and the ghetto were all critical to the formation of the African American experience. But it was the unique combination of fluidity and fixity that all these represented that came to shape African American life.

Movement

While all of the massive migrations were the product of specific circumstances and produced their own dynamic—and hence stand as unique events—their cumulative impact was derived from the power of repetition and the multiple memories they stockpiled. For more than four centuries, people of African descent in the United States have been on the move, reenacting the timeless drama of migration: the abandonment of the familiar, the trauma of transit, the confrontation with the new, the embrace—however reluctantly, tenuously, and, perhaps, unconsciously—of place, the generational struggles that followed, and finally the remembrance of the past, reflecting on what once was and what then became.

Ousted from African homelands and then driven across the North American continent like a great river of humanity, the four great migrations can be divided into many streams, each with its own eddies, whirlpools, ponds, and rills. Whether forced or free, these immense movements of men, women, and children repeatedly fragmented the extant society, smashed domestic relations, broke lifelong friendships, and reduced the familiar to the foreign. Under the best of conditions, these passages by their very nature generated fear and insecurity, as migrants struggled to learn the new protocols through the lens of the old. And the conditions under which black people moved, in slavery or freedom, were rarely the best. Often it was not simply that oppression and exploitation replaced freedom and magnanimity, but that new circumstances replaced the familiar old forms of exploitation and oppression with new ones. For some, no matter how oppressive, the familiar was preferable to the foreign. For others, no matter how liberating, the loss of old ways left unhealable wounds.

Yet, even at its most oppressive, the new society offered new possibilities, for migrations were only partially about geographic transfers and more about the refashioning of consciousness. Whereas some skills were reduced to obsolescence, others were elevated in value. New solidarities emerged from shared constraints and with them a variety of new cultural forms. The insecurities and fears that accompanied the great migrations generated fresh assertions of human dignity and renewed affirmations of the human spirit.

And even at its most liberating, the new society fostered nostalgia for the old. New opportunities and new freedoms could never replace what had been left behind. "There were no chinaberry trees, no pecan trees," recalled Clifton Taulbert in his memoir of his northward transit from rural Mississippi. "The sound of Mama's and Ma Ponk's voices could not find their way through the maze of buildings that separated us. Never again would I pick dewberries or hear the familiar laughter from the field truck."[13] The new landscape was never quite as striking as the old. For Taulbert, as for other migrants, a longing for an idealized past flowered in an imperfect present. Even when the past was not idealized, migrants felt a sense of loss associated with change. They desired, above all else, to connect the present to the past. Their histories can be written at the point of interconnectedness or the connections that were imagined.

But the great migrations created vast chasms in the experience of black people. Addressing these violent ruptures—to the extent they could be addressed—required enormous energy and extraordinary creativity, for these massive migrations eroded established customs that professed ancient pedigrees and unseated long-standing conventions. They dissolved regionalisms and localisms while creating, at the same time, new cosmopolitanisms and then new provincialisms. These new cultures contained possibilities as well as constraints.

Explosions of cultural creativity followed each of the great passages.

Again and again, the protocols and ideas of race were transformed. In the seventeenth and eighteenth centuries, black people learned the meaning of enslavement on the periphery of the North American continent. In the nineteenth century, blackness was remade on the rich loam of black-belt Alabama, taking on meanings unknown on the red clays of Virginia and the swamps of South Carolina. In mid-twentieth-century America, blackness secured yet different meanings in the stockyards of Chicago than it had in the cotton fields of Mississippi. In the late twentieth century, as people of African descent from all over the world converged on the United States, race was interpreted yet anew. At each turn, migrants relearned the constraints and possibilities race allowed, as blackness took on new meaning.

The multiple passages entailed joining worlds that were lost to worlds whose full dimensions could barely be imagined, even by the most prescient. Of necessity, the unfamiliar required innovation. The novel circumstances in which black people again and again found themselves caused them to place a premium on adaptation. These strategies were spun out in endless variety, for the contingencies created by migration challenged old verities and required new truths. Few truths survived long in a landscape of rapid change, as the repeated reinvention of self and society created patterns of thought and action that prized the originality of a John Coltrane riff, a Toni Morrison novel, a Richard Pryor skit, or an LL Cool J rap.

New forms and new structures set the boundaries for new polarities that quickly emerged in the wake of these massive movements: Africans and creoles, slave and free, newcomers and old settlers, homeboys and street dudes. These new forms delineated the societies that emerged in the wake of immense transfers of peoples, but they hardly defined the contours of the new order, whose complicated cultural matrices depended on specific circumstances: who went where and why, the baggage migrants carried, and the nature of their new habitat. The cultures of black peoples in the transit from Africa, across the American continent, from south to north, and then from all parts of the globe to the United States were made and remade not by maintaining the old in some reified form but by creating something new as migrants became natives.

Although the great migrations marked extraordinary discontinuities in the African and African American experience, the frequency with which these massive, periodic transfers occurred caused them to be incorporated seamlessly into everyday life and, in time, to become the backbone of African American history. For some, such movements became routine, if hardly normal or welcome. "The traders was all around," remembered the former slave Lewis Hayden, "the slave pens at hand, and we did not know what time any of us might be in it."[14] The endemic nature of migration—whether the feared arrival of a slave trader, eviction from a tenant shack, or sale to a convict lessee—required men and women to prepare themselves and their loved ones for what could only be seen as inevitable. For much of their history, black people lived not so much in flux—a circumstance endemic to the human condition—but in anticipation of catastrophic change. Husbands and wives, parents and children, kinfolk and neighbors understood that their ties would at some point be severed and that they would be required to reconstruct their lives anew often in radically different circumstances. Such expectations—and the accompanying anxieties—informed black life, for the migrations' reverberations echoed throughout African American communities. They gave rise to rituals that both anticipated and cushioned change, as few were so foolish as to await the moment of departure to consider what the new realities might bring.

Place

Between the great migrations stood periods of deep rootedness.[15] Movement might be omnipresent in the African American experience between the sixteenth and twenty-first centuries, but so too has been a sense of place. Indeed, one of the great ironies of migratory history is that diasporas rooted people in place—sometimes places where people came from and sometimes places where they went.[16] The church, Masonic hall, beauty parlor, barbershop, storefront, and even the street corner and stoop were just as significant to the African American experience as the slave coffle and the Chicken Bone Special, for they were points of sociability where bonds of trust and collaboration were established and maintained. More than an attachment to landscape, the concept of *place* spoke to relationships, often deeply personal, and the institutions that emerged from those relationships.

The linkages created by movement had to be disentangled, decoupled, and fixed socially and culturally as well as geographically.[17] The value of place in African American life seemed to increase with the constancy of movement and its often dire consequences. In time, Africa, the plantation South, and the inner city each became—by turns—a kind of Jerusalem. Although slaves and their mobile descendants were historically characterized as the ultimate outsiders—dismissed as socially dead denizens by some—they quickly made the land their own, mastered the terrain, and created dense networks of kinship and friendships that stretched across the land.[18]

In a word, they were rooted. Frederick Douglass, speaking from his own experience as both slave and free man, contrasted the difference between the expectations of enslaved and free peoples. Free people, declared Douglass, developed no "extravagant attachment to any one place," while the slave "had no choice, no goal but was pegged down to one single spot, and must take root there or die." From Douglass's perspective, the firm connections necessitated by chattel bondage created a profound respect and even affection for place and the men and women connected to those places, even when another place—perhaps any other place—would have been preferred. "Perhaps the most marked trait in the negro character," declared a *New York Times* reporter amid the chaos of the Civil War, "is his love of home and of the localities to which he is accustomed. They all pine for their homes."[19]

Douglass's image of the slave "pegged down" and this imputation of the love of locality as the "most marked trait in the negro character" evoke the figure of a people without motion, of being literally frozen in place. *Rootedness*—at least as employed here—does not refer to immobilization. Much as slaveholders, planter-merchants, and others who followed in their wake wanted to extend their sovereignty over the slave, sharecropper, tenant farmer, or ghetto dweller, they utterly failed to do so, if only because mobility was precisely what made these men and women so valuable. The image of the slave or cropper locked in place belies reality. The plantation regime as it developed in mainland North America and the industrial order that followed it required even the most constrained workers to move, as messengers, wagoners, and sailors, as well as husbands visiting wives, lovers courting sweethearts, and friends calling upon neighbors.

The notion of *rootedness* instead speaks to attachments—personal and material—within a defined geographic frame. Douglass was never "pegged down" on the Lloyds' Great House Farm. When he— like others—spoke of his local connections, he was referring to the people—family and friends—as much as the landscape of a special piece of Maryland's eastern shore. That was Douglass's place, where generations of his family had resided, in which he seized his manhood in the epic battle with the slave breaker Covey, and to which he returned as a free man and international celebrity.

After the war, former slaves' attachment to place manifested itself in a desire for land, the legendary forty acres. The quest for land had many meanings, but few former slaves coveted mere real estate. While they appreciated the independence that land ownership might bring, land ownership was as much a matter of social identity—and the multiple personal relations that entails—as of political economy, for the land they wanted also spoke to deep emotional investments. Often it was the land they had long resided and worked. Sometimes, as a group of former slaves declared, it was "land they had laid their father's bones upon." As one Union officer observed in 1862, "Never was there a people . . . more attached to familiar places than they."[20]

The former slaves' "love of locality" or what yet another federal agent called their "local attachments" resonated in the twentieth century. Reflecting on her youth in Knoxville, Tennessee, poet Nikki Giovanni insisted that it was "a place where no matter what, I belong." Charlayne Hunter-Gault, who as a young woman integrated the University of Georgia, wrote fondly of her Southern home in a memoir she appropriately named *In My Place*. Amid her biographical account of the ugly confrontations with the segregationist educators and epithet-wielding fellow students, Hunter-Gault lovingly recalled the "evocative sights, sounds, and smells of my small-town childhood, the almost overpowering sweet smell of honeysuckle and banana shrub seducing buzzing bumblebees and yellow jackets; the screeching cries of crickets emanating from every shrub and bush; clouds of black starlings producing shadows wherever they flew over the dusty red-clay haze. This was the part of the South that I loved, that made me happy to be a Southerner, that left me unaffected by the seamier side. . . ." "I do believe," echoed Maya Angelou, putting a point on Hunter-Gault's confession, "once a Southerner, always a Southerner."[21]

But if some loved the Southern countryside, others developed equally powerful connections to the gritty cities of the North. Jacob Lawrence, whose work captured the very essence of the twentieth-century abandonment of the South, recalled, "I lived in Harlem. I grew up in Harlem. My life was in the Harlem community."[22]

The allegiances dueled, as yet other refugees from the former slave states held firm to the belief that the South was their place. It was a sensibility articulated by thousands of African Americans who fled north and then, in the wake of the Civil Rights movement, returned to the place of their nativity. "Black people *are* Southerners," emphasized journalist Fred Powledge. "They are of and by and from and for the South . . . and have repeatedly demonstrated . . . their love for and faith in the region."[23] Some suggested that the connection of black people to the South was even an essential element in their nature, going so far as to deny the possibility of transplantation. "The Negro has never been a wanderer," asserted an officer of the Colored Organization of New Jersey on the eve of the exodus from the South. "Fixed ties have ever held for him attractions that have outshone opportunities that lie elsewhere."[24]

In the 1970s, when the third great migration that carried some six million black people from the South to the North had run its course and a counterflow to the South from the North began, economists and sociologists affirmed that migrants and their children and grandchildren remained "strongly tied to historic homeplaces." Many of these ties were those of memories that represented "the intense value put on place and landownership, a value," as noted in a close study of one particular returned migrant, "widely-shared among her generation." Even migrants who had been born in the North felt the pull. They were not returning to their childhood roots, but to roots nurtured through the lives of others augmented by extended family visits, reunions, and family obligations. Still others tied "their homeplace" to their marital connections or simply to the force of belief.[25]

Of course the South was not a single place any more than black Southerners were a single people. The South that Maya Angelou remembered differed from that of Fred Powledge, and Powledge from that of Nikki Giovanni. Their Souths were products of particular geographies and chronologies. What Angelou and others have called "the South"—as in "once a Southerner, always a Southerner"—was reified, frozen in time and in imagination as somehow "the" authentic South. The contending, opposing cultures that continually made and remade Southern society were reduced to a catchall.[26] Much the same would be done for Africa.

While some understood connections to place in essentialist terms, for others *place* had much more prosaic meanings, for it drew upon routines repeated so often that they proceeded without explanation, responsibilities taken without request, and favors exchanged without question. But as a wellspring of solidarity, place also defined the grounds of suspicion; while it embraced some, it excluded others. In drawing the boundaries of community, place defined kinship in the largest sense, creating—for example—a reverence for ancestors never known, whose remains stained ground that had never been seen and whose specters remained a presence long after breath had left their bodies. Over the centuries, African Americans have held reunions that drew thousands, and the constructed genealogies reached back across the Atlantic.[27] Upon exiting his native Mississippi, Richard Wright voiced the sentiment of many other migrants, declaring he could "never really leave the South, for my feelings had already been formed by the South, for there had been slowly instilled into my personality and consciousness, black though I was, the culture of the South."[28]

Place had such a powerful pull that its magnetic force drew in those who had never actually experienced it. Piri Thomas, man of dark-skin and Puerto Rican and Cuban descent growing up in Spanish Harlem felt compelled to visit the South as a way to explore and understand the meaning of his own blackness. A Southern-born friend encouraged him to do so, saying, "It's damn hard leaving the South and harder still goin' back to it. But now that it's come down to it, I'd like to see what's shakin' home." What drew Piri Thomas to the South likewise annually sends perhaps thousands of African Americans back to Africa, a journey that sometimes confirms a connection to Africa, but at other times leads to profound disillusionment.[29]

Of course no one really ever lived *only* in Africa or *only* in the South, just as they never lived *only* in the North or in Chicago. Rather black Southerners were more the product of neighborhoods, well-defined geographic spaces that were bound together by family ties, work patterns, and political alliances, as well as by the peculiarities of the natural and built environments. In such places, men and women knew one another and knew one another's kin and near kin, their religious affiliations, their political ties, and even their dogs. Intimacy made for belonging.[30]

Yet the migrants' embrace of place was also uneasy, tentative, and often probationary, for there was that other place—sometimes half remembered, sometimes totally unknown, and sometimes constructed from the whole cloth—that also commanded allegiance. That distant place was the land of fathers and mothers, grandparents, and ancestry from time immemorial; it was a land of celebrated giants, of men and women of legendary strength and penetrating wit, whose wealth was uncounted, whose deeds were great and whose character was unimpeachable.[31] There, life had been lived to its fullest, free of the weight of subordination and the sting of condescension. Immigrants and often their children thus looked backward as well as forward, formulating their identities and drawing strength from who they once were (or thought they were) as well as who they would become.

Self—individual and collective—was constantly being constructed between movement and place. Black people—as opposed to Angolans, Igbos, and Mandes—discovered their common Africanness had become a race on the western shore of the Atlantic. In much the same manner, African Americans hustled from the seaboard to the interior came to recognize their Virginian or South Carolinian origins in Mississippi, so black Georgians and Mississippians became Southerners in the cities of the North and ancestral places like Barbados and Jamaica, Ghana and Kenya came alive in twenty-first-century America. While the ligaments by which black people constructed their identity had been snapped in the process by which Africans became African Americans, the connections testify to the constant remaking of what had been and what would be. The old or the new might fail to be recognizable in these hybrids, as neither the rearview mirror of history nor the telescope of the future could capture the realities of the new mixtures.

The Contrapuntal Narrative

Over the course of four centuries, the great migrations and the intervening periods of stability have created a culture in which physical movement has been both resisted and embraced and in which identification with place has been alternately espoused and disowned. If those on the move yearned for the stability of place, those chained to place—often literally so—wanted only to move. The great migrations or passages—from Africa to the New World (*the* Middle Passage); from the seaboard to the interior, or black belt (a second "Middle Passage"); from the rural South to the urban North (a third passage); and the global diaspora to American cities (a fourth passage)—provide critical markers in the formation and re-formation of the African American people.[32] Each initiated a reconstruction of black life on new ground, creating new measures of cultural authenticity and new standards of cultural integrity. To be sure, the old ways were incorporated into the new, blending what once was with what would be, and creating an illusion of a seamless, unchanging cultural concord that reached back to antiquity. But not even the most powerful continuities could suppress the arrival of the new, as

31

manifested in the most deeply held beliefs or the most transient fads. Thus, at various times, to be black meant to wear one's hair in an eel skin queue, to conk the kinks straight, to bush au naturel, to plait into tight braids, or to shave the pate clean.[33]

The neck-snapping discontinuities between change and stasis have drawn black people to their past and invested that past with enormous weight, even as they wrestled again with an ever-changing present. At times, such connections with the past have created nostalgic longing for the old country, the old homestead, or the old neighborhood by men and women who—by force or choice—had been uprooted. These themes—the necessity to make life anew and the yearnings for a barely remembered or wholly imagined past—remain the great constants of African American life, echoed in literature, politics, and certainly music. Antebellum colonizationists, post-Reconstruction Exodusters, early twentieth-century Garveyites, and late-twentieth-century street vendors, generation upon generation, articulated a desire to recall, revisit, and sometimes return to the ancestral homelands and reclaim an African, then a seaboard, and even a Southern zion. Such projections suggest why African Americans constructed new histories from the ur-narrative of King Buzzard, the egalitarian guarantee of the Declaration of Independence, the biblical promise of exodus, or the Afrocentric roots of civilization.[34]

Yet the force of change—the serial migrations and repeated cultural reconstructions—made it impossible to recoup the past fully, despite the powerful propensity to freeze identity at a single moment, sometimes defined by ancestry, ideology, or even body image. In truth, the old societies could never be fully reconstructed as they had been, as they were remembered, or even as they were imagined. Indeed, the great passages themselves transformed the old societies. They were felt as much by those left in the seaboard South after their children were sold away as those who remained in the black belt after their neighbors had gone north. The transatlantic slave trade remade black life on the west coast of Africa between the sixteenth and nineteenth centuries; the internal slave trade again remade the settled seaboard South in the nineteenth century; and the movement to the urban North remade the rural South in the mid-twentieth century; and yet again the global diaspora has transformed blackness in the late twentieth and the twenty-first centuries. No matter how strong the identification with the "old country," the world that migrants had left was no more. Immigrants—whether forced or free—might some day return to the old country, but they could not go home.

But if the Old World could not be transferred to the New, it was never entirely forgotten. In making and remaking themselves—first as Africans, then as African Americans—over the course of some four hundred years, black people never turned their backs on the past. Rather, in successive iterations, they incorporated the past into their new selves, not in heroically remembering, but in drawing upon their experience often with a great sense of purpose.

The boundaries between movement and place and the resulting tension grew over time as immigrants faced the necessity of divesting themselves of portions of the past. While transnational languages—pidgins and creole tongues—might temporarily knit the past and the future together, the disjuncture was inevitable, if not for the immigrants themselves then certainly for their progeny.

The cultures of movement and place penetrated one another, in part because change, no matter how revolutionary, was never complete. Old patterns always coexisted and overlapped with new ones. More importantly, the vectors of change did not always point in one direction. Movement did not give birth to place or vice versa any more than the past necessarily summoned the present or than the present automatically fulfills the past. Often languages, religions, cuisine, or music created amid the flux of movement was transported back to the migrants' place of origins as well as forward to their place of arrival.[35]

There have been many bridges between movement and place, linking the sense of what was lost to what was gained: rites of passage, aesthetics of form and color, styles of cooking and dressing, folktales and proverbs, even intonation of voice. None, however, was more manifest than music. Music, as Lawrence Levine has written, "appears to be one of the most conservative of cultural traits." The portability of music and its seeming indestructibility maintained rhythmic patterns—and occasionally melodies and lyrics—even when migrants were stripped naked and denied their every material possession. In connecting shared experience with communal values, music, as Amiri Baraka has observed, has served as one barometer of the African American experience. The transformation of African American music mirrored that of black peoples, as the great passages set them in motion and the new arrivals rooted them in place. Nowhere is the contrapuntal narrative more evident.[36]

But music was not simply a window into African American life; it was a means by which black people understood their circumstances and articulated their deepest beliefs and most powerful yearnings. It provided a way to speak the unspeakable, both to themselves and those who dared to listen. Explaining the return of black Northerners to the Mississippi Delta, one of the poorest parts of the South, contemporary social scientists emphasize the magnetic draw of the "powerful and stark form of blues . . . some of the finest remnants of African American sacred music."[37]

Music also transmuted shared experience into communal solidarity. This was particularly true of the call-and-response that was a unifying element in eighteenth-century shouts, nineteenth-century spirituals, and twentieth-century jazz, as well as other musical genres. Echoing the theme sounded by the leaders, others then elaborated on it—assenting or dissenting to the message and then expanding and modifying it in various ways—thus taking ownership of the message. The voices of captive Africans were still echoed two centuries later in the churches of the Mississippi Delta. "The preacher," remembered Bluesman B. B. King, "says one thing and the congregation says it back, back forth, back forth, until we're rocking together in a rhythm that won't stop. His voice is low and rough and his guitar high and sweet; they seem to sing to each other, conversing in some heavenly language."[38]

While the call-and-response pattern remains an omnipresent hallmark of African American music, there are some others such as particular melodies, cadences, and strategic repetitions. Embellishments that emerged from field hollers, spirituals, the blues, jazz, and rap created grooves which then swung to join musician and audience as one. Each was driven forward by a never-ending process of improvisation that reflected—and marked—the remaking of African American life.

Music was present from the beginning, as slave-ship captains reported the collective voices emanating from below deck. The repetitive choruses, the interplay between leader and congregants, and the improvisational character provided the first evidence of one of the essential elements of what would be the African American repertoire. These features and others—polyrhythmic, tonal, and timbral flexibility, to name a few—became prominent in African American music and remain so in the present day. But if some central forms have remained the same, black musicians constantly reworked the melodic and harmonic ideas with different tempos and rhythmic impulses that reflected both movement and place.[39]

Thomas Jefferson, like many observers since, recognized the special place of music in the lives of black people, even if he—again, like so many after—attributed it to some congenital trait. The continuities of African American music and the lack of accurate description has made it easy to essentialize the sounds that observers like Jefferson attributed to the music of black people. Put another way, those continuities have made it difficult, as Shane White and Graham White noted, "to restore the 'pastness' of past sounds." The history of African American music is often frozen in place, celebrated as a marker of identity for a people whose identity was constantly disparaged. In the process, however, such celebrations often ignore cross-cultural construction first among Africans and then among African Americans, Native Americans, and Europeans in the creation of an ever-changing black musical tradition. Examining how movement and place transformed the evolution of shouts and hollers into spirituals, spirituals into gospel, and country blues into rhythm and blues both historicizes African American music and maintains its ubiquity in the black American experience without presuming these genres had distinctive lineages.[40]

African American music, with its extraordinary variety and multiplicity of forms, rarely follows the "normal" course of any chronology of black life, a chronology whose specific markers remain mired in conjecture and endless debate.[41] Black musicians, enslaved and free, functioning as "griots"—African storytellers—told many tales. The power of invention and reinvention of the black musical tradition overwhelms any attempt to link particular genres to particular moments. Subordination, moreover, discouraged black musicians from speaking directly, so their music was often coded, filled with ironic references, multiple meanings, and veiled imagery. Nonetheless, music speaks profoundly to the transformative dynamic that has constantly remade the experience of black peoples. No history of either movement or place in African and African American life can be fully understood without careful attention to the sounds that accompanied it. Nothing better revealed the larger transformations of African American life— be they cultural, economic, or political—than music.

African and African American Migrants in a Nation of Immigrants

The interplay of movement and place is not unique to black Americans. Americans of all sorts also experienced its whiplash effects, for the history of the United States rests upon movement—first across the oceans and then across the continent—and then the embrace of place. In the hands of historians like Frederick Jackson Turner, the migratory experience became the defining characteristic of American life. His argument was so powerful that even his most determined critics could only emphasize movement, though generally of a different sort. Oscar Handlin, reflecting upon his own work as a historian of American immigration, famously declared, "Once I thought to write a history of the immigrants in America. Then I discovered that the immigrants *were* American history."[42]

Handlin's appreciation of migration as the master narrative of American history strangely was never extended to African Americans. For some, to concede as much was to incorporate them into American history as equal to others. Differences in the nature and timing of the arrival of Africans and Europeans (forced and free) served as a means of excluding people of African descent from the ideology that celebrated the United States as a global sanctuary from oppression and as fostering material improvement for all. Writing in 1920, historian Carl Russell Fish, a pioneer student of American immigration, denied black people a place in the history of the United States for just this reason. Their "enforced migration" precluded the possibilities of self-improvement that were at the heart of the American ethos. Lerone Bennett, writing some forty years later, agreed—although for different reasons. If the new American republic's foundational ideology saw the nation, in the words of its first president, as a refuge for "the oppressed and persecuted of all nations," what place could there be for enslaved peoples of African descent?[43]

For others, the incorporation of African Americans into the master narrative denied the exceptional nature of the black experience: the long, violent nightmare of enslavement, segregation, disfranchisement, and poverty. "African Americans," flatly declared one economist, "are the descendants of slaves, not immigrants." "Unlike the Irish, Poles, Jews or Italians," insisted a careful student of Chicago's ghetto, "Negroes banded together not to enjoy a common linguistic, cultural and religious tradition, but because a systematic pattern of discrimination left them no alternative." Others have dismissed the possibility on principled ground, observing that the employment of the very word "immigrant" for enslaved Africans "strips the language of its symbolic meaning."[44]

The debate concerning the special character of the African American versus the European American experiences has turned nasty at times. The comparison of migrations often became the occasion for invidious matches as to who suffered the greatest hardships, the most wrenching losses, or the most devastating separations. The differences among the "uprooted" counted for more than their shared experience. Perverse competitions as to relative damage meted out by restrictive covenants, redlining, or the barrage of vile epithets—dago, gook, greaser, hunky, kike, and nigger—demonstrate that shared experience breeds contempt as well as camaraderie.

Without question, the organized, systematic removals wrought by the slave trade were categorically different from migrations based on the belly or on fear—no matter whether the fear was generated by political persecution or by environmental disaster. Forced migrants did not make the choice between improving their circumstances in their homeland or someplace else, although they too were subject to the vagaries of the business cycle. The crimp and the labor contractor—like the slave trader—were in the business of labor recruitment. But no matter how rapacious and exploitive they viewed themselves and were viewed by others as different than slave traders, no matter how similar their objectives, methods, or even motives. Similarly, unlike indentured servants, debtors, or redemptioners, who might have conceived a term of servitude as a bargain that exchanged labor for the promise of a better life in the future, those who arrived in slave ships could hardly conjure any advantage derived from their passage.

What can be said for the differences between European free migrants and those black men and women caught in the slave trade also applies to the various movements of black men and women, for here too the distinction between choice and coercion is manifest. The men and women forcibly transported across the Atlantic or across the North American continent differed from those who chose to leave the South for the North in the twentieth century or come to the United States in the twenty-first, no matter how desperate their situation. Africans ensnared in the slave trade were not trying to improve their material circumstance, enrich their social lives, or escape from political oppression. As free men or women, even the most impoverished black sharecroppers fleeing the hellhounds of landlord debt and Klan violence had some choice of destinations and traveling companions. They could imagine a better life in a better place.[45]

Black men and women who evacuated the plantation South for the urban North in the first half of the twentieth century hardly left by choice, although there were many reasons for them to do so. The decision of planters and furnishing merchants, often with the direct assistance of the state, to protect their own profit at the expense of the well-being of black laborers made it impossible for many to remain in the rural South. The men and women who were expelled from the plantations that they, their parents, and perhaps their grandparents had worked on often migrated north with great reluctance. Some left only under threat of bodily harm. They fretted about leaving home, severing the network of kin in which they were enmeshed, and losing the familiar landscape that they knew and loved. They feared the unknown and were skeptical about the promise of freedom and opportunity among white Northerners. But they were also excited about the new possibilities. The joy that radiated from the railroad cars cannot be compared to the misery emanating from slave ships. While observers regularly compared the slave coffle to a funerary train, literally a march toward death, no one—not ever—described the trains and buses that carried black people northward in such a manner. The decisions that shaped the migrations of black men and women who left the South were largely their own, beginning with how and who and where and sometimes when. Traveling on their own or with family, they carried numerous possessions. Whatever pain accompanied the loss of the familiar and whatever anxieties attended the fear of the new, escape from the oppression which had dogged them generated an optimism unimagined by those caught in the slave trade. If the forced migration of both the international and internal trades represented social death, the movement north bespoke life and the possibilities that accompanied smashing the shackles of confinement.

The possibility of return, however distant, also distinguished the free from the forced immigrant. The former lived in a dense network of connections, real or fictive. The latter was isolated and alone in a world permanently truncated.[46] Perhaps more important, free migrations— far more than forced migrations—generated reverse flows. A large portion of those who ventured across the Atlantic and the Pacific sampled life in the New World and turned on their heels and went home.[47] While a handful of enslaved peoples crossed the Atlantic or later the North American continent several times, most did not. Black Southerners who migrated northward, however, commonly returned home, sometimes for short visits, sometimes for an extended stay, and sometimes permanently.

In the late twentieth century, shuttling between Africa, the Caribbean, or other distant places and the United States became even more common, as changes in transportation and communication created new kinds of global connectedness. If the isolation of slaves—their one-way ticket—shaped African American culture during the first three centuries of the history of black America, the mobility of their successors did the same during the last one hundred years. Assessing the circumstances of the men and women who "returned" to the South in the 1970s, anthropologists discovered that returnees had been "born in northern cities, but almost all had been well acquainted with their destination since childhood through school-year and summer residence as well as through repeated visits."[48] Returnees brought the new world back to the old and, in the process, remade the old society. Increasingly, the transmission of culture moved both ways, as movement and place became conjoined in an unbounded process, subverting the notion that culture is formed by a linear process. The new culture, in short, was as much a product as a precipitate of movement.

Those differences reflected the ways in which migrants should be understood. While the motives of forced migrants can be reduced to a function of economic calculus—the market for labor, for example— free migrants have a multitude of reasons for moving beyond that of finding work. The needs of families and kin, the desire to create new societies, and the aspiration for greater political freedom or material prosperity are just some of these. A similar event—war, for example— could have a different effect on both forced and free migrations. While forced migrations created protocols of their own, modern free migrations are governed by all sorts of legal regulations, and affected by many more factors. Migrations of choice—even made under difficult conditions—tended to be much more selective. Forced migrations tend to spew men and women helter-skelter across the countryside.[49] The comparative homogeneity of free migrations suggests the ability of migrants to plan their exodus by seeking out information and joining together with family and friends.

The unique experience of black people as slaves and as free people cannot be reduced to another version of the classic struggle of immigrants for recognition, acceptance, and success. Frederick Douglass was neither John Altgeld nor Carl Schurz, and Bigger Thomas was neither David Levinsky nor Mike Dobrejcak. The centrality of white supremacy has distinguished the history of black people from that of the Germans, Irish, Italians, Japanese, Jews, Mexicans, and others.[50] The former lost their freedom in crossing Atlantic, while the latter often celebrated their arrival in America as an expansion of their liberty; the former's arrival was understood in terms of their unnatural injection into American society and their contested incorporation, while the latter have been seen as a continuous, even natural process of absorption or what some have called assimilation.

The assimilative power of American pluralism apparently had little effect on people of African ancestry. "Ethnics"—a term rarely applied to people of African descent—might be incorporated into the melting pot and given a ticket to full inclusion into American society, but black arrivals were not. The concept of the melting pot (and its close relatives: assimilation, amalgamation, and cultural pluralism), whatever its utility for the study of European and Asian immigration, has been given little weight with respect to the forced arrival of Africans.

Such notions of assimilation fail to accommodate the effervescent diversity of American society or its lack of a single hegemonic core in favor of more complex cultural reciprocities by which American society (or perhaps any society) was continually refashioned. Still, few have applied the idioms of pluralism (Horace Kallen's "democracy of nationality" or Israel Zangwill's "melting pot") to African Americans. The "process of interpenetration and fusion in which persons and groups acquire the memories, sentiments, and attitudes of other persons or groups, and, by sharing their experience and history, are incorporated with them in a common cultural life" is generally not part of the study of African American life, although people of African descent have been "interpenetrated" in American life and "fused" with peoples of Native American, European, and Asian descent. While scholars repeatedly revisit the debate over the assimilation of Europeans and others deemed "white" in terms of ethnicity (a concept invented for just that purpose), religion, or work experience, people of African descent remain of one piece, primordially rooted with a presumed collective identity.[51]

The putative staying power of ethnicity—suggested by the mid-twentieth-century popularity of such books as *Beyond the Melting Pot* or *The Rise of the Unmeltable Ethnics*—has seemingly drawn the experiences of white and black immigrants together.[52] Yet profound differences in the experiences of blacks and whites even in the post–*Brown v. Board* era validate the categories of race and ethnicity, which are often used in opposition to one another.[53] Studies of whiteness affirm that race remains a driving force in understanding American life.[54]

But all human beings share a migratory history. That ubiquity integrates African American experience into world history, modern history, and American history (and vice versa).[55] From the largest historical perspective, the great migrations of African American peoples straddled the great historical divides created by the expansion of Western capitalism and informed—perhaps determined—the lives of peoples in Europe and Asia as well as Africa and the Americas. Between the middle of the fifteenth and the beginning of the eighteenth centuries, most of the men and women crossing the Atlantic were forcibly repeopling the Americas in the wake of the catastrophic destruction of Native American peoples and the reluctance of Europe's underclass to leave their homelands. In a like fashion, the massive expansion of industrial production—and the subsequent demand for foodstuff and other commodities—during the nineteenth century initiated both the surge of Europeans to the Americas and an internal migration (free and forced) within the Americas. The emancipationist century—the years between the 1780s and the 1880s when one Atlantic nation after another proscribed the trade in persons—set loose another massive movement of peoples, as Asians, many of them contracted, indentured, and shanghaied, also found their way to the Americas. In the United States, the dual migration—Europeans settling on the East Coast, Asians on the West—tethered African Americans to the Southern states. Not until the spigot of European and Asian migration shut during the second decade of the twentieth century would black people begin to move north. Finally, most late-twentieth-century migrations reflected both the movement of highly trained technicians and managers from the third world to the first—the so-called brain drain—and the desperate flight of poor people from low-wage to high-wage nations.

From such a global perspective, the seventeenth-century slave trader in El Mina, the eighteenth-century crimp in Bristol, and the nineteenth-century labor contractor in Pozen performed the same function, and the enslaved African, dragooned English sailor, shanghaied Chinese peasant, and desperate Polish peasant likewise stood in a similar relationship to the making and unmaking of a transnational labor force that was driven by the expansion of commodity production. The enslaved African, impressed Chinese coolie, and the Polish peasant found themselves swept up in a process of rural dispossession and urban proletarianization. Moreover, these massive changes in the world economy were often preceded by environmental disasters—droughts and floods, famines and plagues—on one hand, and political violence—civil wars, state-sponsored terrorism, genocide, and ethnic cleansings—on the other, which made life unbearably difficult. These upheavals would eventually reach into every corner of the globe.

The global perspective and the long view of human history call into question distinctions between coerced migrations and voluntary migrations.[56] For while many migrants moved on their own free will,

44

the labor drafts and political discord that accompanied these migrations strained the very meaning of human volition. English peasants driven from the land by enclosures, Irish tenants avoiding starvation, Poles running before Cossacks, Jews escaping pogroms, Armenians dodging Turks, and Native Americans fleeing the U.S. cavalry, or Ugandans, Croats, and Laos escaping the murderous ethnic cleansers could hardly be called free immigrants.[57] Moreover, the process of settlement, integration, and assimilation of free and forced migrations had much in common as men and women whose primary identity had nothing to do with nation-states were transformed into nationals of one sort or another. The processes whereby enslaved Angolans and Wolofs became Africans followed much the same path as Genoese and Tuscans who became Italians or Hausas and Igbos who became Nigerians. Although some moved in chains and others by choice, transplantation transformed networks of kin groups into new peoples.

While the distinction between forced and free migrations cloaks the fact that all migrations involve cultural transformations, these various migrations also mask the essential reality that even the most traumatic uprootings do not necessarily dissolve the migrants' humanity, their sense of self, and their determination to shape their own lives. Forced migrants, like free ones, carried with them ideas about family, work, religion, and much else that they put into practice at the first opportunity, albeit in different circumstances. Emphasizing the distinction between the voluntary and the coerced, moreover, revivifies the myth of stability—the timelessness of premodern society and fixity of peasant life. Such notions may be useful foils for understanding the hyperactivity identified with modernity, but they have long since been exposed as hollow stereotypes. Geographic movement, as students of migration have demonstrated, has been and remains the normal condition of mankind.

The experience of migration that made and remade black life also entwined the lives of black people with that of other Americans. Sometimes they were so intimately connected that a reduction of one enlarged another. When the movement of European indentured servants to the Chesapeake region faltered in the 1660s, the trade in African slaves—and the commitment to slavery—grew. When the constitutional mandate and congressional law closed the transatlantic slave trade to the United States in the early nineteenth century, European migration swelled, whitening the North American continent. When that migration ceased a century later as a result of World War I, black people left the South for the North. Meanwhile, Africans and their descendants mixed with Native Americans and European Americans as they met sometimes allies, sometimes enemies, and sometimes curious bystanders eager to avoid entanglements caught in circumstances not of their own making. The experience of these peoples was likewise tied to vast uprootings, sometimes of their own choosing but often made under duress. Threats of enclosures, horrors of famines, trails of tears, and nightmares of state-sponsored terror drove many of these people from their homelands. To doubt these movements were founded in extreme coercion belies the obvious, and to say that some found opportunity in these changes states nothing new. Following such traumatic uprootings, these migrants also became identified with particular places, be they ghettos, reservations, or suburbs. As they took root, they too constructed their histories from fading memories of the old country, biblical allusions to the promised land, images of the Golden Mountain, transcendent hopes of American life, and certainty that they too were God's chosen people whose destiny was foretold in sacred texts.

Even the violent cultural cleansing whereby European slave masters stripped African slaves of the very signatures of their identity—their names—was not unknown to other immigrants. At Ellis Island, immigration officers regularly renamed the new arrivals, often in the most flippant manner and with the same sorts of ridicule that slave masters applied to their newcomers. Suggesting how the weight of a foreign cultural hegemony bore down upon them, many immigrants needed no prompting in disposing of their ancient appellation, so Sophie Abuza renamed herself Sophie Tucker, just as Asa Yoelson transformed himself into Al Jolson, Harry Lillis into Bing Crosby, and Israel Baline into Irving Berlin.[58] Many peoples, in short, shared the rhythm of movement and rootedness. If the names were different— Hester Street, Swede Town, and Little Italy rather than Drayton Hall, Monticello, and Mount Vernon—the experience was undeniably a common one, and a powerful reminder of what Americans share.

In the end, what distinguishes the African American experience is not merely the difficult distinction between free and forced migrations or the alleged absence of an immigrant past, but rather the collective weight of multiple migrations. Coerced or by choice, repeatedly and—then again—by coersion or choice—people of African descent rooted themselves in the land. In the process, they produced two massive contradictions.

First, the necessity of the periodic reconstruction of black society on new ground created a sense of "we-ness," which joined together black peoples who had vastly different origins, beliefs, and interests across space and time. Bonds created by the terror of the Atlantic passage, the horror of the long march from the James to the Mississippi River, and the hopeful expectations of the train ride from Biloxi to Chicago provided a common experience, which became the basis of a new collective to which newcomers could identify and into which old hands could be incorporated. Men and women who had been utter strangers were joined together by the most elemental of shared experience: survival. African American culture was formed in the holds of slave ships and the necessity of dealing with harsh circumstances beyond their own creation. It was reformed in coffles tramping west, and reformed yet again in the segregated railroad cars that carried black people northward. In deplaning a jet at Kennedy, O'Hare, or

Hartsfield airport, new arrivals in the twenty-first century echo the experience of their forebears who were likewise caught in the maelstrom of a changing world economy.

Yet the experience of migration that made and remade black life also entwined the lives of black people with that of other Americans: Native Americans who had been expelled from the very lands that African Americans would be forced to cultivate or European Americans who would claim ownership of those same grounds. The contrapuntal narrative of movement and place traced the transformation of people of African descent into African American and into Americans.

Here the story becomes even more telling, for culture never develops along a single path. Each iteration of African American culture was a hybrid, and could only be understood as the product of specific historical circumstances; it is always changing. Men and women often tried to freeze those changes as they searched for stability and permanence in a world in constant motion by positing culture—in this case "blackness"—as a timeless structure. But new circumstances eventually demand new understandings. Those understandings—a new narrative or history—tried to explain how and why the new people arrived where they were and became who they were. Sometimes this has been a narrative of reproach: what was done to us. Sometimes this has been a narrative of celebration: what we did for ourselves. These narratives can be further subdivided: narratives of abandonment (why God failed), narratives of salvation (why we were chosen), narratives of edification, and so on. Movement demands a rethinking of identity; hence new stories.

CHAPTER TWO

The Transatlantic Passage

They became Africans in America. The men and women seized by force, dragged across the continent, and herded into the coastal barracoons called themselves by many names, but few if any designated themselves *Africans*. Rather their names derived from their lineages, places of habitation, national affiliations, or various ancient solidarities. As they were stuffed into the holds of waiting slave ships, they gained still other designations, as captains and supercargoes invented new nomenclatures derived in part from their outsiders' knowledge of the continent. Relying on a crude understanding of African geography (and some imaginative projections), slavers labeled their captives by the ports of embarkation or the hinterland they presumed these ports drew upon. Coromantees from Koromanti, Minas from El Mina, and Whydads from Ouidad.[1] At other times, the seaborne merchants of men borrowed labels from the keepers of the barracoons with whom they traded. Still others thought they recognized the language their captives spoke or identified some physical feature from the manner in which men and women wore their hair, marked their bodies, draped their clothing, or carried themselves. But since the captives spoke many languages and bore a variety of markings, the naming and renaming proceeded on uncertain ground. Often it was little more than uninformed conjecture, mixed with hopeful speculations. Hasty judgments based upon the flimsiest evidence—often filtered through barely understood pidgins or jargons—soon became reified in bills of lading and ship manifests. Yet these designations also had little staying power.[2]

As the ships pulled away from the wharves, the captives' identity underwent yet another and more fateful transformation. No longer were the peoples who filled the holds simply Angolans or Efiks, Kongos or Wolofs—labels that spoke more to how outsiders identified them than how they thought of themselves.[3] Instead, they took on new names bereft of any ties to lineage, place of origin, or even port of embarkation. In 1619, noting the arrival of some of the first black men and women in England's Chesapeake settlements, John Rolfe famously observed that "[a]bout the last of August came in a dutch man of warre that sold us twenty Negars." Rolfe's blurt of the not yet benighted N-word would later be made respectable as *negro*; other names followed, such as *colored* and *Anglo-African*, then as *Negro* (appropriately capitalized), *black*, *Afro-American*, and *African American*. Like Rolfe's "negars," these names too announced a new people in the making.[4]

Africans were thus a product of the New World, not the Old. Just as Catalans and Galicians became Spanish when removed from Iberia, the former residents of Abruzzo, Basilicata, Genoa, and Tuscany became Italians outside of Italy, or—more recently—Chileans and Cubans became Hispanics in the United States, so the many peoples of Africa were melded into Africans on the west side of the Atlantic. Like the newly minted Spaniards, Italians, and Hispanics, their identity was not so much a product of who they were but who they would become. The process a making Angolans and Efiks, Kongos and Wolofs into Africans was slow and hardly complete after the captives reached the Americas, where the slaveowners' shallow understanding of Africa further twisted notions of identity. Even those slaveowners who appreciated the differences among the nations of Africa and carefully recorded the origins of their slaves were mystified by the fine distinctions among the many peoples of Africa. Perhaps Kikongo and Kimbundu or Edo and Ijo sounded alike to an unacquainted ear. More likely, slaveholders did not listen very closely. A South Carolina planter conceded that he could "never make out" the derivation of his slave who had been "imported with a cargo of Eboe negroes" some seven years earlier.[5]

Ultimately the mixing of African nations—not the perceptions of European slave traders or American slaveowners—made the many peoples of Africa into Africans. But even self-identification offered little help in the process of naming. People were sometimes defined by the language they spoke, but allegiance to a single authority did not follow from a shared language, genealogy, or history. Autonomous nations in the modern sense—with fixed territorial boundaries and ruled by a singular authority which claimed a monopoly of loyalty— were the exception (like the eighteenth-century Asante) not the rule. Instead, boundaries were ill defined, authority had multiple sources, and loyalty was divided. Moreover, since the peoples of Africa were undergoing vast changes in the era of the slave trade, they took many names for themselves. Partly as a result of the chaos created by the trade—wars, abductions, sales, and resales mixed with various natural and man-made disasters—African peoples moved frantically within the continent. Families, villages, and nations that had been decimated joined with one another, embracing new identities from the fusion of once distinct peoples. The migrants themselves changed—learned new languages, made new friends, adopted new attitudes, and developed new personas—as they trudged across the continent, lodged in barracoons, and prepared to cross the Atlantic. The fluidity of African nationality meant that captives identified themselves in numerous ways, confusing even the most observant of their captors.[6]

Identities, whether assumed or imposed, became increasingly problematic as the inexorable realities of enslavement trumped ideas respecting national origins. As the captives mixed among themselves, blending the languages and habits of diverse African peoples, the slavers' designations forfeited any relationship to reality. Often Angolans who looked like Calabars or arrived with Calabars or behaved in the manner of Calabars were labeled Calabars, although they may never have been in or near Calabar. It was the slave trade itself that created the new designations.[7]

Whatever their origins, the captives had a different understanding of slavery than the men who claimed ownership over them. In sub-Saharan Africa, enslavement—although legitmate in custom and law and a nearly universal practice—had been a dreaded misfortune, but not a catastrophe. Slaves, as one of many forms of dependency, were generally not critical to commerce or production. They worked in households as well as the fields and shops, less a source of labor than of status and wealth. Employed at a variety of domestic tasks, they mattered little to the organization of the state or society. African slavery was a porous, familial, and lineage-based system for much of the seventeenth and eighteenth centuries. Men and women might be enslaved as criminals, debtors, adulterers, sorcerers or witches, or—most commonly—captives of war, who may well have found enslavement preferable to the usual treatment meted out to wartime prisoners. Thereafter, most slaves were employed as domestic or agricultural laborers; their product was for subsistence or local consumption rather than the international market.

Such employment of slaves did not reduce the slaves' worth, and it sometimes protected them from abuse. Since land in most African societies was owned corporatively by kin groups or the state and not easily transferable, slaves became the most valuable form of revenue-producing property, as well as an excellent means of accumulating capital. Control over slaves was a source of wealth and power, for it also allowed for control over land. In endowing slaveholders with high social standing, slavery was more a political than an economic institution. Men of power, deeply invested in slaves, assured that property rights in man would be respected. Slavery had become ubiquitous in African society prior to the advent of the transatlantic trade. The legal forms and social protocols to enslave were well in place, and slavery's legitimacy universally accepted.

But in Africa slavery was rarely linear and hereditary over the course of generations; rather it was often a means of incorporation into family and community. Anointed with rights that protected them from arbitrary transfer by a system of mutual obligations, enslaved men and women enjoyed a place within the social life of their owners' family, village, and community. Many African societies depended upon the incorporation of such enslaved peoples to sustain themselves, which accounted for a distinct preference for females. Some slaves rose to positions of power and distinction as soldiers and administrators—jobs that could only be entrusted to outsiders. From such positions, freedom—not an individualist's independence but full incorporation in the community—was a real possibility.[8]

The door to slavery swung both ways in Africa, making slavery a remarkable permeable institution. If African societies provided the mechanism for enslavement, they also allowed for liberation. While enslavement was common, so too was manumission. Over time, the emancipated were able to attach themselves to their owners' society. They too could rise to positions of eminence and perhaps one day become slaveowners themselves.[9]

That former slaves as well as slaves had a place in African society did not always temper the violent nature of slavery. Slavery in Africa—depending upon circumstance—could be as exploitative and brutal as any. Moreover, just as the slaves' circumstances differed from place to place in Africa, they changed over time. In the centuries after European incursions onto the coast of west Africa, slavery took many forms, especially as new centralized and militarized states arose whose entire concern was the trade in person, either through warfare, kidnapping, or judicially sanctioned captivity. During the eighteenth century, as Islam advanced into west Africa, jihads against non-Muslim peoples added to the number of Africans enslaved. Still, even into the nineteenth century, slavery remained linked to domestic rather than commercial production. Most African societies remained societies with slaves—that is, societies in which slavery was just one form of subordination and generally not the dominant one.[10]

As captive Africans entered continental Europe in the fifteenth and sixteenth centuries, slavery remained largely a domestic institution. Even as the number of African slaves grew in Portugal and Spain, the household—not the field or the workshop—continued to be the primary locus of slave life. Some slaves served as sailors on the very boats that carried them from their homeland, a practice that would be carried over to the Americas. African slaves lived and worked in close proximity to their owners, laboring alongside other Europeans—free and unfree, Christian and Muslim. In time, transplanted Africans spoke Portuguese, Spanish, Dutch, English, or creole tongues; practiced Christian and Islamic faiths; gained familiarity with the trading etiquettes and jurisprudence of the larger Atlantic world; and secured their freedom in substantial numbers. By the middle of the sixteenth century, almost 10 percent of the 10,000 black people residing in Lisbon and a like proportion of the 6,000 in Seville had secured their freedom.[11]

On the Atlantic islands—Madeira, the Azores, the Canaries, and then São Tomé and Príncipe—the Portuguese and Spanish planters introduced slaves to a new, harsh form of chattel bondage. Geared to the production of sugar and other exotic commodities for sale in distant markets, plantation slavery bore little resemblance to its domestic counterpart either in Africa or Europe. Rather it was a labor system in which slaveowners considered their human property little more than units of production. Eager for the profits that sugar mills produced, planters drove their slaves hard, pushing mortality rates to horrific heights and leaving slaves few opportunities to establish families, participate in independent economies, or create lives of their own. In such a system, the possibility of escape from bondage was small and the chance for incorporation into free society nil.

The emergence of the plantation system changed the nature of slavery throughout the Atlantic. In Africa, the demand for slaves fostered the growth of new states whose very being rested upon slavery. Slave raiding and slave trading became the essence of these new states. African elites became less interested in assimilating captives into their households and more concerned with their sale to Europeans in exchange for guns and other weapons of war that enabled them to gain still more slaves.[12]

The increased availability of Africans made it possible to expand the plantation system, and when the plantation crossed the Atlantic to the Americas beginning in the sixteenth century, African slavery accompanied it. Within a century, slavery had become synonymous with people of African descent in the minds of many Europeans; "these two words, Negro and Slave," reported one English clergyman in 1680, had "by custom grown Homogeneous and convertible."[13] Blackness took on a new meaning.

The changed meaning of blackness put a growing number of African peoples in harm's way. Although the initial captives may have been drawn from enslaved adulterers, criminals, debtors, and wartime prisoners, by the eighteenth century—when most Africans arrived in mainland North America—enslaved peoples were rarely guilty of anything more than being in the wrong place at the wrong time. A few may have been sold by desperate or depraved kinsmen and neighbors for some real or invented offense, but Africans rarely sold their own people, as they understood it. "Not a few in our country fondly imagine that Parents here sell their Children, Men their Wives, and one Brother the other," wrote a Dutch trader from the coast of Africa at the beginning of the nineteenth century. "But those who think so deceive themselves." Instead, black people were taken by mercenary armies, bandits, and professional slavers.[14]

Taken from deep within the African interior, Africans faced a long, deadly march to the coast. Traveling sometimes for months, they were passed from group to group, and slaves might find themselves sold and resold many times over. Each time they would be imprisoned in some filthy pen, poked and prodded, and perhaps auctioned off to yet another set of strangers, as many peoples participated in the slave trade. Even before they reached some central distribution point, according to one account, "great numbers perished from cruel usage, want of food, traveling through inhospitable deserts, &c." But whoever drove the captives to their unwanted destiny, the circumstances of their travel were extraordinarily taxing. Ill clothed and ill fed, the captives moved at a feverish pace, only to stop again and languish in some pen, while middlemen bartered over their bodies, sold some, and purchased yet others to add to the sad coffle.

Captives did not go quietly. Resistance that began at the point of capture continued as the enslaved marched to the coast. Rebellions rarely succeeded and, while some captives escaped, most of the fugitives were recaptured; the journey then began again. Conditions improved over time, but in the 1790s one in four slaves taken in central Africa died before reaching the coast. In some places, more than half the slaves perished between their initial capture in the interior and their arrival on the coast. Overall, the movement to the coast was nothing more than a death march for many.[15]

Conditions in coastal factories were, if anything, even more lethal. Often built in low-lying swamps, they were breeding grounds for disease. Captives found themselves packed away in dank dungeons with little ventilation and little concern for the most elementary sanitation. There they could languish for weeks, sometimes months, depending on the nature of the trade. The weak and traumatized fell by the thousands, as epidemics swept through their crowded pens.

The corpses, according to one account, were simply dumped into the surrounding marshes, as a kind of human landfill. Inevitably they reeked of death.[16]

Exhausted and emaciated, the survivors did not simply await their fate. Even at this last moment, captive men and women sought to regain their freedom. Some tried to get word to their families, so they might be ransomed. A few well-connected captives were redeemed. The vast majority of captives with neither the connections nor the resources needed to buy themselves out of bondage sought to escape. However, once they entered the walled castles, flight became increasingly difficult; the handful who succeeded were soon recaptured and returned, as the towns that grew up around the barracoons had little sympathy for the fugitives. Still, the barracoons were rife with conspiracies and insurrections. Revolts and escapes, though rare, punctuated the history of the coastal enclaves, perhaps because the captives' desperation pushed them to risk all. Carried from holding pens to the awaiting slavers, some jumped overboard and swam toward shore. Others, refusing to see their loved ones shipped across the Atlantic, banded together with friends and relatives in order to assault the canoe men. But only a handful of these last gasps for freedom succeeded.[17]

These were the fortunate few. Most captives faced the nightmarish transatlantic crossing. The depths of human misery and the astounding death toll of men and women packed in the stinking hulls shamed the most hard-hearted. Slave traders themselves testified to the deleterious effects of the trade. Even among those who defended slavery, there were those who condemned the Middle Passage as an abomination. But, like all human experiences—even the worst—the Middle Passage was not of one piece. While the vast majority suffered below deck, a few men and women chosen from among the captives helped set the sails, steer the ships, and serve the crews that carried the mass of Africans across the Atlantic. A few were armed to guard the enslaved. Denmark Vesey, the former slave whose alleged conspiracy shook South Carolina in the 1820s, was but one of many slaves who sailed the Atlantic as the personal servant of the ship captains. Some slave ships employed free black sailors among their crews, and a handful sailed with black crews. Others were elevated from the mass of captives to the crew when the ship was shorthanded or required some special service, such as a pilot or translator. Guardian slaves—many of them drawn from the gramettoes who defended the barracoons—continued their collaboration with slavers on board. In addition, "privilege slaves," who were the property of the captain and other officers, were given an indulgence as part of their compensation and mixed with others of no special rank. Such slaves received special treatment, if only to allow their owners to realize this benefit. The Atlantic passage of these captives differed greatly from those stowed below deck.[18]

The Middle Passage differed from place to place and changed over time. While some slave ships shuttled from port to port purchasing and selling slaves to amass the most marketable cargo, others loaded a full complement and proceeded directly across the Atlantic. Once in the Americas, slavers might discharge their entire payload at a single port or travel to different ports, peddling slaves in small lots. Depending upon the port of embarkation and the port of arrival, the transatlantic crossing could take weeks or months. Slave ships, no less than other vessels, suffered the hazards of ocean travel, be they pirates, privateers, or shipwrecks. Seasonal changes in trade winds made a difference, as did the skill of the captain and crew, the nature of maritime technology, and the vessel's construction. In general, the shorter the voyage, the better the slaves' chances of survival—although short journeys under unfavorable circumstances could be more deadly than months at sea.[19]

Slave captains appreciated the benefit of delivering their captives alive and healthy. If they needed a reminder, the great merchants who financed the trade instructed them as to the care of their valuable cargo, issuing orders respecting rationing, exercise, and medical attention. Corpses, after all, found few buyers. But aboard ship the alleged rationality of the market faltered before the irrationality of the trade in human flesh. While captain and crew might be directed to allow slaves "every indulgence Consistent with your own Safety," the safety of the ship and the profits rendered its owners always trumped indulgences granted to slaves, with disastrous results for the captives. Fear of shipboard insurrection induced slave traders to keep captive men cramped below deck for weeks and sometimes months, and pressure to reduce expenses left many slave ships short of provisions, water, and medical supplies. Even the most enlightened captains—whether alert to their own pecuniary interests or mindful of the needs of their captives—often lacked the ability or resources to deliver their cargoes alive and well. Some slave ships were well supplied and directed by seasoned mariners; others lacked proper provisions and were captained by incompetent or simply untested seamen. But the best-supplied ship, directed by the ablest mariners, could suffer disastrous consequences if it ran short of provisions, was struck by disease, or was thrown off course. The highly competitive trade in slaves, with its thin profit margins, fostered the wildest speculation. Some traders took risks that lacked only intent to be criminal. Skimping on food, filling the hold with extra slaves—so-called tightpacking—redounded to great profits for the trader, but they also meant great pain for the traded. The ever-changing mortality rates speak to the fact that the Middle Passage was always a nightmare, but it was not always the same nightmare.[20]

For the captives, however, some things never changed. Fear was omnipresent as the captives, stripped naked and bereft of their every belonging, boarded the ship and met—often for the first time—white men. Brandishing knives, whips, shackles, neck rings, and—perhaps most frightening—hot irons to mark their captives in the most personal way, these "white men with horrible looks, red faces, and long hair" left more than a physical scar. Many enslaved Africans concluded they were in league with the devil, if not devils themselves. For others, their seared skin confirmed that they were bound for the slaughterhouse to be eaten by the cannibals who had stamped them in much the way domesticated animals were marked.[21]

The branding iron was but the first of many instruments of savagery the captives faced. Eighteenth-century ships were violent places where imperious captains ruled with the lash, and the barbarity of maritime life reached even greater heights on the slave ship, where whips, chains, shackles, and thumbscrews were standard equipment. When it came to subduing slaves, the captains' autocratic power was extended to the crew, and men who had been themselves brutalized often felt little compunction in brutalizing others. Indeed, the inability of the captives to defend themselves unleashed the most sadistic impulses, promoting appalling cruelties, as the lines between the callous and the cruel, the cruel and the vicious, and the vicious and the sadistic were fine indeed. Under the best of circumstances, slaves could expect the lash for the slightest infraction and various other punishments for actions that threatened or even appeared to threaten the success of the voyage.

While violence was ubiquitous on the slave ship, it was neither random nor purposeless. Rather it was calculated to intimidate captives in circumstances where there could be few incentives for men and women to submit peacefully. By awing captives with overwhelming power wielded without regard for life or limb, slavers hoped the display of force would convince the captives that resistance was futile. To that end, captives were stripped of the trappings of humanity: denied personal possessions, privacy, and other prerogatives accorded the meanest members of free society. Slavers used every occasion to emphasize the captives' degraded status and utter isolation—indeed their lack of status. The filth and violence dissolved the carefully developed distinctions between the pure and the impure upon which many African societies rested. The humiliation that accompanied such degradation was almost always public, giving the captives little means to maintain their dignity. Among the lessons taught in this systematic debasement was the sacrosanctity of white skin. More than any single place, the origins of white supremacy can be found in the holds of the slave ship. Speaking through a black interpreter, one captain informed his captives that "no one that killed a white man would be spared." Few were.[22]

Equally inescapable was the horror and anguish that accompanied the captives' stark realization of what transport across the Atlantic entailed. Sometime during their journey, in one terrifying moment, they understood that family, friends, and country were gone, never to be seen again. The markers of identity—many of which had been physically inscribed upon their bodies in ritual scarification, tooth filing, body piercing, and tattooing—were denigrated, if not transformed into a source of ridicule. Lineage, the most important source of social cohesion in African society, was dissolved. Sons could no longer follow fathers or daughters their mothers. The captives had been orphaned, and their isolation shook them to the very essence of their being, as they realized they were no longer subordinates within communities of mutual—if unequal—obligations but rather excluded from all communities. Observers universally commented on the captives' consternation—"terrible apprehension," "deepest distress," and, most tellingly, "the terror"—as they confronted the stark reality of death in life.[23]

In like fashion, other critical social distinctions lost their meaning, as the complex hierarchies and webs of dependencies that gave form to African societies were swept away. Unlike Europeans who crossed the Atlantic in the seventeenth and eighteenth centuries—even those coerced as indentured servants, debtors, or criminals—there would be almost no possibility of going back, no connections to relatives and friends in their homeland, and no aspirations for a brighter future. Perhaps for that reason, most shipboard rebellions took place within sight of the African coast. Once land fell from view, the captives' appreciation of their separation from everything they knew and loved deepened. The effect was devastating. As one observer noted, "All cried very much at going away from their home and friends, some of them saying they would kill themselves."[24]

The violence and horror of isolation soon yielded to an even more pervasive companion. As the sharks that trailed the slave ships well knew, death was a universal presence aboard the slave ship. Its ubiquity was matched only by its variety, as men and women sickened from disease, dehydration, and the ever-present effects of the rolling yaw of the ship. Many died. The damp, dank, crowded holds spawned endless varieties of deadly afflictions. Children, whose mortality exceeded that of adults, fared particularly poorly. Although mortality rates of those crossing the Atlantic improved over time, on average more than one in seven Africans who boarded a slave ship did not leave alive. The count was generally higher among men than women and higher still among children of both sexes. Slave ships left a trail of dead bodies across the Atlantic.[25]

For those who survived, few escaped some kind of disability or illness. Fevers from a variety of diseases to which Africans had no immunity as well as crippling dysentery—the feared bloody flux— were a fate shared by almost all aboard the ship at one time or another. The numerous pathogens that accompanied tainted water exacerbated the effects of the various contagions. These, in turn, were multiplied by the primitive medical care offered by the ship's physician, who might be a barber by training. The emaciated condition and deranged psyches of those who disembarked on the west side of the Atlantic were a measure of the frightful costs of the transatlantic slave trade.

After weeks at sea, the routine became familiar. Days and nights blurred in the darkened holds so that the captives could no longer distinguish the two. Packed between decks with hardly enough room to move or even sit, the slaves' muscles stiffened and their minds numbed as the unrelenting odor of sweat, urine, and excrement generated by the dozens—sometimes hundreds—of men and women stuffed into small, unventilated compartments overwhelmed all. The stench was unforgettable. "Such a salutation in my nostrils . . . I had never experienced in my life," remembered one survivor. Equally unsettling were the sounds—the groans of the dying, the snap of the lash, the creak of the ship itself. Amid the ordeal came the daily ration of foul water, hardtack, and nondescript stews of yams and palm oil with a small piece of salted meat hardly made more palatable by a shot of rum. The only break from the putrid air and darkness was few moments on deck, where slaves—squinting at the light and savoring a sea breeze—took a silent count of who had survived yet another day. Then came the forced "dance"—the captain's pathetic attempt to keep the slaves' bodies limber—always under the watchful eye of armed men, fearful that the slaves' brief release from their confinement would spark rebellion.[26]

But if the routine grew familiar, it also grew more depressing, and a deep melancholy blanketed the captives as even the most sanguine became resigned to their fate. The sense of hopelessness increased as the ship sailed west. Some captives—distracted by the violence, weakened by malnutrition, sickened by the primitive sanitation, and crazed by lack of water—were determined to destroy themselves. They waited for the right moment and threw themselves into the sea and the waiting sharks. When the crew—determined to protect its valued cargo—blocked the way with nets and other barriers, slaves starved themselves. The crew force-fed some, employing the *speculum oris*, a diabolical device designed to hold the slave's mouth open while some gruel was poured down his or her throat. Others were beaten into submission. But having lost the will to live, many slaves were determined to die, and they did.[27]

Captive women faced special dangers. Although rarely shackled and often housed above deck, enslaved women found themselves prostituted to their captors. Ottobah Cugoano, who endured the Middle Passage in the eighteenth century, recalled that "it was common for the dirty filthy sailors to take the African women and lie upon their bodies." Officers and crew believed sexual access to the enslaved women to be simply one of their prerogatives. Some captains issued strict orders against dalliances with captives; others partook in the raping, taking multiples "wives" from among the captive women. Vulnerable and available, women, in the words of one captain, "[a]fforded us abundance of recreation." Surrounded by sexual predators, with but small means to protect themselves, they became subject to outrageous abuse on their person. Although women—in large measure because of their superior ability to retain water—survived the Middle Passage better than men, the scars were deep.[28]

At no time in the long history of slavery were slaves more at the mercy of their captors than during the Middle Passage. Yet, linked together by a shared determination to survive, black men and women found small ways to control their own destinies. If the enormous differences in power between themselves and their captors left enslaved Africans little room to negotiate, their very desperation forced them to try. Slaves scrutinized the captain and crew, searching for some evidence of empathy in the hard-bitten men who lorded over them. Slavers, despite their monopoly on force, understood even they could not rely on coercion alone. They searched for collaborators who might serve as the captain's eyes and ears below deck in return for some small shard of privilege. Slavers also enlisted "guardians" chosen from the castle slaves who served a similar function in the barracoons. They purchased others precisely for this purpose, generally from among captive peoples with a long history of animosity against those aboard the slave ship. Slaves from the Gold Coast thus were enrolled to control slaves from the Windward Coast and vice versa. Guardians were dressed in the symbols of European superiority—trousers, blouses, and caps—and given the badges of their office—whips, special foods, and other advantages—to set them apart from those chained below. But like the slaves they lorded over, they too were sold upon reaching the Americas.[29]

The tight quarters pushed captives and crews together and afforded the opportunity to know each other as human beings rather than as master and slave. Occasionally captives found patrons among members of the crew—many of whom had been forcibly impressed into slaving—who may have recognized similarities between the slaves' circumstances and their own. With nothing to offer but themselves, sex became a commodity that might be traded. From such exchanges, slaves secured water, food, or protection that could make the difference between life and death. Relations between captives and crew—however conditional and opportunistic—gave enslaved Africans some inkling of the possible divisions between the crew and their officers, and the officers and their captain. When such divisions manifested themselves, the captives seized the moment, turning them to their advantage as they could. In one instance, slaves joined the crew's mutiny; in another, a ship captain armed the enslaved against marauding pirates or privateers. Captives sometimes benefited from their cooperation, but the advantages were small and fleeting. If they were promised freedom, the promises were rarely kept. Perhaps such cooperation was only a measure of the slaves' desperation.[30]

Enslaved men and women turned to their fellow captives for support, but conditions below deck hardly promoted solidarity. Tempers flared in the tight quarters, as the enslaved struggled among themselves for space, water, and food. Captives squabbled endlessly. Shipboard alliances among men and women of many diverse polities who spoke many languages and who frequently belonged to nations with histories of animosity to one another did not come automatically or easily. Often collaboration with slavers as an informer was easier—and more rewarding—than joining together with one's fellows. Slavers depended upon these collaborators as much as they did their own guns. When "the Jellofes [Jolofs, or perhaps Wolofs] rose," according to one report, "the Bambaras sided with the Master."[31]

But as the inevitability of a common future became clear, the captives found reason to ally themselves. Confederations born of shared anguish and pain made impossible situations more bearable, as captives bolstered each other's spirits, shared food, and nursed one another through bouts of nausea, fever, and dysentery. "I have seen them," reported one ship captain, "when their allowance happened to be short, divide the last morsel of meat amongst each other thread by thread."[32] Small acts of kindness provided the basis for resistance, and a new order slowly took shape below deck. Sullen men and women began to forge a new language, from knowing gestures, a few shared words, and a desperate desire for human companionship. New languages—some of which had emerged from shared vocabularies of various African tongues and the common experience of African enslavement—gave birth to pidgins and then creole languages. Men and women with an ear for language took the lead in this new multilingualism, and others soon followed, as the captives shared a need to communicate.[33]

The talk was not without purpose. The enslaved watched their captors carefully, studying their routines and habits so that they ultimately knew more about their captors than their captors knew about them. They awaited their chance, and when it arrived, they struck their enslavers hard. About one in ten slave ships faced some kind of unrest, and no slave trader—whether captains or crew—lived without fear of revolt. Most such uprisings failed, and punishment was swift and unforgiving. But even those who watched the proceeding in silence learned powerful lessons. Shipboard alliances marked the beginnings of new solidarities.[34]

Nothing more fully reflected the nascent solidarities than the sounds emanating from the ship's bottom. "Men sing their Country Songs," reported one slave captain, "and the Boys dance to amuse them." When they were brought up from below deck, enslaved women joined them singing in the call-and-response pattern that would become a staple of African American music by which performance created collectivity by incorporating all voices. While slavers encouraged singing for their own reasons, the most forthright admitted their ignorance of the meaning of the songs. Those who did, however, identified themes of place and movement, of the loss of a homeland and the migration into the unknown. "In their songs," observed abolitionist Thomas Clarkson, "they call upon their lost Relations and Friends, they bid adieu to their Country, they recount the Luxuriance of their native soil, and the happy Days they have spent there." But then they turned to their future and "their separation from friends and country." Movement and place—the first plaintive utterances of the main themes of African American life—were sounded even before the ships sighted American shores.[35] These first sounds of the contrapuntal narrative would be echoed again and again in the centuries that followed.

The first men and women of African descent arrived in mainland North America in the sixteenth century, often accompanying European explorers. For the next century or so, they trickled onto the continent in small numbers, often not directly from Africa but from Europe, the Caribbean islands, or other parts of the Atlantic littoral. Later they would be dubbed "Atlantic Creoles" because of their origins along the ocean that linked Africa, Europe, and the Americas. Many of these newcomers spoke the language of their enslaver and were familiar with the religions, commercial conventions, and systems of jurisprudence of the various nations of the Atlantic. Entering frontier societies in which many Europeans also labored in some form of unfreedom, black men and women employed their knowledge of the Atlantic world to integrate themselves into the European settlements, working alongside Europeans and Native Americans in a variety of mixed agricultural and artisan production. Likewise, they joined churches, participated in exchange economies, and formed families much like other settlers, free and unfree.[36]

With the advent of the plantation in mainland North America, the nature of slavery changed yet again. The beginnings of plantation production—tobacco in the Chesapeake in the late seventeenth century, rice in the low country in the early eighteenth century, sugar and then cotton in the Southern interior in the nineteenth century—increased the level of violence, exploitation, and brutality. Slaves worked harder, propelling their owners to new, previously unimagined heights of wealth and power. Slaveowners expanded their plantations and demanded more and more slaves, as slaves proved to be an extraordinarily valuable asset in themselves. Not only were they workers, but they reproduced themselves, adding to the owners' wealth. Rather than arriving in ones and twos with other cargo from the Atlantic, boatloads of captives—generally drawn from the African interior—crossed the ocean.[37]

Slaves imported directly from Africa—distinguished from Atlantic Creoles—first landed in large numbers in the Chesapeake during the last decades of the seventeenth century. Following the codification of chattel bondage in the 1660s, the new African arrivals slowly replaced European and African indentured servants as the main source of plantation labor. Between 1675 and 1695, some 3,000 enslaved black men and women arrived in Maryland and Virginia, mostly from Africa. During the last five years of the century, Chesapeake tobacco planters purchased more African slaves than they had in the previous twenty. The number of black people in the Chesapeake region, almost all of them derived directly from Africa, expanded rapidly, particularly on the estates of the great tobacco planters. By the beginning of the eighteenth century, Africans composed a majority of the enslaved population.[38]

The number of Africans in Maryland and Virginia increased rapidly during the first third of the eighteenth century. Chesapeake planters purchased nearly 8,000 African slaves between 1700 and 1710, and the proportion of the Chesapeake's black population born in Africa shot ever upward. Another 13,000 landed in the 1720s, and the transformation of Virginia and Maryland into slave societies sped forward with increasing velocity in the 1730s. During that decade, the number of forced African immigrants averaged over 2,000 annually and sometimes rose to twice that number, so that by 1740 enslaved black people—again, most of them Africans—constituted some 40 percent of the population in parts of the Chesapeake. Although black people never challenged the whites' numerical dominance in the region, they achieved majorities in a few localities. For many European settlers, it seemed like the Chesapeake would "some time or other be confirmed by the name of New Guinea."[39]

By midcentury, the majority of enslaved men and women in the Chesapeake had never seen Africa. Slaves in the Chesapeake, in the words of one European observer, proved "very prolifick among themselves." Despite the long hours of work by slaves, by the 1730s births to slave women outnumbered imports, and the black population was increasing naturally at the annual rate of 3 percent, a rate higher than most contemporary European societies. Although transatlantic slavers continued to deliver their cargoes to the great estuary, the proportion of Africans declined as the indigenous African American population increased. The growth of the African American or creole population reduced the slaveowners' need for African imports, and fewer than 10,000 African slaves entered the region in the 1750s. At the start of the Revolution, the first passage was over in the Chesapeake, and the region was no longer an immigrant society. A native-born people began to sink deep roots into the soils of mainland North America.[40]

The slave trade continued, however, in the low country of South Carolina and Georgia. There the forced migration from Africa followed a trajectory similar to that of the Chesapeake, but it started later and continued longer. As a result, more than twice as many Africans—upward of 250,000—entered the low country than the Chesapeake. Sullivan's Island, a tiny quarantine station in Charlestown harbor, became the Ellis Island of black America.[41]

The entry of Africans began slowly in the low country, as it had in the Chesapeake, but it increased far more rapidly. By the third decade of the eighteenth century, slavers were delivering more Africans to South Carolina than to Virginia, and Africans constituted the majority of the low country's population. African arrivals declined sharply following the Stono Rebellion in 1739, as fears of insurrection led planters to restrict the trade. But greed soon overwhelmed fear, and slave importation resumed during the 1740s and exceeded anything previous. During the 1760s, South Carolina and Georgia planters imported 20,000 slaves. Although importation again slackened during the American Revolution, at war's end the pent-up demand for slaves pushed importation to new heights. Lowland slaveowners purchased more than 100,000 Africans between 1787, when South Carolina reopened the African trade, and 1808, when the legal trade to the United States ended. Thereafter, American planters continued to smuggle slaves into the country, although the illegal imports composed but a small fraction of the slave population.[42]

With the slave trade open and the influx of saltwater slaves—that is, newly imported Africans—nearly continuous, black men and women in the lowlands had great difficulty forming families and raising children. But, as in the Chesapeake, the number of men and women slowly came into balance. By the middle of the eighteenth century, the black population of the low country began to reproduce itself and African Americans began to outnumber Africans. But even as the African American population grew, it did so in tandem with newly arrived Africans. At midcentury, when enslaved black people in the Chesapeake had few opportunities to converse with other Africans, Africans and African Americans knew each other well in the low country. They lived in close proximity, worked together, frequently married, and often stood shoulder to shoulder against their owners. Their intimacy spoke directly to the unique development of African and African American life in the low country.

Slavers also deposited their cargoes in other parts of mainland North America—New England, the Middle Colonies, the Floridas, and the lower Mississippi Valley. Everywhere planters preferred so-called men-boys and women-girls, young adults whom they could put to work immediately and who would reproduce the labor force. "Negroes from 15 to 25 years of Age sute this market best," observed Charlestown's largest slave trader. Among the young, planters desired men over women. The male majority was slightly more pronounced in South Carolina, where men outnumbered women more than two to one, constituting two-thirds of the Africans imported between 1720 and 1774. But the disproportion of men elsewhere on the mainland was not far behind. Although the balance of slave imports changed over time, as long as the trade remained open, the black population remained younger and more male than that of the white population.[43]

The movement of African nationalities was not nearly as obvious. With the regularization of commercial relations between European and African merchants, slave captains studied their markets on both sides of the Atlantic. They repeatedly returned to the same ports, delivering the merchandise Africans desired and purchasing the slaves their American customers preferred. In time, European slave traders became specialists, in some measure to meet the demands of their customers on both sides of the Atlantic whose preferences grew increasingly well defined.

Such preferences meant that the national and familial divisions within African society sometimes survived the Middle Passage. These divisions manifested themselves in the supply that reached deep into the interior of Africa. In local interior markets or fairs, where the enslaved had been initially auctioned, slaves desired on the coast brought higher prices and thus made some individuals targets for enslavement. Warlords—sometimes heads of state and sometimes freebooting thugs—thus chose their victims carefully, with a fine understanding of the market. They also had an appreciation for the vulnerability of certain peoples. Eager to maximize their profits in an increasingly competitive market, they too directed particular peoples to particular ports.[44]

While hardly in a position to control their own fate, Africans—many of them potential captives—also influenced who would be shipped across the Atlantic. From the first, would-be captives resisted, banding together, fortifying villages, and even establishing client relationships with the enemies of their enemy to protect themselves. By playing one slave raider against another, Africans reduced their vulnerability, at least to the degree that raiders left them alone. As the full dimensions of the transatlantic slave trade become known, resistance stiffened. As a general rule, slavers avoided those who fought back.[45]

Slaveowners in the Americas likewise influenced the forced migration, particularly in places where the number of imports was large and the trade remained open for long periods. Having seen tens of thousands of slaves, planters became extraordinarily opinionated about the slaves they wanted, based upon their understanding of the physique, skills, culture, and even food preferences of various African peoples. Yet while these opinions were often shallow stereotypes rest-ing upon crude understandings of African nationality—Angolans ran away; Calabars destroyed themselves; Coromantees revolted— such assumptions nonetheless carried great weight. In the low country, buyers emphasized their preference for Gambian people (whom they called Coromantees) above all others. "Gold Coast or Gambia's are best, next to them the Windward Coast are prefer'd to Angola's," observed a South Carolina slave trader in describing the most salable mixture in 1755. "There must not be a Calabar amongst them."[46]

Pressures and preferences on both sides of the Atlantic determined, to a considerable degree, which enslaved Africans went where and when, populating the mainland with unique combinations of African peoples and creating, in some small measure, distinctive regional variations in the Americas. During the late seventeenth and early eighteenth centuries, captives from Senegambia and the Bight of Biafra (present-day Nigeria) constituted about three-quarters of the slaves entering the Chesapeake. Even within the Chesapeake, various polities came to inhabit different regions, with Africans from north of the Gold Coast (present-day Ghana) disembarking in the Potomac Valley and those from south of the Bight of Biafra in Virginia's York and Upper James river basins. The proportion changed with time, as many more slaves arrived from central Africa. But over the course of the eighteenth century, Igbo peoples constituted the majority of African slaves in Virginia and Maryland, so much so that some historians renamed colonial Virginia "Igbo Land."[47]

A different pattern emerged in low-country South Carolina and Georgia, where slaves from central Africa predominated from the beginning of large-scale importation. Although imports from the Bight of Biafra entered the low country in considerable numbers in the 1740s and those from the Windward Coast in the 1760s, Angolan and Kongo peoples maintained their commanding presence among the forced immigrants even as the slave population of the low country grew more diverse. After the Revolution, the pattern changed again, as central Africans once more dominated the new arrivals. If Virginia was Igbo Land, the low country might be likened to a New Angola.[48]

But the patterns of African settlement never created lasting regional identities. The overall thrust of the slave trade threw different people together in ways that undermined the consistent transfer of any unified culture or lineage. Mainland North America became a jumble of African nationalities. Their interaction—not their homogeneity—created new African American cultures.

The reasons were many. Nationality or ethnicity in Africa did not follow neat geographic boundaries. Even before the beginnings of the transatlantic slave trade, the people of Africa had been on the move. Numerous peoples—many of them multilingual, embracing different beliefs, and engaging in a multiplicity of domestic arrangements—shared the physical space that became catchment areas for slave traders. A raid on a particular village necessarily took many different peoples. On the long march to the coast, some slaves died, others escaped, and still others were sold locally. Meanwhile, traders captured or purchased others, and all added to the heterogeneous mixture of peoples lodged in the seaside barracoons.[49]

As traders transferred slaves from shore to ship, the process of mixing people continued and even intensified. Few ships took on a full contingent in a single port and sailed for the Americas. Most moved from place to place, collecting slaves as they could, rarely purchasing more than a handful at a time. During the eighteenth century, slave ships often cruised along the African coast for months before obtaining a full cargo. Trawling for slaves along the Gold Coast in 1712, the *Sarah Bonadventure* collected some one hundred slaves over five months. Its officers boarded their captives in groups of two to eight, hence creating a diversity in the holds. In 1787, the captain of the *Hudibras* purchased 150 men and women along the coast of west Africa; among them were "fourteen different tribes or nations." The Babel of languages emanating from the ship spoke to the diversity of African peoples that slave traders carried to the Americas.[50]

While most slave traders disembarked from specific African ports to land at specific American ones, they might also stop in numerous places along the way. At these stopovers, commitment to the most lucrative deal encouraged traders to sell a few slaves and purchase others. Jumbling their cargos offered an advantage that slave traders appreciated, for they understood that slaves who spoke the same language and shared the same culture might more easily act in concert.[51]

On the American side of the Atlantic, not all slave purchasers knew or cared much about the origins of their slaves. For many, youth, health, and fitness mattered more than origins. "If they are likely young negroes, it's not a farthing matter where they come from," asserted one Virginia slaveowner in 1725, articulating a view common among Chesapeake tobacco planters. Moreover, even if they wished for specific slaves, the most knowledgeable planters could not bend the international market to their will, as the market for slaves was constantly shifting and beyond the control of even the most powerful. Despite their stated preferences, planters often received precisely the slaves they disliked. While lowland planters desired Gambians from the west coast of Africa, they generally received Angolans and Kongos from central Africa.[52]

The barriers to transatlantic cultural continuity were enormous for slaves sent to mainland North America. Unlike free European immigrants, few kinfolk and fellow villagers followed one another—what historians call "chain migrations"—from points of African departure to American destination. Over time, the slave trade rudely mixed peoples of different geographic origins, nationalities, language groups, and religious beliefs. The predominance of men and teenagers and the absence of family groups further militated against cultural cohesion. Within a given plantation population, newly arrived slaves could at best find fragments of their previous lives. Only on rare occasions might they discover a fellow villager or kinsman, as later European immigrants would find a *paisano* or a landsman. No friend or relative greeted the newly arrived Africans, offered a helping hand, or provided insight into the strange and forbidding world of the plantation.[53]

One shared experience joined them together. It would be central to the restoration of a sense of place. No matter what their sex, age, or nationality, Africans who survived the journey to the New World faced the trauma of enslavement.

Once disembarked, new anxieties compensated for whatever relief African peoples gained from the end of the seaboard journey. Indeed the shock of arrival only repeated the trauma of African enslavement. Staggering to their feet, bodies still bent from their weeks below deck, trembling with apprehension, the captives were again fitted with shackles—a painful welcome to their new homeland. They again confronted the auction block and the prospect of being poked and prodded by strange white men speaking strange languages.

New owners tried to sunder whatever connections survived the Middle Passage and assured that those made anew among shipmates did not survive long. At the docksides, newly arrived Africans were often sold singly or in small groups. When great planters and merchants purchased slaves in large lots, they generally resold them in small ones. That the majority of American slaveholders owned only a handful of slaves assured that the heterogeneous assemblages of peoples who crossed the Atlantic together had little opportunity to remain together. As the new arrivals were dispersed across the North American countryside, they individually confronted men determined to demonstrate their mastery. Having selected from among the frightened, tired men and women who crossed the Atlantic, Robert "King" Carter, perhaps the largest slaveholder in eighteenth-century Virginia, began the process of initiating newly arrived Africans to their American captivity. "I nam'd them here & by their names we can always know what sizes they are of & I am sure we repeated them so often to them that every one knew their names & would readily answer to them." Carter then forwarded his slaves to a satellite plantation or quarter, where his overseer repeated the process, taking "care that the negros both men & women I sent . . . always go by the names we gave them." In the months that followed, the drill continued, with Carter again joining in the process of stripping newly arrived Africans of the signature of their identity and reminding them, at every opportunity, of their subordination.[54]

Marched in chains to some isolated, backwoods plantation, forced to labor long hours at unfamiliar tasks, enslaved black men and women began their lives in mainland North America. It was a grim existence, as their debilitating work regime, drafty shelters, and bland rations invited a familiar visitor. Within months of arrival, many of the new immigrants—ridiculed as "outlandish" by their owners— were dead. In all, perhaps as many as one-quarter to one-third would perish in the first year from overwork, exposure, and diseases to which they had but scant resistance. A few survivors took to the woods and others tried to paddle east in a futile effort to retrace their path across the Atlantic. Still others resisted more directly, assaulting overseers with fists, knives, and axes, burning barns, and occasionally organizing rebellions. Their efforts were met with overwhelming force backed, when necessary, by the local constabulary: the lash and pillory for first-time offenders; dismemberment for those who persisted; death for those who were deemed incorrigible. Against this carnival of violence, many simply collapsed and a few destroyed themselves. Most accepted the grim reality, turned inward, did their owners' bidding, and waited for their moment. The repeated shocks— African enslavement, the Middle Passage, and American captivity— took their toll.[55]

Lonely and disoriented, transplanted Africans lived amid a Babel of languages. Linguistic isolation was especially painful and depressing. His shipmates having been sold, Olaudah Equiano found "no person to speak to that I could understand. In this state, I was constantly grieving and pining, and wishing for death rather than any thing else." Thus many new arrivals struggled for comprehension, not so much to understand the orders shouted by their owner or his representatives—who had their own ways of making their wishes known—but to break the silence that isolated them.

Fluency was achieved in many different ways. Some slaves had an ear for language and became considerable linguists as they mastered various languages of the New World. When he ran off from Philadelphia, one Joseph Boudron, who had been born in Guadeloupe, but lived in New York and Charlestown, spoke "good English, French, Spanish and Portuguese." Others participated in the creation of pidgins or trading languages and later so-called creoles or more formal languages that slaves forged from the cacophony of African, European, and Native American tongues. From just this process the Gullah language emerged in low-country South Carolina. But the creation of full-blown creole languages were rare occurrences; in the case of Gullah, it was the product of the unique circumstances of low-country slavery: the black majority, the open slave trade, the planters' withdrawal to the rice ports, and the isolation of plantation life. Elsewhere on the continent, where the special circumstances of the low country did not exist, African slaves bent to their owners' language, adding their own intonation, vocabulary, and sometimes even syntax to English, Dutch, Spanish, or French, thus making the foreign familiar.[56]

Once the barrier of language had been breached, the business of making the foreign familiar proceeded along a broad front, as Africans began to create a society of their own. Transplanted Africans began to master the countryside, form friendships, and piece together new lineages from real and fictive or adoptive kin. "Families" derived from the occasional blood connections that survived the Atlantic crossing, as well as from shipmates and new friends who were elevated to the status of brothers and sisters. Having learned that members of his nation were held captive on a nearby plantation, a newly arrived South Carolina slave set off "to visit a countryman of his." To these countrymen, others were added as newly arrived Africans joined together. Upon occasion, friendships created in the holds of slave ships conquered old enmities. One Neptune—whose body was scarred by "many small Marks or Dots running from both Shoulders down to his Waistband" and whose teeth were "fil'd sharp"—fled George Washington's Dogue Run Quarter with his shipmate Cupid and another whom Washington called their "Countryman." Runaway advertisements from various parts of the mainland confirm that Kongos fled with Wolofs; Calabars with Coromantees.[57]

The thicket of connections grew as the newly arrived explored their environs, traveling at night or—if released from work on Sunday—in a single day to meet with old friends or make new ones. Before long, such ventures became regular outings. Try as they might, slaveholders could not prevent enslaved men and women from "rambling" and gathering, according to one frustrated master, in "considerable Numbers of Negroes together in some Certain places." Those certain places—plantations with a compliant overseer or hidden forest clearings—became the loci of black life. Funerals became especially important occasions, since the burial of the dead was such an elemental human rite that slaveowners rarely forbade them. But there were other occasions, as men and women from various estates exchanged ideas, shared memories, honored the passing of a respected elder, celebrated weddings, or marked a child's coming of age. Whatever the initial impetus, such occasions came to serve every purpose from the sacred to the profane. If the forced immigrants sometimes reinforced their connections to the Old World by reenacting ancient rites and affirming customs, they were also mixing the many cultures of

Africa, allowing them to emerge in new combinations. The sounds of these gatherings—the mixture of languages and music—signaled the arrival of something new.[58]

From their experiences in the New World and memories of the Old, enslaved Africans dispersed along the periphery of mainland North America constructed African America. The new society took a variety of forms depending upon the transplanted Africans' origins, the time of their arrival, their numbers, and the site of their enslavement—as well as the culture of their owners and the character of their localized American experience. Such differences created distinctive immigrant cultures in the North, the Chesapeake region, low-country Carolina and Georgia, and the Mississippi Valley. Indeed, within these broad regions still finer differences could be found, such as between black life in New England and the Middle Colonies, the backcountry and tidewater of the Chesapeake, and urban New Orleans and its hinterland. Even in the smallest hamlet, black people experienced a different slavery than those who resided in the countryside. Not only did slaves in different regions speak different languages, but even when they spoke the same language they conversed with distinctive regional intonations and dialects. Elijah, a Virginia-born fugitive, spoke "with the accent of that country," and William, another runaway, was reported to have the "Virginia accent." Seally, a slave sold from Maryland to South Carolina, stood out in that he too "spoke the Virginia language."[59]

Slowly, often reluctantly but inexorably, Africans and their African American descendants took root in American soil, as they made their own the land that had been forced upon them. But black people did not embrace some generic America. Rather they were connected to a particular county, parish, or even plantation. During the eighteenth century, generations of slaves lived and died in the same neighborhood and sometimes on the same estate, often surrounded by family and friends. Planters often spoke of their slaves as "born and bred" within their own families. In one Maryland county, fully three-quarters of the slaves remained on the same plantation or farm between 1776 and 1783, despite the turmoil of those years.[60]

Such ties did not constitute immobility. Nowhere in mainland North American were black people frozen in one spot. Within particular locales, they were ever on the move, transacting their owners' business and their own. Even in areas of large plantations, the boundaries of the estates proved to be remarkably porous. As carters and boatmen, they traversed the countryside, often stopping to visit relatives, trade goods, or exchange gossip. Slaveholders, while condemning the subversive effects of slave mobility, inadvertently promoted it by renting or loaning slaves to neighbors, a practice that seemed to grow during the eighteenth century. Others sent them on long-distance errands, delivering goods or messages. Sometimes such journeys kept slaves on the road for days or even weeks. Upon their return, these wayfarers carried their knowledge of the terrain back to their plantation, so that few slaves did not know something about the adjoining countryside and many had a good sense of the geography of their region even if they had never left their owner's estate.[61]

In addition, the ground upon which slaves resided was hardly stable. Eighteenth-century Chesapeake planters, eager to find more productive land, steadily transferred their operations from the tidewater to the piedmont and beyond. In the Carolinas, indigo production, which had once flourished in the low country, moved to the upcountry. Northern farmers opened new lands in the Hudson Valley, northern New Jersey, and western Pennsylvania, and settlements in the Mississippi Valley crept northward. But the absence of transportation and communication between the North American colonies assured that Africans rarely moved from the region in which they had disembarked. To a remarkable degree, their children and grandchildren did not stray very far. According to one estimate, only a minority—about one-fifth—were removed by their owners to the new areas of production or sold to some distant place.[62] While white free men and women became famous for pulling up stakes in search of some new opportunity, slaves remained in place.

Over the course of the eighteenth century, black people became increasingly identified with place. A Maryland slave scheduled to be sold across the Potomac "declar'd Several times that he will Loose his life, or had rather Submit to Death then go to Virginia to leave his Wife and Children." Slaveholders recognized their slaves' attachment to the land of their birth. As Thomas Jefferson noted, the threat of deportation to "any other quarter so distant as never more to be heard of among us" was a far more fearsome weapon than the lash. The peril of physical removal became the most powerful weapon in the masters' arsenal, precisely because they appreciated the slaves' deep attachment to place. Slave masters employed the threat of deportation carefully, saving this terrifying weapon for only the most intractable rebels.[63]

The transfer of black men and women often became a subject of intense negotiations between themselves and their owners. Rather than chance the disruption—and incur the anger—which the movement of established residents entailed, slaveholders generally preferred to send newly arrived Africans to the upcountry quarters. For transplanted Africans and their African American children, the dense web of kinship created over the course of more than a century of American captivity endowed place with an ever-deepening meaning. In low-country Carolina, as the slaveholdings expanded—with estates in the rice region averaging more than a hundred slaves—the plantation often became a series of extended families. In the Chesapeake region and the towns and cities along the Atlantic and Gulf coasts, where units were generally smaller, "broad marriages" became common. Husbands and wives, parents and children lived apart, but they were accorded visiting privileges, often on Saturday and Sunday. Visiting also allowed slaves to sustain more distant kin connections, with aunts, uncles, cousins, nieces, and nephews, as well as with brothers and sisters. By the middle of the eighteenth century, enslaved black people lived surrounded by kin connections.[64]

Patterns of flight revealed the increasingly dense network of kinship and friendship. Fugitives looked first to their relatives. The proclivity of runaways to find refuge with kin forced slaveowners to follow their slaves' family connections. When Cyrus and his wife, Dorinda, fled their South Carolina plantation in 1759, their owner recited Cyrus's genealogy in an advertisement he hoped would lead to their capture. Dorinda "has a mother and a sister at the honourable William Bull, esqr's plantation on the Ashley-river a sister at the late Thomas Hohnan's and several relations at doct. William Elliott's, and many others; amongst whom theire is great reason to believe both are harboured." Slaveholders tried to constrain such networks by forbidding slaves to marry off the plantation, but to little effect.[65]

The dense network of kinship and friendship also became the primary link that fastened slaves to place. By the middle of the eighteenth century, slaves—according to the Quaker John Woolman— "married after their own way." While slave masters claimed the mantle of the patriarch, slave parents took control over their own children. They named their sons and daughters—having wrestled that perogative from their owners—after some worthy forebear, generally a father or grandfather, although sometimes also female relations. Slave parents protected their children and, as best they could, guided their future prospects. A system of inheritance allowed parents to give their children "a start." Slave children also began to follow their parents into trades, so that both sons of Cooper Joe on Charles Carroll's great Doohoregan Manor in Maryland were also barrel makers. In a like fashion, house servants secured positions for their children within the house. Children, for their part, succored their elderly parents, so much so that Landon Carter—one of the wealthiest planters in Virginia—could only envy his elderly slave Nassaw for the respect accorded him by his own children. While Carter received only disdain from his own children, Nassaw's progeny honored their father.[66]

As African American slaves regularized protocols of courtship, marriage, and even divorce during the eighteenth century, ties to place deepened. Marriages between slaves became not simply the joining of two people, but the expansion of a lineage. Members of extended kin groups—which often included fictive as well as blood kin—were expected to assist one another and, when possible, advance a common interest. Such assistance took a variety of forms, from a good word with the master to concealing a fugitive. Where slaves were able to pass their possessions from one generation to another, the material linkages stabilized home life and strengthened neighborhood ties. Slave gardens and provision grounds, handicrafts and other various small bits of property affirmed the slaves' ability to participate in the marketplace, negotiate with free people—including their owners—and, upon occasion, collect wages like free men and women. Acquired at great personal cost, such holdings—although infinitesimal compared to their owners' wealth—created responsibilities and entitlements, which in turn rested on both obligations and expectations. Inheritance bolstered the family relations.

The visible marks of identity also reinforced the deepening sense of place. As filed teeth and ritual scarification disappeared from the slave quarter, other forms of bodily adornment emerged. With limited resources but seemingly limitless ingenuity, enslaved black men and women improvised physical repertoires from the masters' and mistresses' discarded finery and small pieces of metal, glass, leather, and animal bone. Clothing and the way it was draped, hats and kerchiefs and the way they were worn, and—especially—hair and the way it was prepared became reflections of self, markers of social standing, and evidence of the emergence of a variety of African American aesthetics. Most of these developed within the Americas, although they drew on African practices or the memory of African practices. By the middle of the eighteenth century, astute observers could categorize distinctive regionally defined styles much as they identified different African American dialects.[67]

Physical appearance, like kin and property, set the boundaries of neighborhoods and transformed localities into places with which black men and women identified. Such boundaries—social as well as physical—defined community membership, both who was of the community as well as who was not. Slaveowners appreciated the unity and divisions of black society. They exploited existing fissures within the slaves' ranks and instigated new ones by bestowing favor on some slaves at the expense of others. But the owners' understanding paled in comparison to that of the slave.

As Africans and African Americans worked together, and intermarried, the web of friendship and kinship bridged the divide that once separated them. In parts of the Americas, much was made of the differences between *bozales* and *criollos*, and some like the Spanish and Portuguese even set both apart from *ladinos*, men and women of foreign birth who had some knowledge of the masters' culture. According to one keen observer of Barbadian society, black men and women born in the Americas "value themselves much on being born in Barbadoes," "despise" newly arrived Africans, and "hold them in the utmost contempt, stiling them 'salt-water Negroes' and 'Guiney Birds.'" Such differences also appeared on the mainland, along with evidence that Africans returned the condescension as immigrant Africans and native-born African Americans struggled among themselves. On one South Carolina rice plantation, African slaves refused to join a collective singing and instead set to "clapping their hands . . . and distorting their frames into the most unnatural figures . . . emiting the most hideous noises in their dancing." Somewhat later, Charles Ball, a Maryland slave, remembered that his African-born grandfather "always expressed great contempt for his fellow slaves, they being . . . a mean and vulgar race, quite beneath his rank, and the dignity of his former station."[68]

The rapid emergence of an African American majority—even in the low country, where the transatlantic slave trade remained open and active—diminished the distinction between those born on the east side from those born on the west side of the Atlantic. Aside from occasional references to saltwater slaves, such terminology as *bozales* and *criollos* had little relevance in mainland North America, for either slaveholders or slaves. It rarely appears in the utterances of either. The African American majority was quick to incorporate new arrivals into its ranks, integrating them into their families and sharing their knowledge of the peculiar circumstances of their American captivity. Indeed, the rarity of Africans made them an object of veneration among some African Americans. "[A]mong the very old slaves whom he had known as a boy," recalled a survivor of slavery in 1936, were Africans "looked up to, respected, and feared as witches, wizzards, and magic-workers. These either brought their 'learnin' with them from Africa or absorbed it from their immediate African forebears."[69] African and African American had become one.

The music emanating from the slave quarter provided yet another signal that black people had made a place for themselves on the west side of the Atlantic. The haunting groans that slave traders heard rising from the holds of Atlantic transports mixed with the musical forms that have since been identified with west Africa: multipart rhythmic structures, repetitive verses, and call-and-response, in which a lead singer and a chorus addressed one another with a variety of melodic embellishments. These performances were accompanied by drumming, hand clapping, and foot stomping, and often played out in a circle that moved with counterclockwise motion. While slaveholders denigrated them as mere "shouts," black people adopted the name. By the middle of the eighteenth century, and probably before, such west African forms had become inextricably linked with European melodies and European instrumentation, most particularly fiddles and horns of various sorts as well as a stringed instrument that was the precursor to the banjo. A 1736 account of an African American festival in New York described slaves dancing to the "hollow Sound of a Drum, made of the Truck of a hollow Tree . . . the grating rattling Noise of Pebles or Shells in a small Basket"—along with the ever-present "bangers."[70]

The slaves' music was only one indicator of the relationship that the rising generation of African Americans had forged with the land and its people. While newly arrived Africans had been assigned the meanest of drudgery, by the end of the eighteenth century some black men and women—almost always African Americans—escaped mind-numbing field labor. They began to move into positions of responsibility as drivers, foremen, and artisans. Taken as a whole, their skill level increased steadily. In many places, one-quarter to one-third of the slave men labored as skilled workers. Others drove wagons, sailed boats, and guided ferries, allowing them to move freely around the countryside. Their familiarity with the roads and trails, rivers and streams confirms how the strange land had become a familiar one.[71]

As African Americans—men and women who had no direct knowledge of Africa and rarely bore marks of ritual scarification or uttered more than a few words of their parents' native tongue—moved into positions of leadership, black society underwent a profound transformation. Unlike their parents and grandparents, these American-born men and women—"artful," "sensible," and "smooth tongued"—spoke the language of their enslavers, knew the countryside, and often practiced skilled crafts. They understood the slaveowners' religion even when they rejected it, and their laws even when the judicial system was arrayed against them. Linguistic fluency, knowledge of the landscape, and skills enabled African Americans to counter the exploitation and secure a measure of control over their lives. Whether achieving the ability to name their own children or the rights to a garden, such small victories fed the desire to be free of slavery. If their parents and grandparents had survived the shock of African enslavement, the Middle Passage, and captivity in mainland America, the new generation of African Americans wanted something more. As they replaced aging African fathers and mothers at the top of black society, African Americans searched for cracks in the edifice of slavery. They were not long in finding them.

Changes in American society in the last third of the eighteenth century sped the search. Some of these changes derived from the transformation of the American economy, as small grain production replaced tobacco in the Chesapeake region, new techniques of tidal cultivation supplanted old inland production of rice in the low country, and trade and commerce expanded in the Atlantic ports, particularly in the Northern colonies. These changes, although initiated by slaveowners for their own benefit, inadvertently gave slaves additional control over their own lives. The decline of tobacco reduced the need for season-long labor in the Chesapeake region. Wheat and other small grains required systematic labor only at planting and harvest, which in turn created a seeming surplus of enslaved workers. Slaveholders sold some slaves but hired others and permitted yet others to hire themselves. The new economy also required many more skilled workers: carpenters and coopers, boatmen and wagoners, warehouse keepers and wharfingers. Such positions gave slaves new freedoms, even if they did not make them free.

An upsurge of evangelical religion created another breach in the slave regime, opening a new arena for black people to assert themselves. Believing all were equal in the eyes of God and eschewing the austere formalism and racial exclusivity of the established denominations, the sectarians welcomed black people as brothers and sisters in Christ. Many slaves rushed to the evangelical standard, attracted by the evangelicals' egalitarian enthusiasm and the message that "Jesus Christ loved them and died for them, as well as for white people." They soon demanded that the equality of the afterworld be extended to the here and now. To that end, some evangelicals readily joined black men and women in their opposition to slavery and, on occasion, in a commitment to full equality. While egalitarians were always in short supply, slaves nonetheless employed their evangelical connections to gain a measure of independence and occasionally freedom.[72]

But the largest crack in the edifice of slavery came with the outbreak of revolutionary warfare, beginning with the American War for Independence and extending through the French and Haitian revolutions. Each created massive divisions within the slaveholders' ranks, as the planter class split, initially into Patriot and Loyalist factions. Serving in the armies of one belligerent or another, slaves played master against master to their own advantage, eventually inducing commanders of both armies to offer freedom in exchange for military service. Likewise, black men and women seized the language of liberty and the ideology of equality that revolutionaries throughout the Atlantic employed to justify their cause, claiming—as did a group of Massachusetts slaves—"with all other men a Natural and Unalinble Right to that Freedom which the Grat Parent of the Unavers hath Bestowed equally on all menkind and which they have Never foruted by any compact or agreement whatever."[73]

As black people and their white allies denounced the hypocrisy of slavery in the land of liberty, demands for freedom echoed across the new republic. Slaves petitioned legislatures, went to court, and opened direct negotiations with their owners for freedom. Under the unrelenting assault, slavery tottered and in some places it fell, propelling large numbers of black men and women—mostly African Americans—to freedom. The Northern colonies began the liquidation of slavery as one state after another, through constitutional mandates, judicial degrees, and legislation, provided for slavery's eventual demise. But even in the North, slavery lingered, its death delayed by gradualist measures that extended the process of emancipation over years and sometimes decades. Elsewhere freedom arrived at an even more glacial pace, as individual slaves negotiated their release from bondage by securing deeds of manumission, purchasing their liberty and that of their loved ones, or taking flight. The birth of freedom was slow, often painfully so.[74]

Still, over time, the change was nothing less than revolutionary. Free people of African descent had gone from being nearly nonexistent in the early eighteenth century to being the fastest-growing segment of the American population. The number of black people enjoying freedom doubled and doubled again in the decades following the American Revolution. By the beginning of the nineteenth century, more than 100,000 black people—or more than one in ten black Americans—enjoyed freedom. The Revolution broke the coincidence between blackness and slavery. No longer could every black person be presumed a slave.[75]

The sudden and spectacular expansion of the free black population initiated a massive restructuring of black life. Newly freed black people took new names, established new residences, reconstructed their families, found jobs, purchased property, and organized churches, schools, and fraternal orders along with a variety of other associations. As former slaves rebuilt their society in freedom, they revealed the complex culture that had taken root both beyond their masters' eyes and under their noses. The names they chose, the residences in which they lived, the families they assembled, the jobs they took, the churches they attended, the associations they organized, and the music they sang all spoke to the new societies that black people created on the west side of the Atlantic.

Since the process of enslavement had begun with the loss of their

African names, the reverse of this revealed how fully people of African descent had been transformed during their two-hundred-year residence in mainland North America and how deeply black people had sunk their roots into American soil. Once free, black men and women quickly sloughed off the names that identified them as slaves, jettisoning the degrading names that associated them with barnyard animals—Buster and Postilion—and the comic classic names—Hercules and Cato—that ridiculed their lowly status. But, as they searched for new names to stamp on their new identity, newly freed black men and women rarely returned to the names their forebears had carried across the Atlantic. Instead, they tied themselves to their American experience, adopting common American names. Some identified themselves with their work (Barber and Cooper), their color (Brown and Black), their aspirations (Prince and Bishop), their place of residence (Boston and York), or their status (Freeman or Liberty).[76] By the beginning of the nineteenth century, a distinctive African American culture became far more visible, with names no longer always concealed behind the facade of bondage.

To be sure, Africa maintained a presence, but in a radically new guise. While newly liberated black men and women eschewed the names of their Angolan, Kru, or Kongo ancestors, they designated the institutions they created after the continent from whence they came. Former slaves worshipped in *African* churches, attended *African* schools, joined together in *African* lodges, and buried their own in *African* cemeteries. Their two-hundred-year sojourn to mainland North America had reconstituted them into a new people, transforming their identity. In making visible the distinctive culture that had been created clandestinely in bondage, the national or ethnic affiliations enslaved peoples carried to America had disappeared entirely, either through a process of slow attenuation or deliberate termination. Ancestral affinities had no visible impact on the choice of marriage partners, child-rearing practices, funeral ceremonies, or religious affiliations. Ijo, Fulbe, Ga, Kikongo, Mandinka, Soninke, or Temne could rarely be heard on the streets of American cities.[77]

The Christian church quickly became the center of free black life. While most slaves remained strangers to Christianity, free black churchmen and women began the process of bending the biblical narrative to their own purposes, identifying themselves with the Israelites of the Old Testament and the story of their deliverance from bondage. Exodus became the central text of African American Christianity, just as the Declaration of Independence had become the central text of African American politics.[78] But as free people of color embraced Christianity, the absence of the influence of African nationality in black religious life was especially striking. Most African churches were the denominational offspring of European American organizations and followed the polity and the liturgy of their denominational root. Rather than drawing upon particular African nationalities, be they Efik or Igbo, denominational affiliations appeared to follow regional differences in the development of American religious life with black Christians adhering to Protestantism in the English colonies and to Catholicism in the colonies of France and Spain. Within this framework, even more specific connections developed, as black people joined Methodists in the areas where this denomination had a strong following, and they joined Baptists in places where that church predominated. Much the same was true of the host of fraternal and benevolent societies that appeared in cities along the Atlantic seaboard. The "Union" in the African Union Society of Newport referred not to the joining together of Angolans and Wolofs and their descendants, but rather to the uneasy alliance between black Anglicans, Baptists, Congregationalists, and Methodists.[79]

The African churches and the allied institutions affirmed the invention of a new nationality. It represented the place black people had made for themselves in the difficult circumstances of slavery and unequal freedom in the United States. The phalanx of African churches, Masonic temples, and benevolent associations that could be found in the cities that stretched along the periphery of North America from Boston to New Orleans revealed how people of African descent gave institutional form to their American experience. These buildings and meeting halls were not simply places to gather but geographical pinpoints that marked transformation of black life during the nearly two centuries of American captivity. The charismatic leaders, cadres of officers, finely crafted qualifications for membership, diverse constituencies, evolving political agendas, and music emanating from these institutions provided evidence that black people had taken root on the west side of the Atlantic.[80]

African institutions also revealed the complexity of African American society, none more so than the church. In 1801, Richard Allen, the leader of Philadelphia's newly established African Methodist Episcopal Church, published a hymnal for his congregation. While it drew on many standard Methodist hymns, it contained many of Allen's own compositions, which he distinguished from the shouts or hollers that had become identified with black people. There would be no "groaning and shouting" in the African church, as such religion was "only a dream."[81]

Allen's disdain for the music of the slave quarter revealed the growing division within black society that emerged as some black people gained their freedom and sought respectability in the eyes of white Americans. Enslaved African Americans continued to elaborate just the music that Allen would suppress. The field shouts, with their forceful delivery and their individualized and improvisatory forms, mixed the sounds of Africa with those of America, sometimes chanting, sometimes moaning, and sometimes screaming the pain of bondage. In 1817, John Watson, a white Philadelphia minister, taking his cues from Allen's *Hymnal*, launched his own assault on the "practice of singing in our places of worship, merry airs . . . most frequently composed and sung by the illiterate Blacks of the society." Most disturbing to Watson, they "visibly affected the religious manners of some Whites." Yet even as white congregants embraced the new music, the infectious "merry air," often accompanied by rhythmic clapping, was becoming the basis of a new African American genre, the spiritual.[82]

Having successfully—if unwillingly—transplanted Africa to the coast of mainland North America, people of African descent now returned to the larger Atlantic world, initiating an African American diaspora that equaled in significance, although not in numbers, the earlier exodus from Africa. Ironically this movement back to the Atlantic demonstrated how deeply attached to mainland North America people of African descent had become, for the migrants took their language, religion, politics, and music with them.

Many of the immigrants, perhaps a majority, left in chains. Following the Revolution, Loyalist slave masters forced thousands of slaves to follow them to the British West Indies, Spanish Louisiana, the Atlantic islands, and Central America. Betraying the promise of freedom, British soldiers sold others to Barbados, Jamaica, and other sugar islands. In the states that had begun the abolition of slavery, slaveholders—determined to squeeze the last bit of profit from their human property—followed suit, selling slaves to distant places before the emancipationist legislation took effect. Post-Revolutionary movement ironically reinvigorated the slave trade.

But other black men and women traveled as a free people. While individual British officers and soldiers violated the promise of freedom, British commanders honored the commitments made by Lord Dunmore in 1775 and General Henry Clinton in 1779 to exchange military services for liberty. At war's end, some 1,200 former slaves and free blacks retreated with British soldiers from St. Augustine, Charleston, and Savannah to New York, where they joined an additional 1,500 black Loyalists—making the total roughly 3,000—in a mass exodus to the maritime provinces of Canada. Other "Loyal Blacks"—as they soon came to call themselves—followed British troops back to England, adding substantially to the black population of Liverpool, Bristol, and especially London. Still others found homes in such disparate places as Prussia and Bohemia. From there they spread—literally—to the ends of the earth. A few landed in the Australian outback.

Many of the migrants—whose numbers may have totaled some 10,000—did not stop at their first destination. After a short sojourn, these Exodusters set out again, moving in yet new directions, cutting their own path around the Atlantic. Mired in dismal poverty and facing rank discrimination in maritime Canada, some of the Loyal Black refugees migrated to London. Confronted by the same discrimination in England, they left for Africa, where the various streams of migrants—most from Nova Scotia and New Brunswick—merged in Sierra Leone, an enclave for former slaves on the west coast of Africa established by British abolitionists.[83]

As they recrossed the Atlantic, African Americans retraced as free men and women the path their ancestors' had first trod as slaves. In so doing, they transported ideas that had taken root in the Americas into the larger Atlantic world. George Liele carried Afro-Christianity to Jamaica, just as the blind Virginia preacher Moses Wilkerson took it to Nova Scotia and then to Sierra Leone. Thomas Peters and Harry Washington conveyed American political ideas along the same path, while others transported the commonplaces of everyday life.[84]

The encounter with the Atlantic in the maritime provinces of Canada, the islands of the Caribbean, England, and Africa revealed in particularly telling ways the self-defining preferences that distinguished African Americans from those whose ancestors had never left Africa. From the perspective of the greater Atlantic, they saw—perhaps for the first time—the full measure of how their American nativity and experience distinguished them from other peoples, especially peoples who shared their ancestry and their color, but not their culture.[85]

Differences manifested themselves in the most mundane aspects of daily life. The language they spoke, the clothes they wore, and the food they ate—or at least that they preferred to eat—set them apart from the peoples among whom they now resided. African Americans bore European American names and spoke English or occasionally Spanish, French, or Dutch, rarely voicing the language that their forebears had carried to mainland North America. Indeed, few spoke the creole tongue that had become much of the Atlantic's lingua franca. Sporting beaver hats, wearing trousers, carrying umbrellas, and demanding wheaten—rather than corned—bread, they proclaimed their American nationality.[86]

In the townships of Nova Scotia, the plantations of Barbados, the streets of London, and the new settlement of Sierra Leone, other touchstones of American identity could be found. Arriving in Nova Scotia and later Sierra Leone, black refugees built houses much like the ones they had left along the Chesapeake and in the Carolinas, often with appointments that bespoke more an American farm or plantation than the African dwellings in which their ancestors had resided. Generally their houses lined a street, rather than taking the form of an African compound or village. Their furnishings would be likewise familiar to other Americans. On the coast of Africa, transplanted black Americans lived, in one estimation, "according to a pattern that owed its characteristics not only to European or even African models but also to the unique experience they shared since their days as slaves in the American colonies."[87]

While some white Americans saw the society that transplanted African Americans carried with them as merely a darker reflection of their own society—one observer declared it "a burlesqued reflection of white society"—African American returnees, however, wanted no simple imitation of white America. They picked and chose what

they borrowed from the larger American culture of which they themselves had been a part, embracing only what they deemed admirable
or useful. The language of liberty proved to be both. Just as their
petitions for freedom in the United States were loaded with assertions
that "the divine spirit of freedom, seems to fire every humane breast"
and with appeals for "equity and justice," so their petitions to British
administrators in Nova Scotia, Sierra Leone, and elsewhere spoke of
natural rights, liberty, and the promise of equality.[88]

From their own experience—as well as the Revolution, in which
they had been full participants—black people placed great emphasis
on matters of rights. The settlers took great offense at any attempt to
limit their liberties, and they were not above stretching them beyond
the bonds that British authorities found acceptable. According to the
governor of Sierra Leone, the settlers "have a great idea that their
freedom gives them equality." While claiming the protection due His
Majesty's subjects, the Loyal Blacks encased themselves in the rhetoric
of American republican liberty.[89]

Like their political sensibility, the settlers' sacred world also derived
from their American experience. As in the United States and Nova
Scotia, the Black Loyalists' most important institution was the African
church and the leading figures were preachers. Indeed, during the
first years of settlement, African Americans like David George and
Thomas Peters, both refugees from South Carolina through Nova
Scotia, were among the dominant figures in Sierra Leone. The settlers not only drew upon the Christian Bible, but also chanted Christian hymns and organized their churches in a manner most Americans
would recognize. African American society in Sierra Leone rested
upon the diverse denominational allegiances of the immigrants, with
the division between Baptists and Methodists being most prominent.
Difference between them grew as each struggled for land and power
in the new settlement, but the solidarity of African Americans soon
asserted itself with the arrival of black people of a different stripe—

Jamaican maroons—who had no tradition of Christian pietism and little interest in attending church. Their presence reminded African Americans—even when they divided among themselves into warring factions—of their common heritage and their shared mission as bearers of civilization. They soon joined together in tutoring native Africans—with no small sense of condescension—in the importance of trousers and frocks, the sin of polygamy, and the sanctity of the Sabbath.[90]

The post-Revolutionary African American diaspora and the transplantation of the African American culture around the Atlantic demonstrated the deep roots black people had established in what had become the United States of America. This sense of place was represented in every aspect of African American life. The region between the Atlantic and the Alleghenies had become home. When white Americans suggested otherwise, they stated forthrightly, "Here we were born."[91] All that, however, would change with the arrival of a new century.

CHAPTER THREE

The Passage to the Interior

By the beginning of the nineteenth century, people of African descent—having survived the trauma of enslavement, the horror of the Atlantic crossing, and the nightmare of American slavery—had rooted themselves on the west side of the Atlantic. Most were American born. Many had American-born parents, grandparents, and even great-grandparents. Black life took a variety of forms—slave and free, rural and urban, and plantation and farm—and it differed from place to place. But, for the most part, African Americans were confined to the long arc along the North American coast reaching from New England to the Mississippi Valley, with the majority crowded into a narrow strip of land between the Atlantic tidewater and the Appalachian Mountains. There, over the course of the seventeenth and eighteenth centuries, distinctive African American cultures had emerged, a confluence of the diverse heritage of Africa, the American experience, and the unique status of peoples of African descent. Following the American Revolution, African Americans incorporated as many as 100,000 newly arrived Africans into their ranks and challenged slavery directly, often employing the new ideology of American nationality. Those who gained their freedom constructed scores of "African" institutions. Some moved back into the larger Atlantic world as missionaries for their own way of life: republicanism, Christianity, and commercial capitalism. But, for the vast majority still locked in bondage, the world of transplanted Africans and their African American descendants underwent a change of cataclysmic proportions, in a transformation that would ultimately propel millions of African Americans across the continent.

For more than half of the nineteenth century, movement defined African American life under slavery. Then, almost as quickly as it began, the movement stopped, leaving black people again rooted in place.

Between the elections of Thomas Jefferson in 1800 and Abraham Lincoln in 1860, more than one million black people—slave and free—were forced from the homes they and their forebears had created in the most difficult of circumstances. This great migration, really a second Middle Passage, dwarfed the transatlantic slave trade that had carried African peoples to mainland North America. Driven by a seemingly insatiable demand for cotton and an expanding market for sugar, the massive migration sent black people across the continent, assigning the vast majority to another half century of captivity and providing immediate freedom for a few who had somehow escaped bondage. Some of the latter fled northward to the free states or Canada; others reentered the Atlantic from where they or their ancestors had come, completing the diasporic circle. But, for the mass of black migrants, movement only tightened the constraints of bondage. Ousted from their seaboard residence, they were forcibly transported into the American interior as part of slavery's expansion, redefining African American life.

Like those who had been forcibly transported across the Atlantic, the lives of men and women ensnared in the second great migration were changed forever. Husbands and wives were separated and children orphaned. As some families were torn apart, others forged new domestic relations, marrying or remarrying, becoming parents and adoptive parents, and creating yet new lineages and networks of kin. Migrants came to speak new languages, practice new skills, worship new gods, and sing new songs, as thousands of men and women abandoned beliefs of their parents and grandparents and embraced new ideas, even if they held fast to some old ones. In the process, tobacco and rice cultivators came to grow cotton and sugar while some craftsmen lost their skills and a few laborers gained new responsibilities and status.

Those left behind did not escape the impact of this second great migration. In portions of the settled seaboard South, the slave population fell especially precipitously, but in no part of the South did black people escape the nightmarish effects of the massive deportation, as the trauma of loss weighed as heavily on those who remained as on those carried off. Just as those who remained in Africa had to rebuild their lives as fully as those who had been shipped across the great ocean, so those left in the seaboard South were changed. Their families also had to be remade, their communities rebuilt, their leaders chosen anew, and—perhaps most importantly—their social order rethought.[1]

The massive deportation took two forms. Hundreds of thousands of slaves marched west with their owners, their owners' kin, or their agents as the shock troops of the massive expansion of cotton and sugar production in the states of the lower South. Seeing opportunities westward, some prominent planters transferred their entire retinue of slaves to new plantation sites. Others, perhaps a bit more cautious, moved with a few chosen hands—generally young men—to begin the creation of new empires of cotton and cane. Once settled, additional slaves followed.

Through the first two decades of the nineteenth century, planters in transit carried most of their slaves with them to the interior. Having brought their own slaves South, some slave masters—wanting to augment their labor force—journeyed back to the seaboard to purchase others. A few shuttled back and forth, buying a few slaves at every turn. But over time, the westward-moving slaveowners surrendered control of slave transit to a new group of merchants whose sole business became the trade in human beings. Although the balance between the two trades was forever changing, it fell heavily in favor of the slave traders. The number of black-belt and delta planters who returned to the seaboard to purchase slaves declined, leaving slave traders in command. During the course of the nineteenth century, traders carried roughly two-thirds of the slaves from the seaboard to the interior.[2]

This second great migration began slowly in the years following the American Revolution when so-called "Georgia men" transported slaves southward in the wake of emancipation in the northern states and widespread manumission in the northern portions of the seaboard South.[3] On the eve of freedom, black men and women saw liberty snatched from their grasp as slaveholders and slave traders conspired to defeat the promise of post-Revolutionary emancipation. In the rush to transform men and women into cash, Georgia men cared little about the distinction between those enslaved for a term and those enslaved for life, or even the distinction between slavery and freedom. Free people of color found themselves swept into the transcontinental dragnet. Kidnapping increased sharply and remained an omnipresent danger to free black men and women. By the beginning of the nineteenth century, the practice had become so pervasive that it gained a name: "blackbirding." Although many states legislated against it, enforcement proved difficult against the insidious combination of greed and stealth.[4]

As planters—aided by the American soldiers and militiamen— ousted native peoples and took possession of some of the richest land on the continent, the Georgia trade outgrew its name. Increasingly, slaves moved more west than south into Alabama and Mississippi and then across the Mississippi river into Louisiana, Arkansas, and Texas. The internal slave trade became the largest enterprise in the South outside of the plantation itself, rivaling the transatlantic trade of centuries past. It too developed its own language: "prime hands," "bucks," "breeding wenches," and "fancy girls." Its routes were regularized and dotted by pens, jails, and yards that provided hostelries for slave traders and warehouses for slaves. Its seasonality—when best to move slaves and when to retain them—became part of the rhythm of Southern life, much like planting and harvest. Its terminals—Alexandria, Baltimore, Richmond, Norfolk, and Washington at one end and Natchez, New Orleans, and Vicksburg at the other—became infamous. There was hardly a Southern town, no matter how inconsequential, without an auction block, prominently located near the courthouse or the busiest tavern. In all, the slave trade, with its hubs and regional centers, its spurs and circuits, reached into every cranny of Southern society. Forced movement had again become an integral part of black life.

In the half century following the close of the transatlantic slave trade, both planters and traders expanded the transcontinental transfer of black men and women. The cascade of humanity flowing from the seaboard South swelled ever larger. During the second decade of the nineteenth century, traders and owners sent out an estimated 120,000 slaves westward and southward, with the states and territories of Georgia, Tennessee, Alabama, and Louisiana being the largest recipients. That number increased substantially and reached a high point during the following decade. It increased yet again during the 1830s, when slave traders and migrating planters ousted almost 300,000 black men, women, and children. Most of the slaves still came from Maryland and Virginia, but South Carolina and Georgia— once destinations—became points of departure for transporting black people to Alabama and Mississippi. During the 1830s, South Carolina and Georgia each forwarded nearly 100,000 slaves, with most being sent to the rich ribbon of alluvial soil that soon denominated the black belt. Others took up residence along the great rivers of the region: the Alabama, Tombigbee, Tennessee, and Mississippi.

The trade slackened as the Panic of 1837 reduced cotton and sugar production and deflated the price of slaves, giving beleaguered black people on the seaboard a measure of relief. But the respite was momentary. Rather than mark the beginning of the end of the internal slave trade, the Panic only allowed the forces that drove the slave trade to gather strength, as leading members of the planter class added to their holdings and consolidated their place atop Southern society.

The assault on enslaved black families and communities resumed in the 1840s as cotton and sugar prices revived and, with them, the demand for slaves. Black people were again on the move. For the next two decades, the traffic in slaves grew steadily. Nearly a quarter of a million slaves left the seaboard for the interior between 1860 and the beginning of the Civil War, with more than half being shipped west of the Mississippi River. Again slaves were drawn from areas that once had imported slaves, as the exporting region gradually drifted southward and westward. At midcentury, Georgia, Tennessee, and even portions of Alabama were sending their slaves west. The process by which importer states became exporters continued almost until the moment of slavery's demise.

The outbreak of the Civil War hardly ended the deportation of black men and women. Slaveholders on the periphery of the South, fearing that their slaves would escape to the advancing Union army, shipped them inland. Thousands of enslaved black men and women were sent to upland farms and plantations, and many more were sold to Texas and other parts of the trans-Mississippi west as the pace of the trade accelerated.[5]

By the time the Confederate defeat ended the second great migration, the geography of black America had been radically restructured; the center of slave life had shifted from the seaboard South to the interior. In 1790, nearly half of all enslaved African Americans resided in Virginia; on the eve of the Civil War that figure had shriveled to 12 percent. While Virginia's slave population increased just barely during the nineteenth century, Maryland's declined. Meanwhile, the slave populations of Alabama, Mississippi, Arkansas, and Texas swelled beyond recognition. The territory of Mississippi—which encompassed lands that would eventually be part of Mississippi, Alabama, and Florida—contained some 3,000 slaves at the beginning of the nineteenth century. In 1860, well over 400,000 slaves lived in Mississippi alone. On the eve of the Civil War, more than half of the slave population resided in the Southern interior.[6]

Along with the massive movement to the interior was a still larger local trade, where enslaved black people were sold within their neighborhoods, counties, or states. This intrastate trade—which may have exceeded the interstate trade—was often just the beginning of the second great migration, as slaves sold locally were later carried west. Even the trade within a locality—a state certainly and perhaps even a county—could have the same disruptive effect as the long-distance transfer; hence, local trades should be considered part of the second Middle Passage.[7]

This great migration, like the first, reflected the needs of sellers in the slave-exporting region and buyers in the slave-importing region, each of whom carefully considered the age, sex, and productive and reproductive capacity of their human property. Although slavery in the settled South remained profitable, many slaveholders found themselves burdened by a surplus of slaves, as the switch from tobacco to cereal cultivation and mixed farming reduced the need for a year-round labor force. Planters and farmers, who increasingly thought of themselves as employers and not masters, found that hired hands—enslaved as well as free—who might be engaged during planting and harvest were more attractive than workers who required yearlong support. In some places, the preference was for hired slaves; in others, for wage labor, both black and white. "Employment and reward for industry and discharge if otherwise," boomed one border-state defender of the wage-labor system. Similar developments in the region's towns, which grew in number and size during the nineteenth century, increased demand for skilled workers—blacksmiths, carpenters, and coopers as well as wagoners and sometimes boatmen—for urban shops and manufactories. As the demand for brute labor declined, so too did the need for young men and women who had muscle and energy but little knowledge of the work at hand. One in three slaves between the ages of ten and twenty residing in the seaboard South at the beginning of the nineteenth century would be gone by 1860.

Economic changes drove the transformation of the region's demography. The switch to cereal and mixed farming and the growth of manufacturing reflected the declining profitability of plantation agriculture in portions of the settled South. Marginal agriculturalists found themselves sliding toward financial ruin and the region edged toward economic stagnation. In such circumstances, slaves were their owners' most valuable and generally most marketable asset. The sale of slaves not only might stave off bankruptcy, but also would enable slaveowners to purchase the seeds, animals, tools, and machines that could revive their own prospects and, in time, the region's economy.[8]

Slaveowners in the settled South also learned the slave trade was a profitable way to rid themselves of unruly and intransigent slave men and women. During the nineteenth century, the threat of sale became the most potent mechanism of slave discipline, as black people, according to one observer of the transfer of slaves from Maryland to Georgia, "dread nothing on earth so much as this." "They regard the south with perfect horror, and to be sent there is considered as the worst punishment that could be inflicted on them." Slave masters found that selling a few slaves "down the river" had a visible effect on order in the quarter. The fear of sale allowed slaveholders to extort promises of faithful service and pledges of future loyalty from their slaves. Not a few used the threat "to put a slave in their pocket"—

meaning to put cash in their pocket in exchange for the slave—as a means of extracting additional drafts of labor. For slaveowners, sale became not only a source of wealth and a way of discipline, but also a means to destabilize the slave community, stripping it of its most effective leaders and intimidating those who remained. Strangely, putting aside the lash for the threat of sale also allowed planters to claim a new standard of humanity.[9]

Although there was a symbiotic relationship between the needs of the slaveowners in the slave-exporting region and those of would-be slaveowners in the importing region, their interests did not always coincide. Fearful that their plantations would become a dumping ground for slave rebels, black-belt planters tried to bar men and women they considered troublemakers. Some of the first laws enacted by the territorial legislatures of Mississippi and Alabama prohibited the entry of slaves with histories of rebelliousness or criminality. Louisiana required imported slaves to be accompanied by certificates attesting to their "good moral character," although the character test was never defined. At other times, various states prohibited the import or the export of slaves for reasons of state policy, humanitarian and commercial. For example, in 1817, Maryland prohibited the export of slaves who had been promised freedom. Alabama, Mississippi, and Louisiana, at one time or another, barred the importation of slaves when the expanding black population appeared to threaten the state's security or the rising price of slaves threatened the economy. But such moments did not last. Often they were the product of some momentary crisis, as in the panic that followed the Nat Turner rebellion in 1831. Generally, when the panic subsided, the laws were quickly repealed, and when they were not, they fell into disuse. Even then demand for slaves always trumped such legislation.[10]

The handful of slave rebels shipped southwest could not disguise the planters' satisfaction, as they received young men and women whose strength hastened the transformation of a wilderness and whose fecundity assured the continued viability of the plantation workforce. From the slaveholders' perspective, the very old and the very young who could not withstand the rigors of the transcontinental journey were just extra baggage. Young adults composed the mass of those shipped west and, over time, their share of the forced migration increased. In 1810, slaves between age fifteen and thirty made up one-quarter of the deportees. By 1830, they equaled nearly 45 percent.[11]

The forced migration distorted the age and sex balance of the black population in both exporting and importing regions. The Southern interior—like Virginia and South Carolina in the eighteenth century—was an extraordinarily youthful place. Men below the age of twenty-five represented nearly 39 percent of Alabama's slaves in 1820, a higher portion than in Virginia, where young men (similarly defined) made up about 35 percent of all slaves. The proportion was doubtless even higher on the largest plantations, for wealthier planters had the resources to purchase the slaves they believed most useful for the difficult work of creating a new plantation. On the estate of the largest planter in the wealthy panhandle area of Florida, a unit of some 213 slaves in 1830—123 males and 86 females—included no women and only one man over age fifty-five. The old heads, experienced men and women whose knowledge might guide the nascent slave community and subvert the planters' project, were missing.[12]

The youth that characterized the population of the Southern interior was balanced out by the elderly men and women who were left behind, much like the effect on the west coast of Africa during the height of the international slave trade. In 1820, slaves over age forty-five comprised some 11 percent of the population of Virginia, while they made up less than 6 percent of the population of Alabama. A comparison between the Alabama county of Greene, where only four slaves in one hundred had reached the age of forty-five, and the tidewater Virginia county of Surry, where slaves of that age were proportionately four times as numerous, exposes the stark differences in the age structure of the slave-importing states of the interior and the slave-exporting states of the seaboard.[13]

The internal slave trade—like its international predecessor—also warped the sexual balance of the black population, at least for a time. As enslaved men trekked west to build the new plantation economy, the settled seaboard South became a disproportionately female society. The female majority within the slave population fit well with the seaboard South's function as the nursery of the workforce for the Southern interior. Although abolitionists (and, subsequently, historians) found charges of the forced breeding of slaves difficult to substantiate, there was no questioning the slaveholders' appreciation for the value of the slaves' producing children.[14] For some seaboard slave-owners, slave children were their most profitable "crop," and they knew it. They encouraged slave women to have children, offered incentives of free time or even cash and threatened barren women with sale. However, the male majority in the Southern interior did not last long, perhaps because of—as with the first Middle Passage—the higher rates of male mortality. Within a generation of the arrival of the first slaves, a sexually balanced population emerged in the cotton South, both assuring the viability of the planters' labor force and reestablishing a self-sustaining black population.[15]

The complementary needs of buyers and sellers—hard-pressed seaboard farmers and ambitious black-belt planters—reshaped black society in other ways as well. Summing up the conventional wisdom, a veteran of the plantation business advised that "it is better to buy none in families, but to select only choice, first rate, young hands from 14 to 25 years of age, (buying no children or aged negroes)." Indeed, in defining the slave family as women and very young children, slave traders showed little interest in the family groups that they demeaned as "mixed lots." Enslaved black men and women came to appreciate the fragility of the marriage bond, and parents came to understand that their teenage children would disappear, never to be seen again. Sales to the interior shattered approximately one slave marriage in five and separated one-third of children under fourteen from one or both of their parents. The preferences of slaveholders both as sellers and buyers destabilized slave families, ensuring that husbands and wives would be separated and children would be taken from parents. Nothing revealed the full extent of the second Middle Passage so much as this.[16]

Beyond sex and age and the peculiar matter of judging a slave's character, black-belt planters had other preferences that shaped black life during the second great migration. Westward-moving planters frequently took their favorites with them. Those who purchased slaves from traders also made choices. Just as some eighteenth-century slave masters prized Igbos over Angolans, Gambians over Calabars, some of their nineteenth-century counterparts desired Virginians over Carolinians or vice versa. Slave traders made much of the places of origin when they advertised their slaves, playing to the prejudices of their customers.[17]

Viewed as a whole, the internal slave trade, like the international one, mixed people from different regions. A close look at the origins of enslaved black men and women carried to middle Florida in the 1830s reveals that a large share of men and women were drawn from Maryland, Virginia, and North Carolina and over 25 percent from South Carolina and Georgia, but also that others were taken from places as disparate as Kentucky and Louisiana. Even those from Virginia, the most important source of Florida's slaves, came from different parts of the state, with about one-third coming from the tidewater region, another third from the piedmont, and with small numbers from Southside and northern Virginia and a handful drawn from the Shenandoah Valley and the surrounding mountains. Mixing slaves at the point of purchase and sale, as well as during their long trek, made it difficult for planters to exercise their preferences.[18]

The resultant jumbling also made it more difficult for black people to find kin and friends among those sold south. The heterogeneity of the internal slave trade left black migrants isolated and alone, so that the black men and women taken from the seaboard South experienced all the horrors of their ancestors' transatlantic journey. Like their forebears, they too had been forcibly separated from everyone and everything they knew and loved. Their westward journey was also traumatic and often deadly. Even before departing, many experienced the harrowing pain and humiliation of having their persons inspected in the most minute and intimate ways. Once the trade was under way, the grim reality of being separated from everyone they knew and loved became manifest. As with the transatlantic slave trade, slaves ensnared in the internal trade would realize—in one chilling moment—the full implications of their captivity.

Having arrived at what would be their new home, only rarely did they see a familiar face. In the new plantations of the southwest, slaves from the Chesapeake and the low country mingled in the new plantations with slaves smuggled from Africa and the West Indies and free blacks kidnapped from the Northern states. While some slaves bragged of their origins—claiming that "Virginia de best" and South Carolinians "eats cottonseed"—such regional chauvinism soon disappeared. Unlike in the eighteenth century, observers failed to dwell upon the peculiar twang in the voice of Virginia slaves or the lilt in the language of those from the low country. But if older distinctions between Virginians and South Carolinians and Africans and African Americans disappeared, new ones emerged, as the new arrivals were not always welcome by the first-comers.[19]

Still, the shared experience of being bought and sold unified black people as perhaps no other. The destination of most seaboard slaves moved steadily westward with the expansion of the cotton kingdom so that the trek from the interior was arduous and, for many, increasingly long. Coffles trudging at the rate of some fifteen to twenty miles a day could make the trip between tidewater Virginia and the Mississippi Valley in about two months under ideal conditions. But conditions were rarely ideal, and muddy roads and swollen rivers forced slaves to detour and could substantially increase the time slaves spent on the road. In fact, few slaves moved without such delays, for travel was rarely direct. Meandering from town to town, much as African captives moved from village to village, and as their seaborne counterparts in the African trade had earlier sailed from port to port, traders here and there sold a few slaves and purchased others. A trader carried Charles Ball, a Maryland slave, southward to Georgia in a coffle that numbered some fifty slaves. Along the way, he periodically stopped, pitched camp, and peddled slaves in the neighborhood, literally moving from door to door. In the evening he would return, Ball reported, with those "whom he had not disposed of." The others remained tethered to camp, anxiously waiting for their turn.[20] Many—perhaps most—transplanted slaves shared Ball's experience of being sold door-to-door. While most slaves faced the auction block and public sales at one time or another, many moved invisibly in the quiet bargaining between trader and would-be owner, out of public view.

Although the logic of commerce urged that these valued commodities be well fed and housed, logic no more prevailed in the second Middle Passage than it did in the first. Eager to pad their profits, traders—in particular the marginal operators—skimped on the care and feeding of their human property. They bedded their slaves with little protection, forcing them to sleep on the dank ground in open fields or some equally uninviting board floor in drafty buildings. They fed the captives on whatever was available and replaced only the most threadbare garments. If men and women fell ill, they could expect only the most rudimentary medical care, if any, for traders were quick to cut their losses. Fearing that a contagion that had taken the lives of several of his slaves would damage his ongoing business, Isaac Franklin, Natchez's leading slave trader, refused to call a physician to treat his ailing slaves. Instead, he let the slaves suffer and die, and then dumped their bodies in a nearby ravine. The infamous captain of the *Zong*, who threw sickly slaves overboard, had nothing on Isaac Franklin. While the mortality rate for the internal slave trade never approached that of the transatlantic transfer, it surpassed that of those who remained in the seaboard states.[21]

Like the traders, slaveowners in transit were also on the make, bartering old hands for new ones or selling men and women to finance yet other new ventures. Slaves sold along the way rarely remained in place for long and were often resold, thus reliving over and over the horrific protocols of the trade. With their bodies greased to hide blemishes and hair painted to disguise age, slaves found themselves repeatedly placed on the auction block to be poked, prodded, priced, and packed off—perhaps to be sold again. Resale came quickly for some. Others lingered just long enough to establish themselves and gain a degree of comfort with their new surroundings, only to be suddenly uprooted again by the death of their new owner, the settlement of an estate, or an owner's whim. A few were held in a state of limbo, while speculators brokered the most profitable deal. For some black men and women, the auction block and the slave pen became a way of life as well as the symbol of their long ordeal. Many of those caught in the trade did not live to tell the tale. Some—grieving for their past and despairing for their future—took their own lives. Yet others fell when they could not maintain the feverish pace of the march.

Over time the regularization of the slave trade reduced some of the hazards of the long march. Slave traders standardized their routes and adopted new technologies. They relied more on flatboats, steamboats, and eventually railroads, improving the circumstances under which slaves were transferred if only to assure the safe delivery of a valuable commodity. By the 1830s, the great slave traders began to transfer slaves by oceangoing vessels, generally from Alexandria, Baltimore, or Norfolk to New Orleans, which emerged as the nation's largest slave market. Moreover, while the large traders rationalized their operations, small-time, undercapitalized itinerants—scrambling through the backcountry districts and crossroad hamlets to make a few dollars—transported a large proportion of the slaves. Their underfunded operations increased the risk to the black men and women sold westward. Without a stable base and with few connections, they traveled a haphazard path, camping where they could and foraging for food as they might. When successful, such operations might propel these speculators into the ranks of the prosperous; they did just the opposite for slaves.[22]

The similarities between the international and the internal trade could not have been lost on anyone caught in the transit to the Deep South. Another similarity between the two is the fact that occasionally black men—like the so-called guardian slaves in the transatlantic voyage—were recruited to oversee other slaves. William Wells Brown, who escaped from slavery and became a leading abolitionist, worked for a slave trader during his captivity in Missouri, much as Denmark Vesey had labored for a slave captain. But the black men and women shipped by sea shared most directly the experiences with their African forebears. While transatlantic traders established factories along the coast of Africa, American slave traders built or rented pens, or "jails," where slaves could be warehoused, inspected, rehabilitated, and auctioned, sometimes to consignment agents who served as middlemen in the expanding transcontinental enterprise. Although slave traders advertised these places as "commodious residences," there was no disguising that they were hellholes. The close quarters and unsanitary conditions bred disease, occasionally of an epidemic nature.[23] The rationalization of the slave trade may have reduced the slaves' mortality rate, but it did nothing to mitigate the trade's essential brutality.

Slaves, especially young women, found themselves subjected to all manner of sexual abuse. Traders prized light-skinned women or "fancy girls" for the high prices they fetched in New Orleans and other cities where they were forced to work as prostitutes. Traders also took advantage of these women, imposing themselves much as had the officers and sailors on the slave ships in an earlier era. Some in fact looked for young women precisely for that purpose and then boasted of their conquests. "[T]he slave pen," wrote one former slave, "is only another name for a brothel." As in the factories on the west coast of Africa, a few traders moved into settled, perhaps even loving, relationships with slave women. Richard Lumpkin, a Richmond slave trader, married one of his slaves and had their two daughters educated in the North. But relationships with black women and affection for their children did not change the dynamics of the slave trade.[24]

There were other similarities between the two Middle Passages. Like the journey across the Atlantic, movement to the interior was also extraordinarily lonely and dispiriting. Capturing the mournful character of one coffle, an observer characterized it as "a procession of men, women, and children resembling that of a funeral." Indeed, with men and women dying or being sold and resold, slaves—step by step—were being severed from their most intimate human attachments. The despondency and despair that accompanied the first great migration became central features of the second as well. Surrendering to desperation, many deportees had difficulties establishing friendships or even maintaining old ones. After a while, some simply resigned themselves to their fate, turned inward, and became reclusive, trying to maintain their humanity in circumstances that denied it. Others exhibited a sort of manic glee—singing and laughing, perhaps a bit too loudly—to compensate for the cruel fate that had befallen them. "Amid all these distressing circumstances," it was with just such a group of "cheerful and apparently happy creatures" that Abraham Lincoln shared a steamboat ride down the Mississippi.

Unlike the slaves who Lincoln reported "danced, sung, cracked jokes, and played various games with cards," others dropped into a deep depression and determined to march no further. Charles Ball, like Olaudah Equiano nearly a century earlier, "longed to die, and escape from the bonds of my tormentors."[25]

But the searing experience also forged strong friendships, as the westward march was also a time for establishing new relationships. Occasionally, some fell in love and married, as did Judy and Nelson Davis, who were thrown together in a coffle moving from Virginia to Mississippi and had the good fortune of ending up on the same plantation. Others who shared the transcontinental trek formed bonds akin to those established by shipmates on the voyage across the Atlantic. Mutual trust became one of the bases of resistance, which began almost simultaneously with the march.[26]

The coffle—like the barracoons on the coast of Africa—was filled with rumor of revolt. While women and children marched unchained, traders—worried about insurrection—shackled the men together during transit and locked them tight when they stopped. But whatever the level of security and surveillance, it never was enough. Waiting for their first opportunity and calculating their chances carefully, a few slaves broke free and turned on their enslavers. Murder and mayhem made this second great migration almost as dangerous for slave traders as it was for slaves. While in-transit insurrections were both rare and rarely successful, the handful of slave traders maimed or killed by their captives was large enough for traders to manacle their captives and guard them carefully. The slaves' occasional triumph—like the revolt aboard the *Creole* in 1841, in which slaves being shipped from Norfolk to New Orleans seized the ship and forced the captain to sail to the Bahamas—put every trader on guard. Far more common than revolt was flight. Slaves found it easier—and far less perilous—to slip into the night than to confront the heavily armed men who lorded over them.[27]

As with their ancestors' forced transit from Africa, slaves had the greatest chance for escape while they were close to home. Knowing the terrain, the fugitives could find refuge in familiar surroundings. Relying upon kin and friends, they secured shelter and support. They also helped themselves by keeping a careful account of their own movement. Charles Ball endeavored through his whole journey, from the time he crossed the Rappahannock River, to make such observations about the country, the roads he traveled, and the towns he passed through as would enable him, at some future period, to find his way back to Maryland.[28]

Yet for even the most determined fugitives under the most favorable circumstances, freedom was a distant prospect. Successful flights were few, whether to the seeming safety of the North and Canada or to the anonymity of a nearby city. Moreover, since many fugitives simply wanted to return home—as did Ball—if only to say a last good-bye or make a final plea for life to remain as it had been, successful flight denied fugitives their primary goal, which was to recover their old lives, as they despaired severing their ties to home. Slave traders appreciated the slaves' dilemma. They waited for runaways to reappear on the old homestead, seized them, and again began the southward journey.[29]

Countering the forces aligned against them, black men and women tried their best to preempt their sale and deportation, which would separate them from their place. When rumors surfaced that their absentee owner might sell them to Texas from their home in Missouri, slaves Susan and Ersey were quick to remind their owner that they had "become much attached to the place (our Husbands being here)," that they had "a great many friends in this place," and that they could not "bear to go to Texas with a parcel of strangers." But few slaves dared to presume that the power of either argument or supplication could counter their owners' avarice. Instead, they headed for the woods. Some took their families into hiding, not only to protect them but also to disrupt their owners' plans. Others, bolder still, confronted their owners directly. A Virginia slave informed his new owner that he might be sold but he would not stay sold. "Lewis says he will not live with me, but will runaway if I attempt to keep him," declared the astounded slaveowner.[30]

If few slaves were so bold, even the most timorous were emboldened by the horrific implications of the sales from the place they called home. Ever so gingerly and with great trepidation, slaves approached their owners. The amalgam of heartfelt supplications and veiled threats—reminders of old loyalties and hints of future insubordination—occasionally had the desired effect. When his owner put him "on the block and sold him off," one Virginia slave remembered that he "cried and cried till master's brother told me to hush crying and he would get him tomorrow." Eschewing such pleas, one slave mother, when threatened with separation from her newborn, "took the baby by its feet . . . And with the baby's head swinging downward, she vowed to smash its brains out before she'd leave it." The master relented. Yet such reprieves were rarely permanent, for an owner's death or financial reverses were forever putting slaves at risk for further trades.[31]

If their appeals were rejected, slaves tried other tacks. Attempting to save his son from being sold south, one slave father mobilized his resources and found a compliant white man to represent him at the public auction. But when the ruse was discovered, the slave trader rejected the deal, denouncing the hapless father for presuming to think he was "white." Despite this frustrating instance, slaves never surrendered easily to the realities of the trade.[32]

Occasionally these last-minute appeals fell in the slaves' favor. In a few places, custom allowed slaves to choose another master if their present owner placed them for sale. Susan and Ersey, for example, did not think there would "be the least difficulty in getting ourselves sold" locally, but they needed permission to find a new owner so they would "not serparate" from their kin. But others were not so confident.

The grim news that they or some loved one would be put on the auc-tion block created a panic as slaves scrambled to find a surrogate master or pleaded for someone to hire them while they accumulated enough to purchase freedom. Maria Perkins's note alerting her hus-band to the fact that their son had been sold captures something of the desperation of a parent about to lose a child. "I want you to tell dr Hamelton and your master if either will buy me. . . . I don't want a trader to get me. . . . I am quite heart sick."[33]

When at last it became clear that nothing could be done to prevent deportation, slaves began preparations for their new life. Those who had accumulated property in household items, furniture, and barn-yard animals distributed them to relatives and friends or sold them to provide a small cushion of cash to carry to their new homes.[34] The transfer of material possessions was but one of the slaves' concerns at this moment of high crisis. Friends and relatives had to be notified so they could say their last good-byes. "[W]ith much regret" as well as hopes that "if we Shall not meet in this world I hope to meet in heaven," Arena Screven wrote his wife that he had been sold from Georgia to New Orleans, using a language so stiff that it could barely "Express the griffin." That done, slave parents looked for someone who might play the role of fictive parent. Laura Clark recalled that her mother turned to a friend, Julie Powell, who was sold in the same parcel as Laura. "Momma said to old Julie, 'Take kier of my baby Chile . . . and if fen I never sees her no mo' raise her for God.'" Through the tears and the ritual exchange of gifts, slaves passed last-minute advice. Mementos that would represent the hopes of a lifetime had to be presented to the deportees.[35]

Indeed few slaves forgot the terrifying moment when they were taken from their loved ones and sold to a distant and yet unknown place. In reminiscences collected years later, the memory of sale had hardly faded. It was "a day I'll never ferget," the elderly Mary Ferguson recalled in 1936, some seventy years after her sale. How could she, when, after her "crying' an' begin'" was dismissed, she was taken from her family. "I never never seed nor heared tell o' my Ma an' Paw, an' bruthers, an' susters from dat day to dis."[36] The shock that so distressed those who experienced the transatlantic passage haunted the victims of the second Middle Passage as well.

Still, black men and women looked for some ways to maintain connections as the places they had made their own were about to be taken away from them. If the transatlantic passage permanently severed the ties with family, friends, and country, the transcontinental passage left the hope, however slim, that those connections could be maintained. Slaves transported by their owners had the greatest possibility of success. Some appended notes on their owners' correspondence with their own families. "I wish to let you know that I think of you often and wish to see you very bad," Rose wrote from a caravan en route to Alabama via her mistress's letter to North Carolina. Rose's mistress-amanuensis confirmed she had "a great many Messages from the Servants," although most were reported as little more than "all give their love to all their friends and their best service to Master and Mistress." Such bland renditions of the slaves' heartfelt sentiments encouraged those few slaves who could write to, as one put it, "tak my pen in hand."[37]

Literate slaves maintained independent correspondence, and their messages had more bite. Phobia and Cash tried to keep in touch with their kin even as they were transported from Georgia to Louisiana. "Pleas tell my daughter Clarisse and Nancy a heap of how a do," they wrote. Then they reminded Clarisse that her "affectionate mother and Father sends a heap of Love to you and your Husband and my Grand Children Phobia. Magi. & Cleo. John. Judy. Sue." Phobia and Cash observed "that what [food] we have got to t[h]row away now it would be enough to furnish your Plantation for one Season." But even the few literate slaves had difficulty maintaining ties half a continent away. Ten years after she arrived in Alabama from Virginia, Lucy finally found a way to communicate with her family. Most relied on bits of fugitive information of doubtful validity carried by planters and their wives returning from visits to the seaboard South.[38]

These connections and the occasional slaves who returned from their new abodes to their old plantations accompanying their owners or on a sanctioned visit provided slaves in the older slave states with some understanding of where they might be sent. To be sure, such fragments passed in whispered rumors were distorted, but they offered a sense of the world to which captives would be transferred. The presence of such knowledge distinguished the internal migration from the transatlantic one, where Africans had almost no knowledge of the Americas.

But for the vast majority of deportees, the stark reality was that the journey from the seaboard South to the interior, like the transatlantic passage, was a one-way trip. There would be no return, even for the briefest of visits, and there would be no correspondence, even of the most abbreviated messages. Indeed, there would be no news of any sort: nothing of a daughter's marriage, a grandchild's birth, a parent's death. This second Middle Passage, like the first, permanently severed its victims from the life they had once known. Slaves literally could not go home. Interviewed in the 1930s, a former Virginia slave, like the millions caught in the transatlantic trade, "had two brothers sold away an' ain't never seen 'em no mo 'til dis day."[39]

But if they could not go home—and the number of migrants who reversed field and returned to their old homes was infinitesimal—the new arrivals remained intensely interested in and often deeply knowledgeable of their old homes. They renewed and refreshed knowledge of the seaboard and kept earlier arrivals alert to the people they had left behind. Small shards of information—news carried by new arrivals, gossip secured from their owners' table—enlisted memories of the world they had lost but never surrendered. Indeed, the very inability of the migrants to return to their former homes fostered their demand to know more.[40]

Arriving at some dense forest or forbidding clearing, having experienced all the nightmares of the second Middle Passage, deportees rehearsed the experience of the first black arrivals to plantation America. In their topography and geography, flora and fauna, the black-belt prairie or the river bottoms of the great valleys looked nothing like the tidewater or piedmont of Virginia and the swamps of low-country South Carolina and Georgia. The new ecology disoriented the migrants, as they searched for the familiar amid the foreign. Rough frontier conditions, debilitating work regimes, and brutal treatment left men and women psychologically spent as well as physically exhausted. The mortality rate of slaves spiked and fertility rates dropped as the first generation of cotton or sugar cultivators—many barely older than children—confronted an often deadly disease environment.[41]

In the face of frontier dangers, black men and women worked at quick pace—often under the lash—to get the first crops into the ground. Mastering a new crop and confronting slaveowners eager to ratchet up the level of exploitation took a toll. There was "no time off of' de change of de seasons and after de crop was laid by. Dey was allus clearin' mo' lan' or sump'n,'" remembered one former slave. Beyond the workplace, the forced migrants faced endless difficulties during those first years. Exhaustion compounded a deep melancholy that cast a pall over black life. The transplanted suffered from dejection that bordered on despondency. "[E]very time we look back and think 'bout home," recalled one Virginian who had been transported to Texas as a young man, "it make us sad." Spartan circumstances— shabby housing, inadequate nutrition, and bad water—pushed some slaves over the edge.[42]

However, within a generation of their arrival in the Southern interior, black people had recovered their balance and began to make the land their own. They mastered the landscape and the skills the new crops demanded. Like the first generation of Africans in mainland North America, they too created a new life built upon their own experiences and memories. This time, however, their memories were not drawn from Africa, from which they were removed by a century or more of American experience, but the Chesapeake, the low country, or occasionally the North, the world of their parents and often grandparents.

The new society in the interior emerged slowly and unevenly, since the internal slave trade remained open and slave traders continued to import slaves from the seaboard. Moreover, even as portions of the interior matured into settled plantation societies, other areas remained open to settlement. Transplanted slaves, many of them but recently arrived from the seaboard, thus were subject to resale, from Alabama to Mississippi, from Mississippi to Arkansas, or from Arkansas to Texas. The death of an owner, the failure of the plantation, or a sudden surge of planter ambition might send slaves to the auction block.

But if the same terror that gripped Africans caught in the transatlantic trade touched African Americans crossing the North American continent, the latter had one advantage. Shared language and common experiences allowed slave deportees from the seaboard to communicate freely. The new generation of forced migrants escaped the linguistic isolation that so weighted upon black men and women in the first Middle Passage. So too had they escaped the shock of seeing white men—faces reddened and hair wild and stringy—for the first time. Such familiarity enabled them to almost immediately begin reconstructing an African American society in their new location.

Like their forebears who had been shipped across the Atlantic, the black men and women ensnared in the internal slave trade also carried much with them on their transcontinental journey. Although many moved with barely more than the clothes on their backs, they too were nonetheless not without ideas that would shape their lives in the Southern interior. The rapid reemergence of the slaves' economy, the reconstruction of the slave family, and the growth of African American Christianity offer hints as to the cultural baggage that enslaved black men and women brought with them and how it was remade in the course of the transcontinental journey.

The slaves' economy—the complex matrix of customs and laws that allowed slaves to engage in independent economic activities, participate in the marketplace, and accumulate small amounts of property—had been disrupted by the forced movement from the seaboard to the interior. But in time, plantation society matured and slaves revived their economy. As on the seaboard, the independent productive activities grew at the intersection of the complementary interests of masters and slaves. Desperate to expand production, some planters paid their slaves—so-called overwork—for laboring on Sundays and evenings, revealing how the distinction between what was the slave's time and what was master's time had gained some legitimacy in the eyes of both slave and slaveholder. The line was blurred still further when slaves liberated some of their owners' possessions and traded them to white nonslaveholders and others for liquor, tobacco, and other niceties. Slaveowners despised such illicit activities, and, at their behest, lawmakers punished such exchanges severely, but owners often inadvertently encouraged such activities. To avoid the expenses of provisioning their slaves, they provided slaves with land for gardens and the time required to work them if slaves would accept the responsibility of feeding and clothing themselves. Slaves discovered markets for their produce among Native Americans, white nonslaveholders, and even their own masters.

Once slaveholders conceded the slaves' ability to work independently and retain a portion of the product of their labor, there was no turning back. Slaves demanded the right to keep barnyard fowl, maintain gardens and provision grounds, and market their produce. Before long, the slaves' economy metamorphosed from a privilege to an entitlement, much as it had been in the seaboard South. In addition to working the traditional gardens and grounds, slaves sold handicrafts, chopped wood for steamboats, and gathered moss and other marketable commodities. They labored into the night and on Sundays—traditionally the slaves' own time—for overwork payments. With produce to sell, they established ties with white nonslaveholders, many of whom were delighted to purchase the slaves' surplus, along with almost anything slaves could purloin from their owners.

The few dollars slaves earned by their own labor—or the "overplus" gained from the overwork—had great significance. This money supplemented the slaves' diet, allowed them to clothe themselves far better than their masters' dole, and permitted them small luxuries to ease the hard realities of frontier enslavement. "Den each fam'ly have some chickens and sell dem and de eggs and maybe go huntin' and sell de hides and git some money," remembered one former Alabama slave. "Den us buy what am Sunday clothes with dat money, sech as hats and pants and shoes and dresses." The benefits black people derived from their own economies tied them to the land—sometimes directly as they took pride in their gardens and grounds, and sometimes indirectly as the benefits they enjoyed became necessities. The trading networks they established with others—slaves and nonslaves alike—familiarized them with their neighbors, creating family ties, communities of interest, and, before long, political alliances. Such work required that available hands do their share. Charles Ball, sold south from Maryland, gained acceptance among the slaves of his new plantation only when he agreed to contribute his overwork "earnings into the family stock."[43]

As Ball's experience suggests, the slave family reemerged slowly. While planters still relied upon the slave trade to reproduce their labor force, they—like their seaboard counterparts—found value in allowing slaves to maintain their own domestic institutions. Slave masters recognized that the birth of slave children added to their wealth, and they followed the practice established on the seaboard of allowing slave men to visit their "broad wives" and of easing the burden on slave women during the last months of pregnancy.

Despite the lack of legal sanction and enormous practical difficulties, the family once again became the center of slave life. As in the seaboard South, the family served as the locus of education, governance, and occupational training. Families established courting patterns, marriage rituals, and child-rearing practices. The family defined the domestic division of labor and shaped the aspirations of young and old. From cradle to grave, the family was more than a source of love and affection. From the slaves' perspective, the most important role they played was not that of field hand or house servant, but of husband or wife, son or daughter—the precise opposite of their owners' calculation.[44]

New families began to take shape as strangers anointed each other as kin. The pain of loss remained, but black people kept the memories of those losses alive. With their fathers and mothers gone, young men and women selected parents from among the few elderly slaves who had been transported west. "Uncles" and "aunts" became revered figures on the pioneer plantations, for they represented a tie to the world that was lost. While elderly slaves, many of whom had been forcibly separated from husbands or wives, were slow to establish new families, perhaps for fear that new unions would again be broken, young men and women married and soon became parents. Joe Kirkpatrick, separated from his wife and daughters, carried to Florida a five-year-old orphan boy named George Jones and raised him as his son. Jones grew up and eventually married, naming his own daughters after the sisters, Lettice and Nellie, he had known only through the memory of his foster father. The second great migration, like the first, dismantled families, but not the idea of family.[45]

Children soon populated the new plantation region. For enslaved men and women the arrival of a child affirmed their survival as a people. The new children also provided transplanted slaves with the opportunity to link the world that they had lost to the world that had been forced upon them. In naming their children for some loved one left behind, slave parents restored the ties that had been forever severed by the second great migration. In so doing, they reconnected themselves and their children with the ancestors they would never know. Some transplanted slaves reached back beyond their parents' generation to grandparents or other ancestors, suggesting how slavery's long history in mainland North America could be collapsed by a single act.[46]

Along those same pathways flowed other knowledge. Rituals for celebrating marriage, coming of age, breaking bread, and giving last rites to honored elders which had been transferred across the Atlantic and were reconstructed along the coast of mainland North America during the seventeenth and eighteenth centuries were passed on to new ground during the nineteenth. Along with the unfulfilled egalitarian promise of the Age of Revolution and the Great Awakenings, these rites survived in the minds of those forcibly deported from their seaboard homes. Such memories became the building blocks for reconstructing new communities in the black belt, Mississippi delta, trans-Mississippi west, and other parts of the land black men and women were making their own.

As the networks expanded, slave society grew increasingly complicated. Kin connections not only joined men and women together in bonds of mutual support but also created new enmities and alliances. From among various networks of kin, work groups, and acquaintances emerged multiple hierarchies. Differences within the slave community required mediation, if only to prevent slaveowners from entering their disputes, a circumstance that slaves much preferred to avoid. Such responsibilities also fell to a new class of leaders, for the enforcement of the norms established by slaves could not be left to the slave masters.[47]

Along with the new structure of leadership grew a host of new institutions, foremost among which was the African Christian church, which had generally been the province of free blacks prior to the beginning of the nineteenth century. The slaves' commitment to Christianity expanded rapidly during the second great migration. By the eve of emancipation, one-quarter to one-third of the slave population and perhaps an even larger share of the free black population identified themselves as Christians. Although antebellum planters—themselves in the thrall of evangelical Christianity—generally supported the conversion of their slaves, Christianity took on a different meaning in the slave quarter than the Big House. While slave masters dwelled upon the Pauline doctrine of slave obedience as their entrée into Christianity, slaves found a different message in the Old Testament. Anointing themselves as the modern counterparts to the Children of Israel, they appropriated the story of Exodus as a parable of their own deliverance from bondage. The appearance of plantation chapels and the growth of a cadre of preachers and deacons, like the reemergence of the slaves' economy and the slave family, tied black people even more firmly to place. The commitment to Christ added to the slaves' sense of proprietorship over the site of their enslavement.[48]

Another survivor of the transcontinental transfer of people of African descent—and one intimately connected to their embrace of Christianity—was the slaves' music. Like the slave family and economy, the music of the quarter was also transformed by the second great migration, giving rise to a sound whose deep religiosity gained it the name "spiritual" when references to it first appeared in print. Although a recognizable descendant of the shouts of earlier years, spirituals had taken a new form, which some white observers characterized as "extravagant and nonsensical chants . . . and hallelujah songs." They still contained much of the same rhythmic structure, antiphony, atonal forms, and various guttural interjections and were accompanied by hand clapping and foot stomping. They were almost always performed in a circular formation with the singer moving in a counterclockwise direction. But increasingly, Christian imagery and Jesus himself became central to the new music.[49]

While the spirituals carried deep religious meaning and articulated multiple messages—joy and sorrow, hope and despair—as befitted a musical form that emerged from a collectivity, they also spoke both directly and in veiled allusions to the primal experience of people uprooted and forced to create place anew. The pain of separation—motherless children, for example—and the hope for a better life to which men and women might "steal away" were among the spiritual's most persistent images. Movement abounded in references to roads and rivers, chariots and ships, and eventually trains. Slaves sang of running, traveling, and "travelin' on." They crossed rivers, forded streams, and flew "all over God's Heab'n," affirming how enslavement and forced migration had become the central experiences of African American life in the first half of the nineteenth century. Even when such movement was wrapped in the imagery of the Old Testament, the journey of the "weary travelers" was as much a part of this world as the next. But the spirituals—in the same biblical language—also emphasized place: sometimes the nostalgia for a place lost, the desire to be "returned" and "carried home"; sometimes that other place, of final rewards. Like the improvisational character of music itself, black life amid the second great migraton was a process of continuous re-creation.[50]

The movement and place that became so much a part of the slaves' music remained a part of the slaves' life. Black men and women continued to be sold and traded, and planters continued to move. Even in areas that were well established, planters—and their slaves— were constantly in motion. In Jasper County, Georgia, which had been settled for more than a generation by midcentury, nearly 60 percent of the slaveholders present in 1850 had gone elsewhere within the ten years that followed. While rates of persistence were generally higher for large slaveholders, even the grandees were constantly on the move. Planter mobility kept the slave community in flux, so that geographic mobility continued to be a feature of African American life. The origins of black men and women who opened accounts in the Little Rock branch of the Freedman's Bank following the Civil War provide a sense of how the second Middle Passage had scattered black people across the Southern landscape: they traced their origins to some seventeen states, 142 different counties, and three foreign countries.[51]

The arrival of freedom amid civil war changed black life dramatically, altering the relationship between movement and place in African American life. The revolution of emancipation destroyed the sovereignty of the master and put in its place the discipline of the market. While former slaves found that Mr. Cash could be as hard a master as Mr. Lash, they appreciated the difference. There would be no more beatings, no more overseers, and no more intrusions into the most intimate relations between husbands and wives and parents and children. They would escape the endless days of forced sunup-to-sundown labor and enjoyed the right to quit for cause or even whim. Freedpeople celebrated these changes, embracing a new order that allowed them to enjoy the produce of their own labor and promised the opportunity to remake their world—perhaps the world—in accordance to the principles they had nourished as slaves.[52]

Even before the shooting stopped, black men and women began the process of transforming themselves into a free people. They took new names, some of which were borrowed from former masters but most of which harked back to a lineage established by parents and grandparents in the Americas or, occasionally, grandparents and great-grandparents in Africa. They reconstructed families, searching out spouses and children who had been sold to distant parts of the South. Churches and schools that had operated clandestinely emerged from behind the veil of secrecy, and dozens of associations were created. The reinvigoration of African American civil society spawned a new politics as new men and women came to the fore and challenged old leaders. Everywhere freedpeople schemed to find new ways to put their knowledge, skill, and muscle to work to earn a living. Freedom commenced the process whereby black people would become, in the words of one black soldier, a "[p]eople capable of self support."[53]

At first, it appeared that the grand hopes initiated by the war and wartime freedom would be crushed as Andrew Johnson's accession to the presidency empowered the old slaveholding class. But in the spring of 1867, the Radicals in Congress gained control over federal policy toward the South and expanded the rights of black people far beyond those defined by the Johnsonian settlement. In quick order, black men became citizens, voters, and—in some places—officeholders. Although the power of black lawmakers was limited by the covert enmity of their white Republican allies as well as the overt hostility of white Democratic enemies, they helped enact legislation providing black people with access to justice, schools, and a variety of social services. The revolution in black life would stall again, and before long, would move backward, as the Northern interest in remaking the South waned and the old regime reasserted itself. But the transformation that accompanied wartime emancipation changed the lives of black Southerners forever.[54]

Among the most momentous of those changes that followed emancipation was the sudden termination of the second Middle Passage. For more than a half century, black people had been forcibly propelled across the continent, separated from their families and friends, and required to remake their lives anew. Freedom called a halt to the massive, forced deportation. After decades on the move, black people could deepen their roots on the land to which they had been exiled. Move-ment—or at least forced movement—was no longer the defining fea-ture of African American life. In 1860, some 90 percent of the black population resided in the slave states. That figure did not change significantly over the course of the next four decades. At the begin-ning of the twentieth century, nine out of ten African Americans still lived in the South and fully three-quarters of these in the Southern countryside.[55] Once again, place emerged as the dominant force shap-ing African American society.

To be sure, black people were not locked in place, as there was plenty of room to roam within the South. Former slaves prized noth-ing more than the right to travel freely, which they believed to be an essential element of their new freedom, and they exercised it at every opportunity. Everywhere, it seemed, black people were on the move, and yet their patterns of movement revealed both the extent and the limit to African American mobility during that period. Having been tethered to an owner's estate, they demonstrated their liberty by vacat-ing their old homesteads, sometimes permanently, as they reassem-bled families and communities that had been shattered by slavery and then further dispersed in the turmoil of the Civil War. Former slaveholders and some federal officials complained loudly about the freedpeople's "wandering propensities" and the seemingly endless comings and goings, which they interpreted as evidence of anarchy in the countryside and confirmation of the chaotic character of black society. They could do little to stop it.[56]

In the years that followed, black Southerners continued to churn, as men and women tested their freedom of movement, challenging efforts of both former masters and federal officers who would deny them an essential attribute of a free people. For many, it was a desire to leave the place where they had been known as slaves or to escape the presence of former owners who never surrendered their sense of proprietorship or simply to appraise the meaning of their freshly proclaimed liberty. For others, it was the hope of better wages or working conditions and the chance for a new start. Even those who remained on the old plantation or hunkered down in their old neighborhood continued to be on the move. No longer needing a master's permission to travel, they ranged freely over the Southern landscape, visiting relatives and friends, tending to their own business, and exploring a world that they had known previously only on someone else's terms.

When white authorities—whether former slaveholders or federal officers—attempted to constrain their mobility, blacks reasserted their freedom of movement, voting with their feet. No element of the Black Codes enacted by planter-controlled legislatures that had been impaneled under President Johnson in the years immediately after the war met with greater resistance from freedpeople than the vagrancy and anti-enticement laws that had been designed to freeze them in place. They protested with equal vehemence the attempts that federal officers, eager to restore cotton production and fearful that former slaves might migrate to the North, had designed to immobilize them.[57]

The search for new opportunities propelled some black men and women to distant places. Like other Americans, black Southerners drifted toward the underdeveloped periphery—both west and south—as some freedpeople and their children migrated to Florida, the Mississippi Delta, and Texas, where new, unbroken land provided possibilities for working the land or higher wages in the mines, sawmills, and timber camps. The proportion of the black population residing in Southern cities also increased, and some black people moved northward, sparking a small spike in the Northern black population.[58]

Occasionally, this steady flow turned spectacular, particularly as the repressive planter-controlled governments took power. In 1877, following the collapse of Reconstruction, several thousand former slaves fled Mississippi for Kansas in a movement they compared to the biblical exodus. These "Exodusters" marked the most spectacular flight from the failure of racial democracy in the South. A decade later, frustration with the failure of Reconstruction sent many black Southerners to the unorganized Western territory, where they established some two dozen black towns. While some gazed west, others looked east, giving new life to the American Colonization Society's design to remove black people to Africa. Henry McNeal Turner, a former Union army chaplain and AME Bishop, promoted yet another exodus to Liberia. But, all totaled, these and other migratory escapes attracted only a tiny fragment of black Southerners. In the forty years following the Civil War, only 2,500 African Americans settled in Africa. The settlements in Kansas, Oklahoma, Liberia, and dozens of other migratory schemes spoke to the desperation of black Southerners, but many could not leave. Most would not.[59]

Thus, even the most mobile black people did not move far. The number of black people leaving the South for other parts of the United States during the late nineteenth century remained small. Less than 3 percent of black people born in the South—a mere 150,000—lived beyond its borders in 1870, and that proportion changed little over the next three decades. Indicative of the stability of the Southern-born black population, a higher proportion of Northern-born black people lived in the South than black Southerners resided in the North. Only a tiny fraction of the black population—less than 350,000 between 1870 and 1900—left the region of their birth, most in the last decade of the nineteenth century. The vast majority of these derived from the upper South, especially Virginia. In short, between the end of the Civil War and the beginning of the twentieth century, the regional distribution of the black population between North and South hardly changed.[60]

Within the South, the vast majority of black Southerners resided in the state of their birth; this was even more evident in the black belt. In portions of the seaboard South, from which the mass of black people had been forcibly extracted, connections to that place were much deeper among those who had remained. Five hundred of the 584 depositors of the Wilmington, North Carolina, branch of the Freedman's Bank had been born in North Carolina, with more than three hundred of them born in the counties adjacent to Wilmington. At the turn of the century, of the some 132,000 Georgia-born black men and women who lived outside of the state of their birth, only 12,000, or roughly 1 percent of all black Georgians, resided in the North. A decade later, almost 90 percent of black Louisianans had been born in the state of their nativity. The proportion was a bit lower in the upper South, where nearly three-quarters of black Kentuckians resided in the state of their birth, but Mississippi matched Louisiana's total. The demographic pattern in other states followed suit.[61]

Black Southerners also remained in the countryside. Although the number of black city dwellers grew rapidly in the years after emancipation, the proportion of black Southerners residing in cities or towns remained small. At the turn of the new century, better than eight of ten African Americans remained in the rural South. In the states of the lower South, the proportion was much higher, reaching nearly 95 percent in Mississippi. Even in states of the upper South, which had more substantial urban centers like Richmond, Louisville, and Nashville, the black population remained disproportionately rural.[62]

Within the rural South, particularly the plantation South, the geography of African American life had taken on a new form following the Civil War as black people abandoned the plantation, which they identified with the subordination of slavery. Rather than reside in the shadow of the Big House, they spread throughout in their old neighborhoods, often dragging their cabins near the fields they worked, an act which reflected the desire to live apart from the white people who once owned them. Before long, they evolved into small villages. These "little communities in the woods," as one observer called them, with their stores, schools, and churches—although generally too small to be mapped—represented the collective interest of free people.[63]

Whatever the social implications for the spatial reformation of rural life, the new arrangement did not change the contours of African American geography. The reconfiguration of the plantation only tied black people more tightly to the countryside. The pronounced attachment of black Southerners to their place surprised white Northerners, who anticipated movement and perhaps feared a northward exodus. "Never was there a people . . . more attached to familiar places than they," reported a Union army officer in February 1862. Three years later, at war's end, when officers of the Freedmen's Bureau began the process of relocating the men and women who had found refuge in federal contraband camps, they discovered that freedpeople were loath to move, even with higher wages and other incentives in the offing. "There seems to be a great reluctance on the part of the majority," wrote General Charles Howard, the brother of Freedmen's Bureau commissioner O. O. Howard, from Virginia in the summer of 1865, "to leave the miserable homes they have established here, and start forth to parts of the country new and strange to them." Howard's observation was repeated many times by so-called labor agents, some of them former slave traders, who found few takers when they offered free transport and the prospect of high wages to freedpeople willing to move to areas of the southwest that were just coming under cultivation.[64]

These same local attachments shaped freedpeople's principal wartime goal of securing an independent proprietorship of the land their forebears had worked as slaves. "We has a right to the land where we are located," a former slave declared at war's end. "Our wives, our children, our husbands has been sold over and over again to purchase the lands we now locates upon. . . . For just that reason, we have a divine right to the land," he repeated for emphasis. In claiming their "divine right," these former slaves were simply restating what Frederick Law Olmsted had earlier called the "fixed point of the negro's system of ethics": that "the result of labour belongs of rights to the labourer." From the freedpeople's perspective, as one Freedmen's Bureau officer noted, "the negro regards the ownership of land as a privilege that ought to be co-existent with his freedom." But it was not simply that their labor had given it worth; their lives had given it meaning. For this reason, black people did not simply want land, but particular lands—the lands they and their parents had worked, the lands their "fathers' bones were laid upon."[65]

A full half century later, the sense of ownership that derived from the generations who occupied the land and whose labor made it productive continued to resonate with former slaves. When an elderly black South Carolinian named Morris discovered his new landlord, Bernard Baruch, was going to evict him, he restated the connections that had created his sense of place there. "I was born on dis place and I ain't agoin' off," Morris lectured one of the great financiers of the twentieth century. "My Mammy and Daddy worked de rice fields. Dey's buried here. De fust ting I remember are dose rice banks. I growed up in dem from dat high. . . . No Mist' Bernie, you ain't agoin' to run old Morris off dis place." Morris stayed.[66]

Such emotive rendering of the importance of place reflected the centrality of family and community in the lives of former slaves. Husbands and wives, parents and children, and all manner of extended kin had found one another in the aftermath of the war, reconstructing families as they—not their former owners—understood them. No longer sold at their owner's whim, forced to beg permission to visit a wife or sweetheart or live in fear of permanent separation, newly freed men and women cemented the once-precarious relations that bound them together as kin. They savored the creation of domestic life under one roof as many enjoyed, for the first time, what free people took for granted: the ability for husbands and wives to sleep in the same bed and for parents to know their children were safely under the same roof. The enormous energy—psychological and physical—of the reconstruction of black life and the memory of the difficulties they had endured to maintain their families during slavery only reinforced their connection to the land upon which they had grown up, courted, married, raised children, buried their parents, and lived within a web of kin and friends.

While the failure of forty acres and a mule as well as other efforts at land reform had crushed the hopes of black people for an economic independence that they believed to be a necessary element of freedom, it did nothing to reduce their ties to the land. Freedpeople, forced to cultivate the same crops in the same way, were determined to avoid any employment that smacked of slavery. They searched for ways to gain a modicum of landed independence, avoiding—as best they could—the direct supervision of a white overseer, gang labor, and other trappings of the old regime that would place them under the immediate control of white men. For many, wage labor was just another form of coercion and subordination, and the contract—touted by Freedmen's Bureau officers as the basis of equality with their masters-turned-employers—was seen as a snare that would once again reduce them to subordination. Although distinguished from slavery by the direct remuneration they would receive for their exertions, many freedpeople believed—in the words of one former slave—that "the contract system would tend to bring them back into a state of slavery again." These desires for independence reinforced new connections to place.

Conceding what they could not resist, black people tried to piece together independent livelihoods, hunting and fishing, truck gardening, and selling items crafted by their own hands. It was a chancy business, especially as planter-controlled legislatures closed the open range to hunters, required licenses to fish and oyster, and enacted taxes that could only be paid in cash. Few black men and women—particularly those with large families—could secure a competency in this manner. In time, most turned to the work they knew and returned to the fields, reinforcing the ties to the places they knew best.

In the years following the war, a host of arrangements—many of them ad hoc—emerged that allowed freedpeople to secure control over their own lives. The character of these arrangements differed from place to place, depending on the nature of the crop, the quality of the land, and the demands of the planters and merchants who controlled the land. In some places, freedpeople worked by the task, setting their own pace. Elsewhere former slaves exchanged three days of their labor for the right to work independently the other three. Still other freedpeople organized themselves into squads or clubs for purposes to negotiate the terms of their labor.[67]

To escape the shadow of slavery, especially in the cotton South, various systems of tenancy emerged. Black farmers with capital of their own entered into straightforward rental agreements or simple tenancy, gaining access to land for a period of time, supplying their own working stock, feed, tools, seed, and fertilizer. They worked on their own and kept the proceeds of their labor. Those who had similar agricultural accoutrements but lacked the cash to rent land—or could not find planters or merchants who would rent to them directly—negotiated varieties of share tenancies. Under such agreements, they shared with the landowner the proceeds of the sale of their crop according to some agreed-upon formula.

Most black men and women had no resources besides their own labor and that of their family. For them, sharecropping—whereby the landowner supplied land as well as the draft animals, tools, seed, fertilizer, and even at times food and clothing—became the arrangement of necessity. Often landowners held a lien again the crop, which entitled them to the first rights for the return the crops produced. If anything remained, the sharecropper received that, but such surplus rarely amounted to much, thus creating a new cycle that trapped its victims in debt.

Sharecropping also took a variety of forms, differing from place to place, from crop to crop, and from time to time, depending on what precisely the farmer and the landowner supplied. The sharecropper's portion rested upon the size of his family and whether his wife and children worked, as well as his own abilities. In addition, sharecroppers could negotiate rights to take firewood from the forest, fish in the streams, run stock in the woods, or keep a substantial garden. At times, they were subject to rules that regulated everything from their deportment to the number of visitors they might entertain. The mixture of prerogatives and restrictions played out in limitless combinations, so that nearly each sharecropping agreement was unique. Whatever the peculiarities of the particular arrangements, they all operated to tie black people to particular places.[68]

Even when these arrangements were highly restrictive, black men and women saw some benefit in them, at least at first. They allowed impoverished, newly freed slaves to live apart from those who owned the land they worked, permitting them to control their own family life, and—to a degree—their own labor. Antebellum laws and customs had defined sharecropping as a partnership. By law, freedpeople also had a hand in determining what would be grown and how it would be grown. Under such arrangements, sharecropping was a sharp break with the slave economy, in which the slave master fixed the division of labor and determined when and how slaves worked and what they produced.

But if sharecropping allowed black people to avoid the reimposition of the old economic dependency, it was far from the landed independence they had hoped to achieve. Over time, sharecropping—and to a lesser degree share tenancy, and sometimes even simply tenancy—devolved into a system by which landowners directly extracted labor. As the rights of sharecroppers and tenants atrophied, control of the processes of production fell more and more to those who owned the land. The various forms of tenancy and sharecropping that once offered black people opportunities to control their lives became new mechanisms of exploitation.[69]

The transformation of tenancy and sharecropping took place at an uneven pace during the last decades of the nineteenth century, but everywhere they came to resemble wage labor. Landlords determined what tenants and sharecroppers planted, as well as sometimes when and how they planted it. As they took control over the work regimen, they also shifted their costs to tenants and sharecroppers by requiring them to purchase seed, fertilizer, mules, farm implements, and other equipment from their storehouse, as landlords transformed themselves into merchants or storekeepers. Tenants and sharecroppers often found themselves paid in scrip that was redeemable only at that very same store, where the prices for food, clothing, and other necessities were inflated far above those available elsewhere. Adding to the injury, planters charged interest on unpaid balances, often at usurious rates.

Although they resembled wage laborers in many ways, sharecroppers rarely received their remuneration weekly or even monthly. Instead, they were paid at the end of the crop year, a system that allowed planters to deduct the expenses that annually accrued to the sharecropper's account. When the year-end "settling up" arrived, black tenants and sharecroppers generally found they had little to show for their efforts. Many were deeply in debt. Often settling one year's debt with the proceeds of the next, they were entrapped in a cycle of dependence. Those who had a positive return often discovered that they stood in a long line of creditors, as planters and merchants also had many debts, some of which stretched to Northern factors and bankers. These moneyed men enjoyed the advantage of a superior lien— that is, a legal guarantee that gave them rights to proceeds of the sale of the crop. They would be paid before the tenants or sharecroppers. In some states, the entire standing crop fell to the landlord until the tenant's obligations were fulfilled. Tenants, in the words of the Georgia Supreme Court, had "only a right to go on the land to plant, work, and gather the crops."[70] Tenants who attempted to sell any portion of the standing crops could be fined or jailed. While the law spoke in color-blind terms of landlords and tenants, the weight of the new restrictions fell upon black workers.

As the obligations of black tenants and sharecroppers grew, and their rights shrank, many were forced out of the cash economy into a system of long-term mortgages and short-term barter in which their debts accumulated on the landlord's books. Unable to repay, they had no choice but to agree to work yet another year, often at the same terms, for the same landlord, on the same land. If they dared to break the arrangement, workers might be prosecuted under so-called false-pretences laws, which criminalized the breaking of a contract. Black workers saw their right to quit, the fundamental tenet of the free labor system, compromised again and again.

If, by some mixture of extraordinary effort and good fortune, black tenants or croppers turned a profit, planters and merchants were not above cheating them directly. Successful black tenants frequently found themselves stripped of the fruits of their labor. The blatant unfairness of the system broke many men and women. Conceding the realities of planter power, they simply stopped trying.[71]

The deterioration of the political rights of black people made escape from economic subordination ever more difficult. In the heady years of Radical Reconstruction, black farmers and laborers might challenge their landlord's year-end calculations, hoping that an agent of the Freedmen's Bureau or a locally elected sheriff or judge—who might well be a former slave—would lend a sympathetic ear. If the case went to court, they might find black jurors equally supportive. But the collapse of Reconstruction, the dissolution of the Freedmen's Bureau, and the Supreme Court's nullification of the Civil Rights Act left black workers almost defenseless before their enemies. Landlords and planters, seizing their advantage, enacted a host of legal subterfuges to disfranchise black men. Literacy tests, poll taxes, and grand-father clauses—backed by the omnipresent threat of violence—forced black people out of the South's polity. Sympathetic Freedmen's Bureau agents, sheriffs, and judges could no longer be found, and the testimony of black plaintiffs in court—if allowed—carried little weight before juries from which black men had been excluded. Tenants or sharecroppers who dared to challenge the planter's or merchant's bookkeeping—even the grossest frauds—found themselves with no authority to which they might appeal with a reasonable hope of success. Since many of the questionable calculations were based upon oral agreements or agreements written in a form inaccessible to barely literate or illiterate black tenants and sharecroppers, disagreements came down to who said what. In such circumstances, challenging the word of a white landlord could be nothing short of a death sentence.

Paralleling and complementing the loss of political rights was the imposition of legislation designed to immobilize black workers, geographically as well as occupationally. Many of these new laws echoed the Black Codes enacted during Johnsonian Reconstruction. Vagrancy laws—which, when not literally racially specific, were enforced in racially specific ways—required black workers to be employed by a certain date, usually in early January, when they had to contract for the year. Those who failed to do so could be arrested, jailed, and—if unable to pay their fines—hired out. From there they could be rented back to the same planter—or someone just like him—whom they had tried to escape. Convict labor accounted for an increasingly large portion of the Southern labor force and loomed equally large in the experience of African American workers. At the end of the nineteenth century, according to one estimate, convict leasing ensnared more than one-third of black agricultural workers in Alabama, Georgia, and Mississippi at one time or another.[72]

As the imposition of the legal apparatus of white supremacy nailed

African Americans to the base of the social order, constraints on their mobility grew. Rather than loosen the ties of black people to the land, the postwar settlement laced them tighter. Between 1880 and 1910, the number of black sharecroppers increased from 429,000 to 673,000. By the end of the nineteenth century, some 75 percent of black Southerners worked in such relations. For some, the chains of debt came to resemble the chains of slavery, as landowners and merchants assumed a sense of proprietorship over their workers—who they sometimes deemed "their people"—which was much akin to masters' sense of proprietorship over their slaves. In the early twentieth century, when black people would at last begin moving north, would-be migrants discovered their path blocked by their landlords, often backed by the force of law. If my tenant "goes away," declared one landlord, "I just go and get him."[73]

Even those who escaped the cycle of debt, ironically, also found themselves tied to the land. Hard work, shrewd bargaining, and perhaps a measure of luck permitted some black agriculturalists to remain free agents. These ambitious men negotiated year after year for some new and better tenure arrangement—more productive land, a larger share of the crop, or a lower interest rate—which would enable them to move from the ranks of sharecroppers to that of share tenants or perhaps even renters, with hopes of eventually becoming landowners. But ascending the agricultural ladder also constrained their physical mobility. The key to negotiating a better tenure arrangement rested upon having a reputation as a hard worker who asked few questions, made few demands, and at year's end produced a bumper crop. According to one observer of Southern agricultural relations, "Being acceptable here is no empty phrase. It means that he and his family are industrious and his credit is good. It means that he is considered safe by local white people—he knows 'his place' and stays in it."[74]

Even the most obsequious black farmers rarely gained the much-sought prize, but those who secured it did so within the tight confines of neighborhoods where reputations—formed in direct face-to-face relations over decades and sometimes over generations—had been established. Of all commodities, reputations were the least portable. If tenancy and sharecropping kept black farmers on the move looking for better terms, it also assured that they would not move far. Most did not leave their county of residence, and many remained in the same locale. For most black people, the vectors of movement were neither long nor linear but lateral: short movements as black sharecroppers searched out a better deal. Rather the constant motion was a kind of march in place, a churning that changed everything and nothing.[75]

Landed black agriculturalists, whose numbers increased in the late nineteenth century, escaped the snare of sharecropping and tenancy—certainly more so than day laborers. The growth in the number of black landowners added to the stability to black life. In Alabama in 1870, less than one black farmer in one hundred owned the land he worked. The number of propertied black agriculturalists increased steadily in the years that followed, so that almost one in seven owned land. Similar developments could be found throughout the plantation South, so that almost one-fifth of black farmers owned land by the end of the first decade of the twentieth century. Often this land—edging on swamps and the sandy hills—was of such poor quality that it could not provide the independent livelihood black Southerners desired. It did, however, provide a home and a good deal more than symbolic security. Land purchased at the enormous cost of the labor of entire families had special meaning. Black landowners were reluctant to leave the land that it took a generation or more to accumulate.[76]

Many black Southerners found—with no little irony—that their ties to the land had rooted them in the land. Ultimately, their strongest connections to place were not chains of debt or even threats of physical violence but bonds of familiarity and, for many, affection. The growing constraints on black life at century's end persuaded them not to flee but to hunker down. As whites limited the economic opportunities of black people, disfranchised black men, and denied black men and women access to a formal education, black people turned more and more to their own world. Exclusion and segregation quickened the development of a universe of separate churches, schools, associations, and sometimes whole towns. There seemed little choice, as the majority of white people—Northern as well as Southern—embraced white supremacy, with white jurists announcing the doctrine of separate but equal and white intellectuals elaborating theories of racial superiority. While black people bridled at the imputations of inferiority that accompanied exclusion from the larger public sphere and protested the constraints it placed upon them, they took pride in their distinctive institutions. Black churches, schools, fraternal orders, and benevolent and political associations provided a buffer from the dismal poverty and shelter from the increasingly vicious racial depredations and savage racial violence. Black towns demonstrated that black people could govern themselves, a point affirmed by black churches, schools, and associations as well. The advantages of avoiding commerce with white Southerners and their gratuitous insults encouraged black Southerners to keep to themselves. Increasingly, black life turned inward and black men and women established a place where they could act with authority, intelligence, and independence, where the presumption of black incompetence had no weight, where their successes could be rewarded, and—perhaps most importantly—where the authority of black people was recognized.

The strategy bore both success and yet greater trials. As the number of black landowners increased, so also did other measures of success. One such measure was the expansion of black literacy, which grew from under 20 percent to over 60 percent during the last half of the nineteenth century. Yet success aroused fear and spurred the anger of white Southerners. Violence against black people grew, as measured by the increase in the grisly crime of lynching. Often white Southerners aimed their anger precisely at those who had succeeded in contradicting the stereotypes of African American incompetence. Such hideous violence pushed black men and women increasingly into their own world.[77]

No part of this separate universe was more important than the church. Usually a small, whitewashed building of modest dimensions located at some well-traveled crossroads and often presided over by an itinerant whose responsibilities extended to several congregations, the church remained—as it had been in slave times—the center of rural black life. Its minister's message rarely veered from a close reading of the gospel and, in his official pronouncements, almost always steered away from anything that could be deemed offensive to the white planters and merchants whose shadows loomed over the lives of his congregants. The weekly sermons presented a stern but loving God who would balance the scales of justice and offered hope not only for the next world but also for the here and now: as He had promised, faith had delivered His people from slavery and it would deliver them from the current injustices. Meanwhile, the weekly gatherings became the occasion for the believers—and not a few skeptics—to nourish their stomachs as well as their souls, bind themselves together as a community, recognize their frailties, gather their courage, and affirm their worth. The torrent of emotions renewed the faith of people who had little else but faith, reassuring them that they were God's children and that He had not forsaken them.[78]

As reflected in their most important institution, the dangers that everywhere surrounded black Southerners nurtured a deeply conservative bent in postemancipation black life. With the possibilities of falling outweighing those of rising, black men and women became increasingly defensive as they protected what little they had. To counter the endless intrusion of white people in their lives, they painstakingly preserved those aspects of their past that they had created at great cost during slavery and its immediate aftermath. Family, church, and community rooted them in the South. Within this realm, nothing revealed a greater sense of attachment to place than the music that emerged in the broad swath of the postwar plantation South that stretched from upcountry Georgia to Texas.

While the roots of gospel, ragtime, and jazz could be found in this musical renaissance, none more fully captured the black experience in the postbellum countryside than the blues. In its plaintive moans, wails, and cries along with its assertions of suffering and hardship, the blues evoked the pain of the continued constraints on black life. Although it often focused on the travail of individual men and women, in its larger dimensions it was a musical response to white supremacy. Like black churches, schools, and towns, the blues also represented an inward turn—a separate world in which whites could not enter. The blues employed traditional American instrumentation—the piano, guitar, and harmonica, along with washboards, spoons, and jugs—and it drew upon long-established African American rhythmic and tonal patterns. At times, it echoed the field shouts and spirituals. And like them, the blues exhibited extraordinary flexibility and range, calling for—indeed demanding—creativity. Although in time the three-line couplet followed by a one-line refrain—the AAB pattern—became the standard blues form, blues men and women prized improvisation and spontaneity, so that no two performances—even by the same singer—were alike.[79]

Blues singers would eventually gain national and even international reputations and would play for presidents and royalty in grand concert halls, but the blues had its origins in crossroad juke joints, front porches, back rooms, and prison cells where impoverished itinerants—generally men—sang a familiar story to other equally impoverished men and women. They sang of a people betrayed and beaten. Many of these betrayals were personal—cheating men and unfaithful women—but the weight of white domination was ever present. Crooked sheriffs jailed honest men and women, greedy planters cheated hardworking croppers, and rampaging mobs showed no mercy.[80] "They arrest me for murder, and I ain't never harm a man," sang blueman Furry Lewis.[81]

> *They arrest me for murder, I ain't never harmed a man*
> *Women hollered murder and I ain't raised my hand. . . .*

But whatever injustice stalked the South, blues men and women refused to concede their place. The South remained home, their home, as much a source of solace as a place of violence. So blues men sang of in "Clarksdale Moan."

> *Clarksdale's in the South, and lays heavy on my mind*
> *I can have a good time there, if I ain't got but one lousy dime*

John Hurt struck a similar note in "Mississippi Road Trip" (1928).

> *Avalon my home town, always on my mind*
> *Pretty mamas in Avalon want me there all the time*

Later, when black people evacuated the plantation, they made it clear the South itself would forever be theirs, as in Bill Broonzy's lines:

> *I'm going to Jackson, Greenwood is where I belong*
> *Anywhere in Mississippi is my native home*

As the new music suggested, black people—having survived the second great migration—had regained their footing in the late-nineteenth-century South. Rootedness, once again, had become the primary characteristic of black life, as most black Southerners remained in the state and often in the same county and sometimes in the same neighborhood of their birth.[82] The musical, religious, familial, and communal ties grew more distinctive with time. By the beginning of the twentieth century, their peculiar character became a matter of common repute among visitors to the region. When a young W. E. B. DuBois, a black Yankee wrapped in Harvard doctorate and brimming with Germanic ideas respecting national and racial character, traveled south, he saw a world radically different from his native New England. Rural black Southerners—almost all of them farmers, working under one form of tenure or another—had created a universe different from anything he had known. Rooted in the land they worked, black people still had a special relationship to place. They were no longer separated by walls of status but by rules requiring physical separation in every aspect of life, from the hospitals where they were born (if indeed they could enter such places) to the cemeteries in which they were buried. Between birth and death, black people were educated in separate schools, prayed in separate churches, drank from separate water fountains, and used separate "necessaries." The rigid segregation—the desire to keep black people in their place—in fact did much to create a sense of place.

That sense of place was reinforced by the absence of other possibilities. If black people looked to the North or the West, they saw little chance to find employment or enjoy a richer social life. Those who ventured outside the region found few clues that the North was a promised land. Indeed, revanchist racism reversed the expansion of civil rights that had followed the Civil War. State and municipal civil rights legislation that had passed in the North during Reconstruction fell into disuse. Black Northerners found their role in Northern politics shrinking, as black elected officials disappeared and the number of patronage appointments shrank. Their place in the Northern economy followed the same downward course, as black professionals lost their constituencies and black shopkeepers their clientele. At the end of the nineteenth century, black Southerners had greater access to skilled work than did black workers in the North, where employers denied them employment in the manufacturing sector and were forcing them out of craftwork. Those who ignored these daunting obstacles often faced the implacable opposition of Northern black leaders who denounced Southern migrants as "a floating, shiftless and depraved element."[83] If black Southerners faced desperate times, they saw precious little reason to decamp to the North.

By the beginning of the twentieth century, DuBois's depiction of black Southerners as rural, agricultural peasants played out in infinite variations in literature, politics, and music. Visitors, contemporary social scientists, and later historians expanded on DuBois's theme, reiterating that "the sight and sounds of the working of the South had changed but little, as if time had passed over the landscape. Generations of blacks inherited the same routines, the same provisions, the same houses, and same obligations, the same compensation."[84]

Yet what once stood still was about to move. In 1895, sensing the quakes that would again remake African American life, Booker T. Washington urged black people to "cast down [their] bucket" and remain in their ancestral home. Others added their own plea. Robert Abbott, a yet-unknown journalist, affirmed Washington's call, declaring that "it is best ninety and nine percent of our people to remain in the southland."[85] They were, however, too late. Black life was about to change again. Abbott, as editor of the *Chicago Defender*, would become a ferocious advocate of Northern immigration. Blues men and women, who once sang about their native South, would soon add new themes to their repertoire. Songs of place would soon be replaced by songs of movement.[86]

I'm goin' to Detroit, get myself a good job,
Tired of stayin' 'round here with the starvation mob.

CHAPTER FOUR

The Passage to the North

At the beginning of the twentieth century, the epicenter of black life remained firmly located in the farms and plantations of the Deep South. The Northern black population—particularly in the cities— had received an influx of migrants in the last two decades of the nineteenth century, but although the proportional increase was large, the real increase remained small. Black Northerners totaled less than 10 percent of the nation's nine million African Americans. A substantial number of black Southerners resided in the old seaboard states, the hilly interior, and the cities that ringed the South. However, the vast majority—some seven million black Americans—still lived in the rural South. Most of these could be found in the so-called black belt, a band of rich alluvial land that stretched from upcountry South Carolina across Georgia, Alabama, and Mississippi to the Mississippi River, and then ran north and south along the banks of the great river. Having celebrated the freedom that accompanied wartime emancipation and the enfranchisement of Radical Reconstruction, black Southerners had seen their revolution run backward. During the last decades of the nineteenth century, rights were lost, freedoms shriveled, and opportunities dwindled. Ex-Confederates and their sympathizers—styling themselves "Redeemers"—regained their place atop Southern society, stripping black people of the suffrage and locking them in a position of economic dependency and social inferiority. While slavery was not reimposed, new forms of political domination and labor extraction emerged. For many black people, the weight of debt and the omnipresent threat of violence made escape all but impossible.

Even at this desperate moment, black men and women were not without resources. Knit together by kin and community, black Southerners looked inward, drawing strength from their rooted communities. If legal ownership eluded most black Southerners, they had nonetheless made the land their own, so much so that the black belt originally named for the color of the soil had become identified with the color of the people who worked it. To many outsider observers, and to a generation of scholars, these black Southerners seemed a peasantry, tied to the land and governed by the timeless verities of soil and season that had endured since slave time. Their language, families, religion, music, and much else drew strength from the connections with the land. The sense of permanence was tangible.

Then, amid seemingly endless commentaries on the immutability of African American life in the rural South, everything changed. Within a bit more than a half century—between 1915 and 1970—the black belt was depopulated as black tenants, sharecroppers, and laborers fled their old homes. By 1970, a near majority of black Americans resided in the North and the West, almost entirely in cities. Less than one black person in five remained on a Southern farm or plantation. The South had gone north and movement ousted place as the central feature of African American life. Yet again, black people began the reconstruction of their society.

By midcentury, and sometimes before, the outline of the new society had taken hold. Black life no longer spoke with a rural drawl but to the quick beat of an urban tongue. Northern cities had become the dynamic center of African American society, generating wealth, creating leaders, and producing a way of life whose many manifestations were reflected in its music, to name just one important form of cultural expression. The spirituals morphed into gospel. The blues of the Delta developed an urban analog, and a new musical form with the unlikely name of jazz became a signature of African American culture.[1]

The interplay of movement and place, which had taken African peoples across the Atlantic and then had taken African American peoples across the breadth of the American South, was repeated yet again. While the movement was different—voluntary rather than forced—and the place was different—urban rather than rural—the contrapuntal narrative of earlier centuries was easily recognizable.

Contemporaries called the massive exodus of black people from the South the "Great Migration"; in fact, it was only the beginning of a third passage.[2] It began with World War I and concluded in the decades following the end of World War II, and sent millions from the South to the North and from the countryside to the city. If greatness is measured by size, the Great Migration was great indeed. Between America's entry into the European war and the stock market crash in 1929, black men and women left the South at an average rate of 500 per day, or more than 15,000 per month. The evacuation of the black belt was particularly striking. In 1910, more than 300,000 black people resided in the Alabama black belt. Ten years later, their numbers had declined to 255,000 and would continue to fall in the years that followed. By the end of the third decade of the twentieth century, when a massive economic depression slowed the movement north, a half million black people had abandoned the region of their birth. By 1930, more than 1.3 million resided outside the South, nearly triple the number at the turn of the century.[3]

The flow of black migrants that began with the Great Migration slowed in the 1930s. Three of four black Americans stayed in the South, with most remaining in the countryside, and many commentators believed the northward movement had run its course. In fact the third passage had only begun to gain momentum. The impact of the third great migration had only begun to be felt.

With the onset of World War II and the return of prosperity, black Southerners moved northward in ever-greater numbers, so that the midcentury migrations overwhelmed the earlier flight. The Great Migration would pale in comparison to the massive exodus that accompanied World War II and the postwar period. In 1940, still less than one-quarter of black Americans resided outside the South; that proportion would double by 1970, as the northward rush emptied portions of the rural South. The 1.5 million black migrants who departed the region during the 1940s more than equaled the sum total of those who had left the South during the previous three decades, and the migration continued in the decades that followed. Black men and women also headed west as well as north, as California particularly became a magnet for migrants from Arkansas, Louisiana, and Texas. The wave of immigrants did not stop with the return of peace. Instead, gathering speed with time, it continued unabated for another two decades. The three million black men and women who exited the South between 1940 and 1960 almost doubled the number who left between 1910 and 1930.[4]

During the 1960s and 1970s, the exodus of black Southerners again slowed, and in the 1980s it reversed field. The number of black Northerners moving south increased from 100,000 between 1965 and 1970 to more than 300,000 between 1970 and 1975. The number increased sharply thereafter, as black people—for the first time in the twentieth century—were returning to the South in greater numbers than they were leaving. The growth of the black population residing in the North and West continued to slow, and the number of northward migrants declined for the rest of the century.[5]

All totaled, between 1900 and 1970, some six million black men and women fled the Southern states.[6] The proportion of black

Americans residing in the South slipped from 93 percent in 1900 to 68 percent in 1950 and would fall again to 53 by 1970. In that year, about one-third of Southern-born black people resided in the North and some 70 percent of black Northerners had their origins in the Southern states.[7]

The South had gone north. By the mid-twentieth century, the South had become the old country, much as Africa had become for black peoples transported across the Atlantic in the seventeenth and eighteenth centuries and Virginia and South Carolina had become for those shipped across the continent in the nineteenth.

This third passage not only transferred black people from south to north but also made urbanites out of country folk. While black Southerners moved to nearly every corner of the North, most settled in cities. The black population of Chicago grew from 44,000 in 1910 to 234,000 in 1930. Thirty years later it stood at nearly half a million. Black Detroit enjoyed an even more explosive growth, with the number of black residents increasing from about 6,000 in 1910 to 120,000 twenty years later. In 1950, it stood at over 300,000. A similar pattern could be found in Boston, New York, Philadelphia, Pittsburgh, and a host of smaller cities from Hartford to Oakland. By 1960, almost three-quarters of the nation's black population resided in cities, a proportion that was topped in the North, where fully 90 percent of black people lived in cities and generally in the largest ones. Seven metropoles (New York–Newark, Philadelphia–Camden, Chicago–Gary, Detroit–Cleveland, St. Louis, Los Angeles–Long Beach, and San Francisco–Oakland) housed two-thirds of the blacks residing outside the South. In 1900, the proportion of the American population living in cities was about half as great for black people as for white ones. At midcentury, the nation's most rural people had become its most urban. Nearly all black Northerners (96 percent) and some 90 percent of black Westerners resided in cities. No group of Americans was more identified with urban life.[8]

Northern cities also became blacker in progressions that were more geometric than arithmetic. Nearly everywhere, the influx of black immigrants far surpassed the growth of the white population, as restrictive legislation and war choked off European immigration and the lure of the suburbs drew white natives. While only 2 percent of Chicago's population was black in 1910, black people totaled 6 percent in 1930, 14 percent in 1950, and 33 percent in 1970. Hardly more than 1 percent of Detroit's population was black in 1910, but black Detroiters equaled some 8 percent in 1930 and over 16 percent twenty years later than that. At midcentury, black people comprised one-third or more of numerous Northern cities, and the black population was more urbanized than the white one. The plantation was becoming a distant memory for black Americans. The earthy connections to the land had all but disappeared. A peasantry became a proletariat.[9]

This third great migration dwarfed all previous migrations of black people. It carried more than ten times the number transferred from Africa to mainland North America in the transatlantic slave trade and six times the number of those shipped from the seaboard South to the interior by continental slavers. Such a vast movement necessarily had many sources, which shifted over the course of the twentieth century and differed from place to place, as the velocity and vectors of the migration changed.[10]

The original impetus, however, could be found at the end of the nineteenth century, when a small beetle invaded Texas and devastated the state's cotton crop. As the boll weevil moved eastward to an even greater feast, the South's cotton economy collapsed in the face of the massive infestation. Some planters turned to other crops. These were generally less labor intensive than cotton, and black workers found themselves ousted from their old homes. Meanwhile, the boll weevil continued on its way. When it retreated, disasters—natural and man made—pressed upon black agriculturalists, adding to the omnipresent burden of poverty and exploitation engineered by white planters to maintain a labor force that was readily available and cheap, if not always as compliant as they would like.

The outbreak of war in Europe eliminated a most important market for Southern cotton and depressed prices. Even when the market revived, the boll weevil continued to make its presence felt. With no cotton to harvest and little hope that the next year's crop would be better, black tenants and sharecroppers took to the road. Trying to stay one step ahead of the dreaded beetle, they moved from areas of infestation to those where the pest had yet to arrive. There they worked at a feverish pace, increasing cotton production in hopes of escaping debts accumulated as a result of previous crop failures. But these harvests, swollen by the workers' extraordinary exertions, only drove prices down and further impoverished black workers.

The entry of the United States into World War I offered opportunities to desperate men and women to remake their lives on new ground. The war created a severe labor shortage in the industrial North. European immigrants—the men and women who had stoked American industrial expansion for almost a century—could no longer cross the war-time Atlantic. Military conscription subtracted yet other white workingmen from the labor force and exacerbated the labor shortage. Taken together, the decline of European immigration and the escalation of the draft made room for black men in Northern factories, dry docks, and railroad yards, allowing them to enter manufactories from which they had previously been barred.

The federal officials and Northern industrialists, eager to assure a ready supply of labor, added to the northward pull. The Department of Labor established the Division of Negro Economics and corporations sent representatives into the South to recruit black workers. Labor agents—some of them deeply idealistic in promoting black life outside the South and others crudely opportunistic in exploiting the migrant's insecurity—urged black Southerners to seize the moment. So too did some black leaders, most famously Robert Abbott, the militant editor of the *Chicago Defender*. Seeing the possibilities of racial advancement—along with a larger readership for his journal—Abbott wielded the biblical imagery of an Egyptian-style exodus and a promised land to promote the advantages of black life in the North. While the deterioration of the cotton economy pushed black Southerners to migrate, offers of free transportation, guarantees of regular employment, and assurances of "a better world" pulled black Southerners north.[11]

Still black men and women were reluctant to sever ties of kinship and fellowship generations in the making. What had been established at great cost would not be surrendered easily. Black Southerners also remained deeply skeptical that the white North was fundamentally different than the white South and doubted they would be allowed to compete as equals for employment in the urban marketplace. They worried about tales of the cold, forbidding Northern climate and equally icy religion. A fear born of the belief that they would lose what little they had deterred many black Southerners from leaving the devil they knew for one they could only imagine. Movement from the rural South would proceed with great care.

But no love of tradition or ingrained peasant conservatism tied black people to the land. The movement from the South had its origins in movement within the South. As the cotton crop, which had once drawn them to the black belt as slaves and held them there as a freed people, at last loosened its grip, black men and women had already begun leaving the land and crowding into Southern hamlets and villages. At first they arrived as sojourners or birds of passage, eager to earn some cash during the slack season in order to maintain their place in the countryside. Before long, the occasional sojourns became seasonal, and then the seasonal sojourns became regular events. At last, the country folk broke with their rural roots. In the first two decades of the twentieth century, the proportion of Alabama's black population residing in cities doubled, so that by 1920 one black person in five lived in urban Alabama. A similar exodus from the countryside could be found throughout the cotton South. Until the 1930s, more black people resided in Southern than in Northern cities and much of the south-to-north movement would be a city-to-city migration.[12]

Southern towns, timber camps, and mine villages offered black people little in the way of prosperity. Black men and women found themselves barred from skilled work and—except in a few places, like Birmingham's steel mills—from most industrial work. Instead, black workers found themselves consigned to a broad category denominated "casual labor," which provided neither a living wage nor regular employment. Employers mobilized these irregular arrivals from the countryside—many of them single men, unskilled and without resources—to drive down wages, even for longtime white residents and skilled workers. Black men labored long hours under brutal conditions with scant remuneration. Married men generally avoided such work; those entering were chary about importing their families, and often lived in boarding houses or sex-segregated barracks. For black workers, the towns and camps became lonely places. To reunite with wives and children and to make ends meet, they returned to the countryside seasonally to plant and harvest. But the steady shrinkage of cotton acreage and the low wages paid to seasonal agricultural labor doomed this strategy. The shuttle between town and countryside, industrial or quasi-industrial employment in camps and mines and work in the fields frayed the commitment of black people to their ancestral homes.

While men and women with families left the countryside only reluctantly, young men and women saw a different vision of the town and country. The "town," observed sociologist E. Franklin Frazier, offered "freedom from the restraints imposed by rural churches. In dance halls, [they] could give free rein to their repressed impulses without incurring the censure of the elders for 'their sinful conduct' . . . [H]aving caught a glimpse of the world beyond . . . these men and women were lured to a world beyond the small towns where they might enjoy even greater freedom and more exciting adventures." In the words of another observer, "Negroes were churning about in the South, seeking a vent." What they learned in the towns and villages, coal mines, sawmills, and timber camps informed them of yet other possibilities.[13]

The young black men and women who were already on the move within the South were among the first to leave the region altogether. Tired of the constraints of life in the South, they saw the possibilities of higher wages and better prospects for themselves and their children in the North. Writing in 1919, an investigator for the Department of Labor declared flatly, "the mere fact of a Negro's having moved out of his former home is no evidence that he had moved to a Northern city. It was the town Negroes who left the region." Having spent time in some crossroad village and relocated to a regional center, and then perhaps moving on to Atlanta, Mobile, New Orleans, or Richmond, the men and women who reached the North could hardly be considered peasantry, and the solidarity and community of the peasant village had long since dissolved—if it ever existed—in the urban South. They had learned much from their stay in the urban South. "I had some boys working in Birmingham," remembered one Alabama farmer who had migrated north, "so I went there first. Everything looked pretty good so I decided to bring the old lady to Birmingham, which I did. We got along pretty good there, but I heard about work up here, so me and my sons came up here, and after we got all settled, sent back for my wife and daughter."[14]

As the trickle of black migrants became a flood, plantation owners and merchants sniffed "a plan to relieve the South out of its well-behaved, able-bodied labor," and so they retaliated. Reviving old regulations designed to immobilize black workers—anti-enticement laws, controls on labor agents, and even legislation against hitchhiking—

Southern planters tried to prevent black workers from leaving. But the old barriers against movement no longer held. Attempts at intimidating sharecroppers, sequestering copies of the *Chicago Defender*, and stopping trains only convinced would-be migrants that the rumors of better times in the North must be true. Finding their paths blocked by sheriffs and hooded vigilantes, migrants fled under the cover of darkness, finally having the last laugh on the agents of their oppression. Planters and merchants continued to speak of "their Negroes," but black people dismissed the possessive.[15]

The fabric of Southern society continued to unravel in the 1930s as the system of cultivation that relied upon tenants and sharecroppers—shaken during the first three decades of the twentieth century—collapsed entirely. Attempts by an increasingly activist state to save the old regime only hastened its decline, leaving black country folk in an ever more precarious position. In subsidizing acreage reduction, crop diversification, and mechanization, various federal New Deal programs further reduced the need for agricultural labor. The great planters enlarged and consolidated their holdings, pushing sharecroppers and tenants from the land and creating massive underemployment and unemployment for black wageworkers. Their actions amounted to a Southern enclosure movement funded by the federal government. While landowners themselves—no more than one-quarter of black agriculturalists in the cotton belt—might be able to subsist along with their families, black tenants and sharecroppers had no work and no livelihood. Planters and furnishing merchants who once schemed to tie black people to the land now only wanted them gone. The number of black sharecroppers fell from about 400,000 in 1930 to fewer than 300,000 in 1940 and to fewer than 200,000 a decade later, as the agricultural ladder of laborer, cropper, tenant, and landowner that had been created following the Civil War collapsed.[16]

Black Southerners fared no better in the cities of the region. Racial solidarity led Southern employers, almost always white, to award scarce jobs to white men, even if it meant letting a black employee go. "Niggers, back to the Cotton fields, city jobs are for white folks," the slogan of the fascist Atlanta Black Shirts, suggests the pressure that would send black urbanities to the North.[17]

The outbreak of a second war in Europe and then in Asia, and the American entry into those conflicts, greatly accelerated the northward and cityward movement, as velocity of the out-migration increased manyfold. The expansion of industrial production and the removal of millions of men to fight in the European and Pacific theaters again created opportunities for Southern-born black workers, just as the transformation in Southern agriculture was forcing black people off the land as workers and owners. By the 1950s, the cotton economy had been remade: tractors roamed the fields where sharecroppers had once followed mules and herbicides did the work of an army of hoe hands. Before long, mechanical cotton pickers swept the fields clean. As the pace of mechanization quickened, Southern agriculture turned from a labor-intensive to a capital-intensive enterprise. The demand for agricultural workers shrank, and black people quit the land in growing numbers. Those who did not leave voluntarily often faced eviction. By the mid-twentieth century, only 73,000 sharecroppers remained in the South. Black landowners fared no better. Thousands of black men and women exited the old plantations, some by choice but others under duress.[18]

Behind the hammer blows of economic change stood the region's seemingly immutable commitment to white supremacy. Represented most horrifically by the broken, mutilated bodies that swayed from a lynch noose, the protocols of white supremacy were embedded in the most commonplace acts of everyday life. From the ritual tip of the hat to Mr. Charlie to the scramble to yield the sidewalk before Miss Anne, black men and women faced lifelong humiliation, political impotence, and impoverishment. Denied the rights of manhood and womanhood, they were "boys" and "girls" until they were old enough to become "uncles" and "aunts." Denied the rights of citizenship, they were barred from participation in the decisions that shaped their lives. During the first decades of the twentieth century, Southern legislators extended the Jim Crow system, adding the force of law to practice, officially sanctioning the segregation of parks, schools, libraries, hotels, theaters, restaurants, restrooms, and drinking fountains. Hardly a public doorway in the South did not bear a sign indicating WHITE or COLORED. Challenges to the supremacist regime—even of the trivial sort—could unleash furious rampages enacted by hooded thugs who generally took their cues from men and women who claimed impeccable respectability. Everywhere black Southerners found themselves forced to play out the galling rituals of subordination. "Ain't make nothing, don't speck nothing no more till I die," one black-belt farmer told sociologist Charles Johnson in 1930, summing up the despair endemic to Southern black life.[19]

The heavy hand of racial subordination fell hardest on those who dared to contravene the logic of white supremacy. Challenging racial stereotypes provoked the ire of Klansmen and whitecappers. "Whenever the colored man prospered too fast in this country under the old rulins," lamented one sharecropper, "they worked every figure to cut you down, cut your britches off you." The northward migration drew precisely from those determined to wear their trousers at full length. For such black men and women, the South offered few prospects for advancement, either in educational opportunities or access to political power.[20] The possibilities of life in the North never appeared as good as when they were compared to the constraints of Southern life. As violence against blacks increased—lynching, a grisly indicator of white terror, peaked in the early twentieth century—so too was the willingness of black men and women to risk everything in the North. Behind the pushes and pulls of economic opportunity were men and women who wanted to stand tall and, at last, enjoy the full fruits of republican citizenship promised in the revolutions of July 4, 1776 and January 1, 1863.

As opportunities in the North presented themselves, black men and women seized the moment to flee the omnipresent racism. "I want to get my family out of this cursed south land down here a negro man is not as good as a white man's dog," declared one black Mississippian. The dreary landscape of limited opportunities seemed even more disheartening to the veterans of the great war against Fascism. Flush with Rooseveltian rhetoric of democratic pluralism—as well as the frustrations of fighting in a segregated army—they had no desire to once again don the familiar straightjacket of white supremacy. The wish to escape the suffocating racial restrictions sent many more black Southerners northward. In the years following World War II, military service offered a passport from the white supremacist regime, and many took it. In 1970, over 40 percent of Southern-born veterans resided outside of the South.[21]

Still, black migrants faced a chancy future. Opportunities for employment in the North ebbed and flowed much like the agricultural crisis in the South. The relationship between these two vectors—the pushes and the pulls—was unstable, always changing over time. Sometimes they complemented one another, enlarging and speeding the migratory flow; sometimes they conflicted, slowing or even reversing the movement of black men and women. Even when they worked in tandem, the pushes and pulls never functioned evenly, making some regions the sites of intense migratory activity and leaving others almost untouched. For example, the return of peace following World War I and the resumption of European immigration weakened the northward pull and in some places reversed it. The postwar depression had much the same effect. When Pittsburgh's economy collapsed following World War I, some 40 percent of the region's black population deserted the city. But by the middle third of the twentieth century, black Southerners had established a foothold in the North and, when another worldwide conflict again swelled industrial production, the exodus resumed. Even before the Japanese attack on Pearl Harbor brought the United States into World War II, the demand for workers—stoked by the ubiquitous labor agents—beckoned black men and women to Northern factories in ever-greater numbers and with ever-greater rapidity. American entrance into World War II would increase those opportunities many times over.[22]

The same interplay of agricultural collapse in the South and industrial opportunities in the North also influenced the character of the migrants. At various times and in various places, it changed the balance between men and women, between young and old, and between individuals and families, both nuclear and extended. At times, migrants came from the city and other times from the countryside; some of them were propertied and some propertyless.

In general, as one South Carolina migrant remembered, "the mens left first and the womens followed," as young men unencumbered with families and much desired in heavy industry generally took the lead. During the 1920s, more than one-third of the black men between the ages of fifteen and thirty left Georgia, a pattern reproduced in subsequent decades. But women were quick to follow, and sometimes they led, for they had reasons of their own to flee the South. Within their own households, they often found themselves doing the work of both mother and breadwinner, cooking and cleaning for their own family and laboring for a white family as well. Outside their own households, domestic work—the most common employment for black women—left them vulnerable to sexual abuse along with the usual regimen of economic exploitation. The sexual balance of most urban black populations, which had historically leaned heavily toward women, began to move in favor of men.[23]

Always, however, migration favored the young, who were at once less attached to the South, more willing to take their chances in the

North, and eager to escape the constraints that had shaped their parents' lives. The wholesale evacuation by young people grew steadily over the course of this third passage, so that between 1940 and 1950 Georgia and Alabama lost nearly one-third of their black populations between the ages of fourteen and thirty-four, and Mississippi lost nearly a half. These young men and women had an equally powerful effect on the population of the North. In a pattern typical of many Northern cities, young men and women composed two-thirds of Cleveland's black population in 1930, as the third great migration reduced the proportion of the very young and the very old and skewed the Northern black population toward young adults.[24] Northern cities, like the Southern interior a century earlier or tidewater Virginia in the eighteenth century, were youthful places.

The character of the migrants differed according to their age, sex, and family status. The first wave of northward-moving black Southerners, many of whom had already made the transit from rural to urban and from field to factory in the South, were generally more skilled and literate than those they left behind. They moved north with confidence, experience, and, at times, material resources. But fast on the heels of these black urbanites were country folks who had little experience with city life. As the cotton economy collapsed and as word of the possibilities in the North spread, migrants increasingly derived from the countryside. Penniless, displaced tenants or share-croppers innocent of urban life and carrying all their belongings in cardboard suitcases replaced men and women familiar with urban life, wage work, and industrial employment. Over time, the northward migration again became increasingly selective, drawing the urban and the educated who had long before been pushed off the farms and plantations and into the cities of the South. In 1940, less than one-quarter of the black Southerners residing in the North had lived on a farm five years earlier. By their education and occupation, many stood atop black society in the South. Fully one-fifth of the adult black migrants carried with them a high school diploma, a proportion four times that of the Southern black population generally. Among those traveling north were the South's best and brightest ministers, lawyers, businessmen, and not a few musicians.[25]

The circumstances under which black Southerners traveled also changed over time. While conditions never resembled anything like that of the slave trade, they nonetheless could be grim. No whip-wielding merchants of men lorded over the migrants, to be sure, but they confronted surly ticket agents and cantankerous conductors aplenty. Likewise, while the northbound migrants never faced the nightmare of tightpacking, they were herded into the "straight-backed seats filled with the dust and grime of neglect." One migrant remembered that the "negro cars . . . were little more than box cars fitted out with benches." They generally stood at the end of the train, catching the fumes and sucking up the cinders from the rail beds. Sanitary facilities, to the extent they existed, were of the most primitive sort. After long hours inhaling the noxious fumes, covered with soot and forced into an impossible posture, the travelers could be forgiven if they recalled their ancestors' transit across the Atlantic even as they streamed north on the *Sunshine Special*.[26]

But if the cramped, constrained quarters echoed earlier migrations, the food migrants carried made it clear that this was a movement of free men and women. While those transported across the Atlantic and the continent survived on tasteless gruels and mush, northward migrants often moved amid a culinary feast, exchanging biscuits, fried chicken, and other homemade treats. Louis Armstrong, who arrived in Chicago from New Orleans in 1922, recalled, "colored persons going North crammed their baskets full of everything but the kitchen stove."[27]

Still, this was no joy ride. The price of the ticket added to the migrants' woes. Free passes grandly promised by labor recruiters soon disappeared—if they ever existed—and the migrants were on their own. Travel was expensive in relation to the migrants' meager incomes. To finance the move, many sold what property they had and depleted their savings. If they were not poor before they left the South, they were likely to be poor by the time they reached the North.[28]

Along with the financial uncertainties came a host of less tangible concerns. The long ride to the North was the first time on a train for many black Southerners, and for nearly all it was the farthest they had traveled from home. The giant locomotives presented a bewildering spectacle, leaving many migrants as apprehensive and fearful at this smoke-belching beast as their African ancestors would have been by a multisailed caravel. The unknown multiplied such concerns. Departing Memphis, where he had migrated less than two years previous, the Chicago-bound Richard Wright "was seized by doubt." His anxieties hardly subsided when he reached his destination. He wondered if he had made the right decision, bracing himself for the worst even as he hoped for the best. "I had fled a known terror, and perhaps I could cope with this unknown terror."[29] However faintly, the shivers of fear first felt aboard the slave ships echo across the centuries.

Unlike with the forced migration that had moved their ancestors, black people took control of the movement north. As the first arrivals settled in their new homes, they invited families and friends to join them. Whereas Africans and African Americans migrating as slaves had been transported as isolated individuals, separated from family and friends, free black men and women moved north as families, or they soon reconstructed their families and joined neighbors—people with whom they had lived and worked. When they arrived at their destinations, most did not have to invent fictive kin or reestablish social networks, as the family and friends preceding them had. If the first and second passages had broken families and dismembered communities, the third passage had just the opposite effect. A survey of some five hundred black men living in Pittsburgh in 1918 found that most were married, more than one-third lived with their wives, and another third planned to bring their families north.[30]

Nothing distinguishes the third passage from the earlier, forced migrations more than the existence of what scholars—with a strange sensitivity to the implications of such language—have called "chains." Like other free people, individuals, families, and sometimes entire black communities were retracing the paths that relatives and friends had blazed. Many of these first arrivals returned to the South to explain precisely the nature of the opportunities—and the liabilities— that Northern life presented. Occasionally, these ambassadors from the North—returning south with their city clothes and metropolitan swagger—lectured at local churches, although more frequently they held forth in barbershops or juke joints. They told of simple acts of entering the same door as white people, not having to yield the side- walk to anyone, and voting. Pullman car porters, who worked on the North–South runs, were yet another source of information for would- be immigrants, as was the U.S. mail. The grapevine telegraph of word-of-mouth communication, whose history reached back into slave times, regained its viability in freedom. While enslaved Africans and African Americans lost their ability to communicate with their loved ones, messages between northward migrants and their kin filled mail- boxes, telegraph wires, and, in time, telephone lines. Eventually, a host of social service agencies, church-based associations, and frater- nal societies supplemented these personal communications to ease the migrants' passage.[31] The informal groups of kin and neighbors and the formal associations created by black people reflected the fun- damental difference between the third great migration and the earlier ones. African Americans were now taking control over the levers of change and—to the extent anyone could guide the massive movement of people—were directing the movement north.

Still, the transit was not easy. Northward migration required black Southerners to pool their resources, shuffling familial responsibilities and sending one or two family members who had the wherewithal to earn a living in the North. These scouts reported back and prepared the larger family for the northward trek. Over time, families composed a larger and larger share of the migrants, and the number of individuals traveling alone declined.

In some places, entire communities mobilized, forming emigration clubs, sharing knowledge, sending a few men and women ahead to establish a beachhead, and then—when all seemed secure—calling for family and friends to join them. Church congregations and congeries of neighbors also collectively agreed upon how, when, and where they would move. In various places, they transported themselves and took up residence in the same neighborhood or even the same tenement building. For many, doing so fulfilled the entire purpose of the move—maintaining the sanctity of familial and communal ties that had been threatened by the transformation of the Southern economy. Unlike earlier, forced migrations across the Atlantic or to the interior of the South, the movement north became the occasion to restore, rather than destroy, family and community life.[32]

Such connections represented yet another distinction between the third passage and the earlier, forced transatlantic and transcontinental migrations: the movement north was not a one-way trip. While many black people left the South without looking back, others maintained their ties to their old country. Having moved piecemeal, the first-arriving family members prepared to receive others. Migrants regularly returned home not merely to visit families and friends, but to gather their kin and neighbors and carry them north. Still others shuttled back and forth, sending children south during their summer vacations to visit with grandparents and accepting nieces and nephews eager to see the big city. As men and women—in increasing numbers—moved between the South and the North, such bidirectional transit made the urban North almost as familiar as the rural

South to many would-be migrants. Movement became a familiar, even natural, part of their lives.[33]

Every new arrival in the North seemed to add a link to the chain that connected North and South, so that by midcentury and often before, few black Southerners did not travel north without some knowledge of the communities into which they were entering. No longer was it necessary to send scouts to explore an unknown territory. Many knew precisely which employers would hire black workers and which landlords accepted black tenants. A few had jobs and housing waiting for them. Networks of kin and community that bound black people together in the South thus extended northward, not only substantially reducing the material costs of migration but also easing the psychological burden as well.

Chain migrations also made the third passage more homogeneous than either the transatlantic or the transcontinental slave trade. Existing transport routes—often the particular railroads and bus lines— that carried migrants northward reinforced the familiarity of the migration and the transfer of Southern regionalism. Migrants from Mississippi took the Illinois Central Railroad to St. Louis, Chicago, Milwaukee, and Minneapolis. Those traveling from Georgia and the Carolinas followed the Seaboard Air Line (a railroad) along the Atlantic coast to Washington, Baltimore, Philadelphia, New York, and Boston. Other patterns could be found. Those traveling from Kentucky, Tennessee, and Alabama tended to settle down in Cleveland and Detroit, and, during World War II, the trans-Mississippi migration carried black people from Arkansas, Louisiana, and Texas to California, Oregon, and Washington. Far more than the Chesapeake had become Igbo Land or South Carolina a New Angola in the eighteenth century, Cleveland became Alabama North and Oakland became Louisiana West in the twentieth.[34]

Though the starting and ending points were fixed, the movement north was hardly linear or direct. Just as the transit from Africa to

America or from the seaboard to the interior was made in a series of small jumps—so-called stage migration—so too was the movement from south to north. Rather than travel from the Southern countryside to some Northern metropolis, black Southerners—perhaps a majority—migrated northward in series of small, irregular steps. Richard Wright left Jackson for Memphis, found a room and a job, and was joined by his brother. Then they "began to save toward the trip north," as he later noted, "plotting our time, setting tentative dates for departure." Madame C. J. Walker, who started life in rural Mississippi as Sarah Breedlove, migrated to St. Louis, Denver, and Indianapolis, before settling in New York City. Ida B. Wells left Holly Springs for Memphis and then Chicago. But unlike the earlier, forced migrations, the repeat migrations of free men and women took another form, as some migrants moved on to new communities while others retraced their steps back to their place of origin.[35]

Once the migrants arrived in the North, they did not stop. One pattern seemed to have been a sort of ladder, where migrants moved from countryside to town, then from town to city, generally in a south to north direction. Having earlier left the countryside for a small Southern town, black men and women journeyed to a larger town, and then began the northward trek in the same way. For many, arrival in some Northern metropolis was not the end of the journey, but often only the beginning. Rather than settle permanently, they retraced their steps back to that small way station in which they had first alighted or moved on to yet another place with more promising opportunities. Jacob Lawrence's family stopped in so many places that the individual towns and cities faded from memory. The "last two cities I can remember before moving to New York," he noted in his memoir, "were Easton, Pennsylvania and Philadelphia." The rest remained a blur.[36]

In time, the movement north took on a life of its own. The northward routes became well-worn grooves in which many traveled. Transportation was increasingly available and inexpensive, as the bus replaced the train and as the automobile—no matter how dilapitated—became an option. Every would-be migrant seemed to have relatives or friends who would welcome them at the end of their journey. The ability of black people to manage the move from the South mitigated the worst features of the earlier, forced migrations. As free men and women, they traveled with a degree of comfort that their enthralled ancestors never experienced. In addition, an increasing number of governmental offices, private agencies, and religious organizations assisted the new arrivals in finding employment and housing while dispensing large doses of advice about urban living.

With the regularization of movement north, the third great migration—like earlier ones—developed a seasonal rhythm. In some places, migration followed the ebb and flow of the agricultural calendar, as migrants awaited the completion of the annual settling up. Elsewhere, the yearly departure of young men and women was incorporated into the academic calendar, as the graduates—with diplomas in hand—bid farewell to friends and relatives. In the weeks that followed, they collected small gifts and weighty advice. Then, with a neatly packed box of goodies, they boarded a train that became known as the "Chicken Bone Special," ready to seize the opportunities they could not hope to enjoy at home.[37]

As the Southern countryside emptied, there seemed fewer reasons for staying and more reasons for going. Abandoned tenant shacks and sagging barns were no match for the promises of the big city. No one wanted to be the last remaining black man or woman. "Ain't enough people I know left to give me a decent funeral," sighed one migrant as she departed Mississippi.[38] The migration fever that touched so many black Southerners during the second decade of the twentieth century morphed into a persistent virus that left few black Southerners untouched during the fifty years that followed.

But if, in time, more and more black Southerners followed the path established by their predecessors, new variations continually emerged as the links between North and South solidified, some opportunities grew and others declined, and the nature of transport changed. But no matter how they traveled, the spirit emanating from the transports was nothing like the brutal violence that had accompanied the transatlantic trade or the dismal funeral marches that were the slave coffles moving across the continent. Rather the mood was a yeasty mixture of high jinks and quiet contemplation as men and women dwelled upon what, for most, was the most important decision of their lives. While migrants missed their family and friends and some were homesick, few suffered the kinds of despondency and depression that had accompanied the permanent separation of the slave trade.

Blues musicians like Otis Hicks—"standin' at the Greyhound bus station"—captured the contrapuntal moment, as place ousted movement as the central feature of African American life—as he was "just standin' there thinking."[39]

Arrival in the North was an event in itself. As with the cruel separations from families and friends that had accompanied earlier migrations, few men and women would forget the rush that accompanied their entry into the North's great metropoles. Richard Wright captured the mixed emotions as well as any. "My first glimpses of the flat black stretches of Chicago depressed and dismayed me, mocked all my fantasies," recalled Wright. Chicago "seemed an unreal city whose mythical houses were built on slabs of black coal wreathed in palls of gray smoke, houses whose foundations were sinking slowly into the dank prairie." Most newcomers, however, hardly had time for Wright's sober reflections. Peering at the phalanx of humanity that gathered at the train or bus station—perhaps the largest assemblage they had ever witnessed—they searched for that familiar face that had promised to meet them while carefully avoiding eye contact with the hustlers who seemed to lurk everywhere. When at last that long-sought-after relative or friend hove into view, the new arrivals simultaneously breathed a sigh of relief and enjoyed a moment of jubilation. A firm hand guided the wide-eyed newcomer into the unknown.[40]

For many, the new world was as different from what they had known in the South as was frontier Alabama from their ancestors' Virginia or as low-country Carolina was from their forebears' Angola. The giant brick buildings, screeching streetcars, and neon lights were larger, louder, and brighter than anything they had known. Men and women scurried in all directions, seemingly heedless of one another and oblivious to the carefully choreographed racial protocols that governed every aspect of Southern life. Black men did not tip their hats to white men or scramble off the sidewalk to avoid a passing white woman. The previously ubiquitous COLORED ONLY signs were nowhere to be found.[41]

To be sure, the grand hopes for a better future were tempered by a deep understanding of the historic realities of race relations in the United States. The migrants were not surprised to learn that racial subordination would be as much a part of life in the North as it was in the South, although they would be shocked by the intensity, persistence, and novel forms it took. Eventually, some would conclude that the journey north changed nothing but the weather. But, upon arrival, the migrants looked forward to freedoms they had never known, from the simple act of taking their seat of choice in a public conveyance or having their vote courted. The promise of steady work, reasonable pay, and equal treatment seemed so utterly different from the ritual condescension and gross exploitation that they had known that it provided reason to celebrate.

Wonder at the marvels and possibilities of life in the North soon gave way to first purposes: to find regular, remunerative employment. While some migrants had jobs waiting, most began their stay in the North by searching for work. As they did, they entered into new terrain. For nearly a century, black men and women had been denied a place in the North's industrial revolution, except in the occasional role as strikebreakers. Barred from factories by an unholy alliance of white employers who disparaged their abilities and white employees (and their unions) who disparaged their persons, the vast majority—fully two-thirds in most Northern cities at the turn of the twentieth century—labored irregularly either as menials, shouldering a shovel or pushing a broom, or as domestics, cooking, cleaning, driving coaches, and minding the children of white Northerners. As W. E. B. DuBois noted in his 1899 study of Philadelphia, "[n]o matter how well trained a Negro may be . . . he cannot in the ordinary course of competition hope to be much more than a menial servant." Since they had been barred from apprenticeship programs, they rarely had a chance to compete. Occupational patterns of black life in other cities confirm DuBois's observation. In 1910, nearly half of black men in Chicago worked in four occupations—janitor, porter, servant, or waiter—and some two-thirds of employed black women labored as cooks, laundresses, maids, and other domestic servants. Everywhere in the North black workers were confined to hard, unremunerative, and often demeaning jobs—when they could find work in the first place.[42]

A small number of black people escaped the servility and insecurity of what was politely called "negro work." As a proportion of the population, the black men and women working as professionals, proprietors, or skilled workers never amounted to more than 3 percent of the black workforce. Although their claim to status often rested as much upon their tawny color and assertions of respectability as upon their occupation or wealth, this select few had established lucrative niches within the service trades as barbers, caterers, and waiters. An even smaller number practiced medicine and law, held elective and appointive office, or ministered the Gospel. Except for the clergy, the customers and constituents of these black entrepreneurs, professionals, and politicians were almost always white, as the North's black population was too small and too poor to support a black business and professional class.[43]

But even as immigrants arrived from the South, the elite's always-precarious position within Northern society was collapsing. New technologies and changing styles accounted for some of the decline, as when the advent of the safety razor eroded the standing barbers and new family-style restaurant service reduced the need for waiters. But the entrepreneurs who operated the palatial barbershops in the best hotels, catered the grand soirees, and directed small armies of servers and busboys in the poshest restaurants did not succumb merely to changes in technology and style. Everywhere black trades-men and professionals found their historic businesses shriveling before the force of racial exclusion. "Between 1895 and 1905," according to one black leader, "colored people of Chicago have lost nearly every occupation they once had almost a monopoly." Those same forces barred the entry of black men and women into the new white-collar occupations as stenographers and typewriters, confining them to the most menial work. Disappearing along with their occupational niches were the small shards of patronage black politicians once enjoyed, as lily white Republicans had surrendered an earlier genera-tion's egalitarian commitments.[44]

If members of the old elite were losing ground, they did not yield their place at the top of black society easily. Their pride of place, sometimes reaching back to post-Revolutionary emancipation, rested upon the embrace of bourgeois ideals of self-improvement through education, religious orthodoxy—often Anglican and Presbyterian—and values of industry, frugality, and temperance. To support these ideals—as well as to demonstrate that they deserved a position within the great American middle class—blacks created a host of exclusive associations, like New York's Century Club, Chicago's Appomattox Club, Cleveland's Caterers Club, and Detroit's Oak and Ivy Club. Membership in these societies was carefully regulated not only by tests of means but also by reputations that rested upon tightly braided business relations and marriages that often made the elite appear more like an extended family than a social class.

The elite celebrated their lineage as often as their ideals. Many of their forebears had led the struggle against slavery alongside white abolitionists, whose descendents served as patrons and political allies. They shared much with these old-line reformers, including the genteel lifestyle, courtly manners, and friendship nurtured over generations. The elite gloried in the name of "Old Settlers."[45]

The new arrivals challenged the Old Settlers—not so much for their place atop black society; that would come later—but with their seeming difference in lifestyle and values. Their strange accents, garish dress, loud music, religious enthusiasm, and country manners—along with their poverty and sometimes color (black as opposed to buff)—threatened the image the Old Settlers had cultivated so carefully. Some blamed their own decline on the entry of black Southerners into Northern society. While the decline had more to do with economic changes and the accompanying rise of new racial ideologies, the elite looked inward. They attempted to elevate the newcomers to their own standards of dress and deportment. Admonitions not to "appear on the street with old dust caps, dirty aprons, and ragged clothes and above all, Keep your mouth shut, please!" hardly made for good intraracial relations. When the new arrivals returned the elite's condescension in kind, the tension between the two grew, much as it had between Africans and African Americans in the seventeenth and eighteenth centuries or with newcomers and established residents of the black-belt plantations in the nineteenth century. In time the conflict would cool, as the Old Settlers and new arrivals found common ground, but at first the new arrivals confronted opposition from black as well as white Northerners.[46]

While the wartime years and the postwar decade that followed were not the most propitious moment to enter Northern society, the pressing need for labor allowed the new arrivals—and many older residents—to break the industrial color line. Almost immediately the migrants took places on the assembly lines from which black workers had long been excluded. By the 1920s, more than two-thirds of Cleveland's black men labored in factories and other industrial sites, whereas prior to World War I less than one-quarter had worked at such jobs. At the same time, the proportion engaged in domestic or service labor fell to 12 percent from a prewar total of almost one-third. A similar pattern could be found in other Northern cities, although the entry of black workers into industrial employment took a different course from city to city and even from industry to industry.

Still, the new arrivals struggled against the traditional opposition of white employers who had long maintained that black workers were socially and psychologically unfit for any but the most menial tasks and white workers who deeply resented laboring alongside black men and women. In some places they made little headway, and the black unemployment rate remained higher than that of whites. But, as in Cleveland, the number of black men on factory assembly lines continued to climb, so that by the 1940s the industrial sector was the single largest employer of black men. Black women also made some advances, and they too began to find a place in Northern factories. Between 1910 and 1920, the proportion of women working in factories doubled, while the proportion laboring as domestics began a slow decline.[47]

To be sure, black workers remained at the bottom of the industrial hierarchy, as white employers continued to shunt them into the meanest jobs and white workers barred them from their unions. The most skilled and lucrative industrial employment remained off limits, and the factories they entered—like slaughterhouses, foundries, brickyards, and other heavy industry—relied largely on the application of brute force. Even within these factories, unorganized black workers were generally confined to the dirtiest, most dangerous, and least remunerative jobs. Black men might butcher animals, feed blast furnaces, and mold bricks while the most skilled trades remained the property of white men. The grim circumstances under which black workers labored placed them in harm's way, and they subsequently suffered higher rates of injury and death than white workers. But the healthiest and strongest black men and women had no assurance of job security. Economic downturns continued to drive black workers from their jobs. When prosperity returned, the first fired were always the last hired. Those who found steady employment discovered the ladder of advancement—from worker to foreman, foreman to steward, and steward to supervisor—blocked. Only rarely did black workers supervise any but their own color.[48]

Black women workers found it particularly difficult to break the industrial color line. Even when factory work became available, they continued to be funneled into domestic employment and other low-status, low-paying jobs with little chance of advancement. Instead of moving up the occupational ladder, many of the women who had left jobs as teachers in the South found themselves cleaning houses in the North. Northern racism—generally de facto rather than de jure—proved as durable as the Southern version. When industrial production plummeted in the 1930s, black men and women lost many of their earlier gains. Even those who maintained their toehold in the industrial sector faced cuts in wages and periodic layoffs. The lack of job security remained a constant in the lives of black workers. For all their striving, nearly nine of ten black families lived below the federal poverty line as late as 1940. On the eve of World War II, the economic standing of most Southern migrants had hardly improved.[49]

The first arrivals in the North needed places to live, as well as jobs. Although they might lodge with a relative or friend for a while, the cramped quarters in which most black people resided hardly left space for permanent guests. During most of the nineteenth century, black people had lived scattered across Northern cities. Generally these were less desirable neighborhoods around docks, railroad yards, and factories, but these same neighborhoods also housed white families— usually of the same class as their black neighbors—with whom black people shared the same alleys, blocks, and even buildings. The movement of black people into the urban North during the late nineteenth century, although small in number when compared to what would follow, reshaped racial residential patterns, creating areas in which black people composed a large portion of the residents. While few cities had such a district, residential segregation was on the rise prior to the third great migration. The process that would eventually create the ghetto had begun prior to the Great Migration.

In general black Southerners had no particular desire to live near white people, although they did hope to escape the segregation that had defined their lives. However, as they entered the North, they were funneled into areas that were composed disproportionately of African Americans. White residents hastily evacuated these areas, often at the behest of white real estate agents. The newcomers found themselves living in neighborhoods composed almost entirely of people of their own color. If they looked elsewhere for housing, they confronted formal and informal prohibitions—restrictive covenants, zoning regulations, and so-called civic associations—employed by white residents to halt the "invasion" of their homelands. This formidable phalanx, in league with bomb-planting vigilantes and often backed by legally constituted authorities, discouraged trespasses across what had become insuperable racial barriers. Residential segregation increased steadily during the twentieth century.[50]

As the concentration of black people increased and the black areas of the city became blacker, ghettos emerged. By the third decade of the twentieth century—and sometimes even earlier—these well-defined enclaves could be found in every Northern city. During the next half century, the ghettos grew, expanding in paroxysms of violence—sometimes angry eyeball-to-eyeball confrontations and sometimes full-scale race riots—as growing black communities pressed against white neighborhoods. When unable to expand, satellite communities sometimes appeared, often in some distant and generally undesirable section of the city. But they too underwent the same process of expansion, increasing in density far beyond any other areas. In time, these satellite communities—which also became uniformly black—merged with the main area of black residence, as black arrivals filled the interstices.

Black people could not live safely beyond the borders of these enclaves. Whatever their liabilities, ghettos became the destinations of thousands of black Southerners, many of whom knew little of Chicago, Detroit, Pittsburgh, or New York but knew all about the South Side, Paradise Valley, Little Africa, or Harlem. If eighteenth-century observers thought the influx of Africans would transform portions of mainland North America into "New Guineas," twentieth-century commentators, like the distinguished Howard University professor Kelly Miller, declared that Northern cities were becoming like "the heart of Hayti or Liberia."[51]

Ghettoization not only restructured relationships between white and black, but also among black people. The expanding ghettos swallowed all people of African descent. No matter what their lineage, deportment, education, wealth, or social standing, black men and women found it all but impossible to reside outside the areas that whites had designated for black people. The differences in wealth and status along with fine distinctions of color, hair, and other physiological features that the Old Settlers had employed to distinguish themselves from the mass of black people mattered less and less—at least to white people.

Old residents and new arrivals, forced to create a city within a city, soon found excitement in the places where they could locate their own food, religion, and music. Ghettos hummed with familiar smells and sounds, as restaurants serving black-eyed peas and ham hocks,

clubs and theaters featuring down-home music, and churches preach-
ing the old-time gospel appeared everywhere. These places attracted
ambitious black men and women, since businessmen, preachers, nov-
elists, musicians, and artists of all sorts found comfort and dollars
in the black audience. The most famous of these cultural enclaves—
New York's Harlem and Chicago's Bronzeville—left a lasting mark
on African American and American culture. But nearly every Northern city had a similar area. Like the explosions of cultural creativity
that accompanied the movement of African peoples across the Atlantic in the seventeenth and eighteenth centuries and African American
people across the continent in the nineteenth century, the renascences
of the twentieth century generated a sense of pride which eventually
was captured in the word *soul*, an indefinable quality that spoke to
the essence of African American life. The swagger that could be found
among the residents of the inner city revealed that black people had
taken ownership. The inner city ceased to be a place of confinement
but a familiar terrain and even a home turf.[52]

By the 1930s—perhaps before—the inner city was also becoming
a source of political power. Employing the suffrage which had been
denied them in the South, migrants joined with the Old Settlers to
create a new politics. To be sure, it built upon an old protest tradition
that reached back to the Revolution and was reinforced by post–Civil
War Republican ascendancy. But it also reflected the new assertive-
ness of men and women Alain Locke captured in the name "New
Negroes": "self respecting, educated, prosperous, race-proud, self
dependent, deserving and demanding full citizenship." Emerging
from churches, social service agencies, women's clubs, labor unions,
neighborhood organizations, the Communist and Socialist parties,
as well as fuller participation in both the Republican and Democratic
parties—the new politics was quick to seize the celebratory rhetoric
of American democracy and turn it against the American apartheid
system. Black men and women organized boycotts and rent strikes;

they demanded equal pay for equal work and warred against exclusion and segregation in schools, restaurants, theaters, and the workplace. Their efforts were supported by a growing network of newspapers—numbering well over one hundred by the 1930s—that sprang up as black people filled Northern cities. Most were local sheets, but some, like Chicago's *Defender*, New York's *Amsterdam News*, and Pittsburgh's *Courier*, enjoyed a larger reach, knitting local struggles into a national movement. Before long, black men began appearing in municipal and state legislatures. In 1928, Oscar De Priest took a seat in Congress as the representative from Chicago, and others would follow. With them came a growing political clout.

Over time, black voters became an increasingly important part of the Northern electorate. Turning away from the party of Lincoln, they became an active element in the New Deal coalition. In many districts in the North, black voters—at least according to their advocates—held the balance of power, a claim at least some white politicians took seriously. Once in office, black officials and those white officials beholden to black voters pressed for new civil rights legislation and the enforcement of long-ignored laws. Perhaps more significant, political activism swelled beyond the boundaries of partisan politics, as a new, more militant civil rights movement demanded full equality.[53]

In 1940, American mobilization for war provided new leverage for civil rights advocates. They demanded, among other things, a desegregation of the armed forces and equal access to employment in the expanding defense industries. When it became evident that those opportunities would not be forthcoming, protests began. Under the leadership of A. Philip Randolph, president of the Brotherhood of Sleeping Car Porters, militants threatened a massive march of black people on Washington, shaking the Roosevelt administration. Although Randolph's March on Washington Movement eventually withdrew its demand for desegregation of the military, in June 1941 a reluctant President Roosevelt issued an executive order providing "full and equitable participation of all workers in defense industries" and establishing the Fair Employment Practices Commission to root out discrimination. The success of the March on Washington Movement fueled political activism, confirming the notion that only mass action could end the policy of exclusion and separation. Activists launched the Double V campaign; the membership of the National Association for the Advancement of Colored People grew by a thousand percent; and new, even more militant organizations, like the Committee of Racial Equality, began to protest segregation in restaurants, theaters, and other public places.[54]

While the larger structure of white supremacy hardly budged, the tremors were felt, not least in the workplace. Employers—pressured by the massive expansion of industrial production—opened their doors to black women as well as men. Aided by their incorporation into the new industrial labor unions, black men and women enlarged their toehold in industrial America. Between December 1941 and August 1942, the number of black men employed in manufacturing jumped from 500,000 to 1.2 million. Over the course of the decade, the share of black men working as "operatives"—the census designation for factory workers—doubled, making up over one-fifth of the black workforce. Representative of changes in other industrial cities, the proportion of black workers employed in Detroit's auto industry increased from 4 to 15 percent between 1942 and the war's end. Black men—particularly those who had put down roots in the North—at last began to climb the ladder of industrial employment, moving from unskilled to skilled labor, from a place on the line into the ranks of stewards and foremen. The number of black women operatives also increased, so that nearly one-fifth of employed black women worked in factories.[55]

Still, advances in industrial employment were fitful and frustratingly slow. The Fair Employment Practices Commission sometimes successfully pressured obdurate corporate employers, particularly those dependent upon wartime contracts. But just as often the commission's directives were ignored, and racially exclusive policies remained in place. The commission had even less success with smaller, proprietary firms that feared that the introduction of black workers would stir discord. Although usually just a pretext for maintaining a lily white labor force, the threat was real enough. Some of the largest and most powerful labor unions—especially in the building trades—continued to exclude black workers from membership, and the members themselves were more than willing to protect white privilege with force, as a rash of "hate strikes" confirmed. Long after major corporate employers and labor unions formally committed themselves to equal opportunity in the workplace, the familiar pattern of black workers being assigned to dangerous, dirty work remained much in evidence.

By the 1940s, a full generation after the beginning of the third passage, the place of black men and women in the most dynamic sector of the American economy remained precarious. Unemployment among black men and women was at least twice as high for black as for white workers, and discrimination—indeed outright exclusion—was common. Entry into white-collar work was near impossible. The first arrivals could do little to bend the prejudices of Northern employers—no matter what their credentials. Prior to World War II, few black men and women—6 percent compared to 37 percent of whites—could be found behind an office desk or a department store counter earning wages as salespersons, bookkeepers, accountants, or clerks. Exploring American race relations in the 1940s, Gunnar Myrdal and his associates concluded, "the North is almost as strict as the South in excluding Negroes from middle class jobs. . . ."[56]

Again the war made a difference. The shortage of workers allowed black men and women to secure employment in jobs previously reserved for whites. Many—some of them the children of Southern immigrants—gained their positions as civil servants in expanding federal, state, and municipal bureaucracies, as teachers, postal workers, middle managers, and clerks of all sorts. Others secured employment in the private sector. While rank discrimination remained, the advances were real, particularly in the defense industry.[57] An expanding cadre of black men and women exchanged their blue collars for white and enjoyed greater stability of employment, a chance for regular salary increases, access to health care, and pensions at retirement, all the while escaping from the exhausting labor of the assembly line. Their presence began to change African American life.[58]

As the wages of black workers increased—growing to many times what they would have been in the rural South—other opportunities arose. With money in their pockets, black men and women became eager consumers. Black entrepreneurs moved quickly to address their needs, opening beauty salons, barber shops, grocery stores, restaurants, dance halls, theaters, and—ultimately—funeral parlors to serve the greatly enlarged Northern black population. Some grew beyond these petty enterprises and began working in banking, insurance, publishing, and manufacturing. They fielded sports teams, manufactured cosmetics, produced records, and shot movies. Promoting the notion that benefits would accrue to all black people from the expansion of "race businesses," they urged black customers to "buy black." For their part, white storekeepers, eager to maintain the patronage of black customers, became susceptible to the pressure of "don't shop where you can't work" campaigns.[59]

Wartime prosperity not only enlarged black communities but also made them more diverse. Like the plantation or cropper villages of earlier times, the inner city's social geography housed a well-defined society that reflected the changes set in motion by the third great migration. Old Settlers faded—although hardly disappeared—pushed aside by a new, Southern-born elite, as some of the new arrivals, seizing the main chance, gained prominence as entrepreneurs, professionals, politicians, and preachers—sometimes all four at once.

At the forefront, occupying positions of community leadership and pressing the case for equality, was a solid class of working people: factory operatives along with schoolteachers, civil service employees, and petty proprietors, as well as laborers and domestics. They distinguished themselves not so much by the size of their bank accounts, but by their dress, deportment, and associational memberships that together made a visible claim to respectability. That claim was sometimes reinforced by residence, as members of the black middle class—much like their white counterparts—separated themselves from the poor, as they nurtured their claim to middle-class decency.

The strongest evidence of respectability derived from church membership. The most prestigious black churches had pedigrees that dated back to the early nineteenth century with the emergence of freedom in the North. These long-tailed institutions with established congregations supported all manner of organizations, from schools to boys and girls clubs, debating societies and reading rooms, and even so-called intelligence offices that functioned as employment bureaus. Their prestige attracted some newcomers from the South, but their formal, high-toned services discomforted others. For these men and women, Holiness or Pentecostal congregations, often operating out of storefronts, became the churches of choice. Their ministers, many Southern born, professed a muscular Christianity and dispensed with the staid decorum and intellectualized gospel that the new arrivals found objectionable. Religious choices not only spoke to the gap between Old Settlers and new arrivals but also to the differences within a society of growing complexity, as upwardly mobile black men and women gravitated to churches that claimed greater respectability. If the ghetto represented in interracial terms a separation of the races, it also manifested in intraracial terms a separation of the classes.[60]

The ghetto was not only a complex institution, but also a changing one. Following World War II, the black inner city underwent its own transformation, as the black population grew in number and density. While blockbusting real estate agents sent skittish white homeowners fleeing to the expanding suburbs, federal policymakers, joined by redlining bankers and mortgage brokers—both determined to maintain racial homogeneity—kept black people penned in decaying urban neighborhoods, denying them access to homeownership in the new suburbs by endorsing race restrictive covenants and rejecting would-be black homeowners applications for mortgage insurance. "If a neighborhood is to retain stability," declared the official Federal Housing Administration's handbook, "it is necessary that all properties shall continue to be occupied by the same social class." While federal policymakers removed the racial rules from their FHA handbook in the 1940s, they continued to enforce them for another twenty years, quietly maintaining the principle of "racial compatibility." Other federal programs, most prominently the GI Bill, which offered returning soldiers financial help to become part of a nation of suburban homeowners, were similarly color-coded. Denying black veterans access to these loans left them and their families locked in the meanest part of American cities. In the decades following the war, the level of urban residential segregation increased until the indexes of dissimilarity—which measured the degree of segregation—reached 90 percent, meaning that almost the entire population would have to move to achieve a random distribution of whites and blacks.[61]

Other changes reshaped African American life in postwar America. While black people could do little to break the vice grip of residential segregation, their growing political presence and economic prosperity stoked the struggle for equality. White supremacy—weakened by legal assaults—began to waver. In 1948, the Democratic Party included a Civil Rights plank in its platform, and President Harry Truman issued an executive order desegregating the army.[62]

While the fiercest battles remained to be fought in the South, black Northerners provided much of the political leverage against the old order and reaped some of the benefits as well.

Centuries-old employment practices that had throttled the advancement of black people withered under the glare of national publicity, the enforcement of long-ignored antidiscrimination laws, and the imposition of affirmative action programs. Employers who once openly rejected black applicants hurried to hire at least a token black man or woman to demonstrate their commitment to a newly invigorated egalitarianism, or at least to comply with federal—and sometimes state—law. The rush to meet the new ideal allowed some black women to find a place behind a reception desk, and some men gained access to a clerkship, but tokenism itself soon became exposed as a form of obstructionism. Between 1940 and 1960, the number of black women clerical and sales workers increased from less than 2 percent to almost 11 percent. Employers, who once denied black workers any sort of visibility lest they too be tainted, suddenly placed black men and women in the most visible positions. Banks, hotels, and department stores advertised the presence of black tellers and clerks. A black receptionist became de rigueur in many corporate offices.

New openings greatly expanded the black middle class. Black stockmen and charwomen emerged from the back rooms and basements and took their places on sales floors or offices as salespersons, bookkeepers, and accountants. A growing number of black teachers, black police officers, black social workers, and black real estate agents swelled the ranks of those who did not have to labor with their hands. Between 1940 and 1960, the proportion of black men and women employed in white-collar jobs doubled.[63]

During the 1960s, the long-term changes set in motion by the third great migration and by the immediate effects of the Civil Rights movement decisively altered the economic structure of black society. The number of black men and women working at white-collar jobs increased by 80 percent over the course of the decade. The proportion of black men working in professional and managerial positions more than doubled during the 1960s. By the end of the decade, the share of the black population nominally defined as middle class increased from one in eight to one in four. A general prosperity allowed large numbers of black people to escape the confines of menial labor. If the years accompanying World War I had seen black men and women enter the industrial working class for the first time, the 1960s witnessed their arrival in the American middle class. No longer confined to the old positions of clergy, postal or social workers, teachers, or a variety of petty proprietors, middle-class black men and women could increasingly be found working alongside white architects, engineers, physicians, managers, and other professionals. Some struck out on their own to become successful entrepreneurs. The structure of black America began to approach that of white, even if its wealth did not.

The black middle class continued to prosper as never before. The number of black families earning $10,000 or more (in constant dollars) more than doubled the years between 1960 and 1969. The growth rate of the black middle class declined during the next decade, but it nonetheless continued to expand by nearly 60 percent over the previous decade's total. Similar growth occurred in the years that followed, so that the number of black families earning more than $50,000 increased by a factor of two. Although its resources remained shallow and its place precarious, the black middle class—aided in part by affirmative action programs—nonetheless continued to grow steadily in the decades that followed.[64]

But while the black middle class gained ground at midcentury, black industrial workers lost it, as the ladder of industrial employment collapsed, and with it the possibilities of rising within the industrial hierarchy. The reorganization of the American economy left many black men and women without access to employment as factories— lured by low taxes, better roads, access to new markets, and nonunion labor—abandoned Northern cities for the suburbs, then left the suburbs for the South, and then the South for foreign destinations. Many factories closed, never to open again. Disproportionately, these were in heavy industries—automobile production, rubber processing, and steelmaking—just the industries where black workers had enjoyed a substantial presence. With these industries went the "good jobs," and the pensions, health insurance, and security that came with seniority. Unions, into which black workers had at long last been incorporated, lost their ability to protect seniority and guard against discrimination.

The black men and women of the third great migraton, who had secured a toehold in the industrial working class during World War II and enjoyed the postwar prosperity, saw their grip slipping as the structure of American manufacturing shook in the 1960s and after. The skills of those experienced in the old smokestack manufactories did not transfer easily to the new high-tech industries. Even when black men and women had the qualifications, the new jobs had been removed to the distant suburbs, out of reach of inner-city black residents. The automation of production added to the dangers black workers—still concentrated in the ranks of the unskilled—faced. When the layoffs came, whether as a result of periodic downturns in the economy or of more permanent structural changes, black workers were the first sent home. The Civil Rights movement did little to improve the material conditions of black people in the inner city. One in three lived below the poverty line. Between 1975 and 1980, black unemployment increased by 200,000, as more and more black men and women were excluded from the labor market. The combination of ghetto residence and a sour economy locked black people in poverty.

Once again, excluded from the dynamic sector of the American economy, buffeted by the changing nature of production, and tied to the most vulnerable industries, black men and women saw their connections to regular work unraveling. Many of those who had found prosperity and security working in a unionized factory could only find hourly work flipping burgers. Deindustrialization left many black workers stranded in the inner city without good jobs and left many others without any remunerative employment. They had joined the industrial working class just when a substantial portion was being discarded as obsolete.[65]

The absence of regular employment and a living wage demoralized working people, particularly young men and women. Black families, which had survived slavery and segregation, frayed, as men—without access to work—had difficulties supporting their wives and children. Between 1960 and 1975, the number of black households without male wage earners increased from 22 to 35 percent. Along with the disappearance of black men from family life came a dramatic increase in the number of households with children born out of wedlock. Although adept at creating new forms of domestic life—piecing together a livelihood from part-time employment and assigning larger roles to grandparents—the absence of male breadwinners impoverished black people, particularly as household solvency came to depend upon the income of two breadwinners. Many black men and women found themselves confined to an alienated proletariat without the skills or education to secure regular employment, even when it became available. With a living wage increasingly beyond reach, some became dependent on welfare to make ends meet. Others turned to an underground economy of drugs and crime. Desperation only worsened the problem, with an increasing proportion of young men and women facing incarceration.[66]

The infrastructure of the inner city deteriorated along with the lives of its inhabitants. Attempts to attract new investments failed, as urban officials backed by municipal planners defined black neighborhoods as substandard blight. Rather than rehabilitate old neighborhoods, they scheduled them for destruction, a process sped up by the construction of highways designed to carry white workers between downtown employment and suburban homes. The rows of sterile high-rises—"the projects" in the lingo of the day—that replaced dilapidated but functioning neighborhoods only increased the density of the inner city and undermined stable communities. The close quarters and large numbers packed into these buildings soon denuded the surrounding courtyards, transforming them into barren wastelands, often littered with broken bottles and other debris. Within the buildings, corridors and elevators became sites of all sorts of mayhem, so that the residents avoided them when they could, barricading themselves behind steel doors with multiple locks. Even amid these difficult circumstances, communities often flowered. The same barren projects that gave birth to violent drug gangs also seeded the welfare rights movement. Still, many residents, particularly those with aspirations and resources for a better life, fled. A growing number of impoverished blacks took their place.[67]

Changes set in motion by the Civil Rights movement—the dismantling of legal segregation and the new growth of the black middle class—allowed some black people to leave the inner city. Most moved to close-in suburbs which soon became as segregated as the inner city. The number of black men and women living in suburbs totaled some seven million by the middle of the 1980s, more than double the number a decade earlier. Those who remained in the inner city did not always resemble the respectable, churchgoing men and women who had once composed the core of black communities. Instead, many were impoverished and chronically underemployed or unemployed. Their family life was in shambles, characterized by female-headed households, out-of-wedlock children, welfare dependency, and the prevalence of drug use. Sociologists and other social scientists pointed to the spatial mismatch between work and residence and debated the so-called cultural and structural causes of the various urban disorders.[68]

Life in the inner city, whether in ramshackle buildings or soulless towers, gained a reputation as being rife with disease and criminality. White suburbanites—viewing the ghetto from a distance—saw it as evidence of the moral deficiency and intellectual inferiority of its residents. As citizenship was redefined by home ownership and patterns of consumption, black people—denied access to credit—found themselves excluded from the postwar prosperity. The white exodus from the city continued with ever-increasing speed at midcentury. By 1968, when a series of riots following the assassination of Martin Luther King, Jr., decimated numerous black neighborhoods, black people were fully identified with urban life.

The rise of the black middle class and the decline of black workers into what some had begun to call an "underclass" left African American society sharply divided. This division was also reflected in the profound alteration of the social geography of African American life over the course of the twentieth century, a process that defined a new sense of place for black people.[69]

The characterization of black society at the end of the twentieth century—new middle class and underclass—recalled earlier examinations of the effects of antebellum enslavement and postbellum rural impoverishment on black people. They vastly understated the diversity of black life in favor of an emphasis on the pathologies of the inner-city. They emphasized street hustlers over wage earners, those who invested in numbers over those who saved for the future, and those who shot dope over those who shot hoops, creating seemingly indelible stereotypes. What was clear, however, was the full identification of black life with the city, a coincidence affirmed by the regular return of black suburbanites to their old neighborhoods to attend church, dine in a home-style restaurant, or listen to music with friends in a familiar club. During the last third of the twentieth century, the inner city became what the plantation had been in the seventeenth and eighteenth centuries and what the sharecropper plot had been in the late nineteenth. After more than a half century of movement, black people had again found place.

The surety of place spawned a new confidence. It was expressed in a variety of ways, most prominently in a series of overlapping nationalistic movements that celebrated blackness. While some were political and demanded Black Power and others were economic and asserted black control over production and consumption, all spoke of Black Pride. Each, by turns, might connote armed self-defense or participation in partisan politics, black capitalism or the creation of a black aesthetic, the commemoration of old heroes or the creation of new ones. Clothed in dashikis, sporting Afros, and holding high, clenched fists, the new movement asserted "Black is Beautiful" in a manner that reflected ownership of the inner city.[70]

Once again, nothing so traced the transformation of black life during the third great migration than the evolution of black music. The migration northward and cityward altered some musical forms and created entirely new ones, a process sped up by the commercialization of various popular amusements. The spirituals morphed into gospel at the hands of Southern migrants like Thomas Dorsey. In his carefully orchestrated chorals, Dorsey, a former blues singer from Georgia who claimed the title of "father of gospel," excised the hand clapping and foot stomping that characterized the spirituals but incorporated the spiritual's syncopated rhythms and repetitions. In the voices of Roberta Martin and Mahalia Jackson, gospel music took on a sophisticated urban patina. Although members of the rising middle class embraced the new sound only reluctantly, by midcentury gospel had found a home in the black church. An active and profitable gospel circuit had been established.[71]

The blues also changed as it moved north, mutating in ways that made it hardly recognizable. Leaving the rough, communal settings of the rural roadhouse, it too became increasingly formalized and stylized, less the product of improvisation and more of careful arrangement. Performed in clubs and theaters rather than crossroad juke joints, it too was increasingly structured by a growing commercial market. Performers changed, as women vocalists like "Ma" Rainey and Bessie Smith replaced men as the main attraction, and instrumental ensembles numbering a half dozen ousted the lone guitar, harmonica, or washboard. The music, cut to the demands of a paying audience or a 78-rpm record, was played for an audience that included whites as well as blacks—and sometimes was limited to whites.[72]

The commercial success of the urbanized Southern import, however, was only one aspect of the development of the blues. In the cities of the North, many black migrants found the new, stylized music unrecognizable and the setting in which it was performed uncomfortable. Yet another brand of the blues—so-called urban blues—was much more to their liking. Although a more direct import from the Southern countryside, it was no simple copy of its rural forebears, for it too had changed with the northward migration, often adding acoustic instruments and with them a new range of sounds. While it also differed from place to place—St. Louis blues had a different sound than that heard in Chicago or Philadelphia—the repertoire was much more familiar to the newcomers.[73]

Together the new sounds of gospel and the urban blues inspired the emergence of rhythm and blues and later rock and roll. Ray Charles and especially Sam Cooke, among the leading architects of the new sounds, were two extraordinary musical talents and shrewd businessmen who not only deftly mixed the older forms but also promoted their own music. Cooke made his own bookings and eventually established his own record label. But no one could control the pedigree of the rapidly changing musical forms, especially under the intense pressure of commercialization. R&B, with its insistent beat and infectious lyrics, was repackaged in countless ways, often to make it attractive to a white audience even when performed by black musicians, and adopted by white musicians to play to black audiences.

Still, there was no denying its origins. The Civil Rights movement marched to its beat and Motown became an emblem of Black Pride.[74]

The commercial success of rock and roll blurred the themes of movement and place, although they remained especially clear in the plaintive wail of the blues. Blind Blake's "Detroit Bound Blues," Bessie Smith's "Chicago Bound Blues," and Henry Townsend's "A Ramblin' Mind" were among the songs that expressed wrenching pain and an eager desire to leave the South, just as Lizzie Miles's "Cotton Belt Blues," Tommy McClennan's "Cotton Patch Blues," and Roosevelt Sykes's "Southern Blues" echoed the sense of loss that accompanied the third passage. Others—like Ben Lorre's "Roamin' Blues"—captured the continuous motion of northward movement:

Left Chicago in the summer, New York in the fall,
Detroit in the winter didn't prove a thing at all

But still others captured the emotional attachments to place, as in Robert Johnson's "Sweet Home Chicago":

Oh, baby, don't you want to go?
Back to the land of California, to my sweet home, Chicago.

Indeed, no part of the migratory experience escaped the blues men and women: the aspiration for change, the frustrations of life in the North, and the desire to return home—as in Memphis Minnie's and Joe McCoy's "I'm Going Back Home."[75]

Ironically, jazz—the musical signature of the third passage—only occasionally spoke the words of movement and place, but it captured their contrapuntal relationship not in its lyrics but in its instrumentality. Jazz too emerged from the plantation South and its capital city, New Orleans, where a variety of native musical traditions mixed with those of the Caribbean and then traveled north, much like the people themselves, moving in small jumps from city to city: New Orleans to St. Louis to Chicago, and then points east—Philadelphia and New York—or west—San Francisco and Los Angeles.[76]

Like gospel and the blues, jazz (in some ways instrumental blues) also drew on the long tradition of improvisation and syncopation and utilized the call-and-response form. But jazz expanded the range of harmonic complexity and placed the emphasis on the instrumental rather than the vocal, and the vocal form most associated with jazz—scat—seemed oblivious to either movement or place. Still, the familiar references could be found in pieces from Jelly Roll Morton's "Black Bottom" in 1926 to Wynton Marsalis's "Congo Square" in 2006. Duke Ellington's theme, "Take the 'A' Train," which was written by his friend and musical collaborator Billy Strayhorn, guided newcomers directly to the center of the new African American world, Harlem's Sugar Hill.

You must take the "A" Train to Sugar Hill
Way up in Harlem

By the 1960s, as the third great migration drew to a close, African American music seemed to be shaking free from its historical moorings. Black people were both in place and everyplace. Yet, as in times past, the stasis in black life would not last long. During the last third of the twentieth century, black life would again be remade, as a new diaspora brought millions of people of African descent to the United States and, with it, a new music.

CHAPTER FIVE

Global Passages

By the third quarter of the twentieth century, African American people were firmly entrenched in urban America. The epic transcontinental journey had been completed, and nearly as many black people resided in the Northern and Western states as in the Southern ones. Their Northern base provided the political leverage to overthrow the system of de jure segregation, remaking black life and the nation along with it. The transformation of American society allowed some of the children and grandchildren of those who had fled the South to reverse field and return to the land of their ancestors. It too had been transformed, so that, as in the North, black Southerners identified as fully with the city as they once had with the countryside. The agricultural past that had been central to African American life for more than three centuries was a distant memory for black people. Like most Americans, they worked in offices and shops rather than in fields and factories. Rather than follow mule-turned furrows, black people navigated the streets and alleys of the inner city. The most visible black men and women were no longer sharecroppers and washerwomen, but athletes, entertainers, public intellectuals, and not a few aspiring politicians. Hip-hop and MTV had replaced spirituals and juke joints.

Shaped by the forces unleashed by the fall of Jim Crow and the collapse of industrial America, the structure of black society was radically altered. The Old Settlers, with their dependence on white patrons, were long gone, as was the new elite with its captive black clientele. In their place stood a professional and managerial class whose education and occupations differed little from that of other upward-striving Americans. Their ambitions, patterns of consumption, and lifestyle so followed that of bourgeoisies the world over that some commentators spoke of the declining significance of race.

But if much had changed in African American life, much remained the same. Race had taken a new form, but had not disappeared or even been attenuated. Black people remained disproportionately at the bottom of American society, denied access to good jobs, condemned to the worst housing, and locked in poverty. The majority of black Americans had yet to enter the much-heralded new black middle class. Those who did—like their predecessors—had just a fraction of the material resources of their white counterparts. Members of the black middle class lived on the edge, ever fearful of losing their privileged place and sliding into a swollen proletariat. As in centuries past, commentators and politicos defined black life by its most vulnerable members. Whereas once they dwelled upon the benighted slave and the eternal peasant, now they emphasized the urban underclass's seemingly immutable culture of poverty.

Lost among the attributes that allegedly defined black Americans was another seemingly immutable characteristic: their overwhelmingly American nativity. While white America had been continually reconstructed by waves of European immigrants, the vast majority of black people—perhaps more than any other group of Americans, save for Native Americans—could trace their ancestry to the seventeenth and eighteenth centuries. For more than 150 years between the official close of the transatlantic slave trade in 1808 and the passage of the Immigration and Nationality Act in 1965, few black Africans or foreign-born people of African descent had augmented the African American population. During the late nineteenth and the twentieth centuries, when Europeans totaling in the millions annually flooded into the United States, African immigrants could be counted in the hundreds. Most of these were fair-skinned peoples who derived from Egypt, Morocco, and South Africa, along with a small contingent of Afro-Portuguese from the Cape Verde Islands. In 1900, only 20,000 black people of foreign birth resided in the United States. A short-lived influx from the circum-Caribbean during the first decades of the twentieth century remained the striking exception. Set in motion by the construction of the Panama Canal, some 150,000 Barbadians, Jamaicans, Trinidadians, and other black Antilleans entered the United States under rules that allowed unlimited entry from the Western Hemisphere. In 1924, new national-origins restrictions limited immigration from the Caribbean, although some West Indians continued to gain entry under the British quota. That codicil was eliminated and then briefly reinstated during World War II, when the United States government issued short-term visas to Jamaican agricultural workers. Still, at midcentury, the foreign-born black population totaled 114,000. Even these exceptions proved the rule. "[T]here was relatively little in the way of new black in-migration to the United States since well before the end of slavery," explained a distinguished demographer in a 1978 survey, "and because black emigration from the nation has not been significant in number, the assumption of a closed population is not too unrealistic."[1]

Then, with the suddenness of the earlier transfers of black peoples from Africa to America, from the seaboard South to the interior, and from the rural South to the urban North, all began to change. During the last third of the twentieth century, dark-skinned peoples of African descent from all over the world descended upon the United States. The influx of people of African descent initiated yet another transformation of black society. Still under way at the beginning of the twenty-first century, this fourth great migration—like the earlier three—promises to remake African American life, much as rappers had begun to remake African American music.

While earlier passages began with the crack of a whip, the slam of an auctioneer's gavel, or the whispered promise of a better job, the new migration had its origins in a fit of absentmindedness. The congressmen who authored the Immigration and Nationality Act of 1965 evinced no particular desire to enlarge the black population, let alone repeople the United States with foreign-born men and women of African descent. Yet making skilled-based merit and family ties, rather than national origins, the criteria for entry into the United States jarred the door open for peoples of African descent. Allowing independent states a quota of 20,000 immigrants, not including the immediate family members of American citizens, threw it open. Subsequent modifications to the 1965 law—particularly the 1986 Immigration and Control Act, which granted the possibility of amnesty to numerous illegal immigrants and introduced the so-called lottery system—only enlarged the portal. Still others gained entry as political refugees and asylees.[2]

During the next forty years, black men and women poured into the United States at an ever-increasing rate. Nations whose citizens had been denied entry or limited to quotas in the hundreds sent thousands. As Caribbean and African colonies gained independence, the number of such places multiplied; newly independent nations, which previously had not been recognized as places of embarkation, became sources of large-scale immigration.

The new American laws and regulations made entry into the United States possible, but, as with earlier passages, the matter of labor—both the need for labor and the needs of laborers—was never far from the surface. For American employers, the dynamics of a global marketplace—both for cheap, unskilled labor and for highly skilled workers—were becoming increasingly evident. For workers, particularly those residing in the low-wage, low-standard-of-living portions of the greater Caribbean and continental Africa, the United States was an increasingly attractive destination. Post–World War II decolonization had been accompanied by promises of prosperity and democracy. During the 1960s, the initial success of many newly established Caribbean and African states waned amid hurricanes and droughts, falling commodity prices, poor planning, and rampant corruption. Economic collapse ignited political turmoil in the form of military coups that empowered repressive regimes, eroded civil society, and initiated civil wars, expulsions, and genocide. Hundreds of thousands, eventually millions, of desperate men and women scrambled to find safe harbors from natural disasters, impoverishment, predatory regimes, and ethnic cleansers. Reclaiming the nation's heritage as a global sanctuary, American presidents—with varying degrees of enthusiasm—offered asylum to these desperate men and women. An increasingly assertive Congressional Black Caucus lobbied to assure that Caribbean and African asylees received the protection of these executive orders. As refugees were not subject to the numerical quotas governing immigration, they added to the total number entering the United States.[3]

The presidential edicts and new legislation hardly met needs of the men and women set adrift. But the possibility of entry into the United States encouraged many to try, legally if possible and illegally if not. Some, having entered on short-term visas, stayed without official certification. As their numbers and desperation grew, amnesty programs legitimated their standing. Those not granted amnesty often had their stay extended by congressionally mandated Temporary Protected Status, allowing illegal entries time to secure asylum. Still others took advantage of the 1990 Diversity Immigrant Visa Program designed to incorporate émigrés from nations with previously low rates of immigration to the United States. But many of those who failed to secure the protection of these programs simply remained illegally.[4]

During the 1970s, the number of black people of foreign birth entering the United States increased at an ever-faster rate, as the United States became a destination for the African diaspora. In the decades that followed, the rate continued to accelerate; more arrived in the 1980s than in the 1970s and even more in 1990s than in the 1980s. Their numbers continue to swell into the twenty-first century, so that the black population closed for centuries, opened to increase from the outside. During the last decade of the twentieth century immigrants accounted for fully one-quarter of the growth of the African American population.[5]

While the diverse definitions of race and the vagaries of counting by national origin make it impossible to calculate the precise number of black arrivals, several million men and women of African descent entered the United States in the last third of the twentieth century and the first years of the twenty-first. Although they were but a small part of the massive migration that followed the 1965 reform of immigration, the newcomers transformed black society. Whereas less than one black person in one hundred was foreign born prior to 1965, by 2000 the proportion was one in twenty. By the early twenty-first century, one-tenth of all black Americans were immigrants or the children of immigrants.[6]

People of African descent arrived from all parts of the globe. Among the new arrivals were black Britons, some of whom descended from the Loyal Blacks who had taken refuge in England in the years that followed the American Revolution. Others were the children of black American soldiers who had served in places as disparate as Germany, Korea, and Vietnam. Yet others came from Australasia and the Middle East, but the vast majority of the newcomers derived from the Caribbean and Africa.

Unlike most of the new black arrivals, Caribbean peoples had established a presence in the United States early in the twentieth century. In the intervening years, many had obtained American citizenship, making it possible for them to sponsor members of their immediate families. Some of the new arrivals drew on these kin connections, but most entered on their own. Among the first were English-speaking immigrants from former British colonies, whose ties with their old colonial overlord had withered after Britain closed its borders to its former subjects. Jamaicans were the most numerous, but many black newcomers originated in smaller West Indian islands like Antigua, Barbados, Montserrat, and St. Lucia. These black men and women were soon joined by an influx of refugees from the larger Caribbean— Cuba, El Salvador, Guyana, and Nicaragua—many of whom were black at least by the conventions established in the United States.[7] The largest group of black refugees whose native language was not English arrived from Haiti. Desperately trying to escape endemic poverty and the heavy, dictatorial hand of the Duvalier family and its equally despotic successors, they were intercepted by the American Coast Guard, interned, demonized as diseased and politically subversive, and then returned to their homeland. Still, they continued their massive exodus until their desperate plight could not be ignored. All totaled, over two million black migrants arrived from the greater Caribbean after 1965, with more than 900,000 entering American borders in the 1990s. The influx hardly slackened during the first years of the twenty-first century, as many of the earlier immigrants, now American citizens, began to sponsor family members.[8]

The African entries followed a similar pattern, with the mixture of immigrants and refugees growing steadily during the last two decades of the twentieth century and the first years of the twenty-first. Their numbers had exploded with the turmoil in Africa, beginning in the early 1960s with the Biafran civil war and continuing through conflicts in Ethiopia, Rwanda, Liberia, Sierra Leone, and Sudan. Between 1980 and 2000, the number of immigrants from sub-Saharan Africa doubled and doubled again. In the last decade of the twentieth century, an average of around 40,000 Africans annually entered the United States, and foreign-born Africans increased from 400,000 in 1990 to some 700,000 in 2000. By then, the first arrivals had gained American citizenship and they too could sponsor family members. In 2001, more than half of the 54,000 African immigrants fell under programs that granted preference to the families of American citizens. Most African immigrants originated in Nigeria, whose nationals in the United States totaled some 140,000 at the beginning of the twenty-first century. But the number of Ethiopians, Ghanaians, Kenyans, Liberians, and Somalis were not far behind.

At the beginning of the twenty-first century, persons of African birth in the United States totaled around one million, according to official federal census totals.[9] The actual number may have been much larger. Some arrived illegally, and others entered legally and stayed illegally. But even legal immigrants often avoided census takers and other governmental officials. The 1990 census counted 2,287 Senegalese residing in the United States, although at least 10,000 were living in New York City.[10]

Not all of the new arrivals intended to settle permanently. Some newcomers were reluctant immigrants, forced from their country by events beyond their control. Also among the new arrivals were thousands of visitors, including students eager for an American education and entrepreneurs equally desirous to make a few dollars. Such sojourners had been many among the black men and women moving from south to north during the third passage, but the forces of late-twentieth-century globalization changed the nature of migration by linking distant places more closely than ever before. The availability and speed of transportation and communication had shrunk the distance between the United States and even the most distant immigrant homelands. Cell phones and the Internet permitted immigrants to keep in touch with family and friends. Jet planes allowed men and women to shuttle back and forth. Whereas migrants once depended upon rumors to learn about the society to which they might be shipped and upon chance encounters to recover information about the societies they had left, late-twentieth-century migrants could maintain continual contact between the two worlds simply by putting a cell phone to their ear. Migrants returned to their countries of origin for the death of a loved one, the marriage of friends, or just a brief respite. During the 1990s, some 90 percent of African immigrants visited their native land at least once after entering the United States and more than half visited home at least once every three years. Like sojourners from the South earlier in the twentieth century, they often sent their children home for summer vacations and hosted visiting relatives and friends, many of whom joined the ranks of the immigrants. Many men and women became comfortable in their old homelands and their new homes, literally transnationals.[11]

Others made a choice. They had no intention of remaining in the United States. Political refugees just waited for a change of regime to return to their homelands. Vendors who plied their wares on the streets of nearly every major American city stayed just long enough to earn a small nest egg and then return home. Other sojourners found advantages in maintaining multiple residences and formalized these arrangements with dual citizenship.

Inevitably, however, some of these short-term migrations lasted longer than originally planned. While sojourners remained determined to return home, life intervened. They married, had children, and embraced an American way of life. Many discovered they earned much more than they could in their native lands. Some found the stability of the United States preferable to the social disorder of their nativity. Return trips became less frequent and remittances to their homeland grew smaller. The possibilities of return dwindled, and in time they settled permanently. Speaking of Haitian refugees, an investigator writing at the beginning of the twenty-first century noted that many migrants "who saw themselves as sojourners or 'birds of passage,' who came to work in the United States to save money to return home, are now buying retirement homes in Florida." While not all sojourners purchased vacation homes, many were transformed into permanent residents.[12]

Whatever the mode or motives for migrating, black newcomers were an extraordinarily diverse group. As with the earlier passages— forced and free—adults composed the vast majority of black immigrants. At the beginning of the twenty-first century, some 70 percent of Africans and nearly 60 percent of Caribbean migrants were between the ages of twenty-five and fifty. But among these immigrants, the sexual balance of the new arrivals differed sharply. While men made up the greater proportion of migrants from Africa, with a sex ratio—or number of men per 100 women—of 140, women composed the bulk of migrants from the Caribbean, with a sex ratio of 85.[13]

Ethnic, linguistic, religious, and economic distinctions compounded the difference between Caribbean and African migrants, as well as among them. Caribbean peoples derived from places as different as mainland Belize and Guyana to island nations big and small. They spoke English and French, Spanish and Dutch, as well as a variety of creole tongues. Coming from a continent almost three times the size of the United States, African migrants were even more diverse: Ghanaians and Nigerians from the west coast of Africa, Rwandans and Ugandans from central Africa, and Ethiopians and Somalis from Africa's Horn. Moreover, such national designations masked an even larger diversity. Nigerians were Hausas, Igbos, and Yorubas, just as Ghanaians were Akan, Ewe, and Fante. Among the various ethnic lineages were Americo-Liberians and Sierra Leonean Creoles, whose forebears had been transported and transported themselves across the Atlantic several times during the last three hundred years. Africans, like their Caribbean counterparts, were also multilingual, not only speaking the languages of the old colonial metropoles but also numerous indigenous tongues, from Amharic in east Africa to Ga in the Niger Valley. Their religious differences included various brands of Christianity practiced by the Caribbean émigrés as well as Islam and Coptic Orthodoxy in Africa.[14]

The immigrants' social standing was as diverse as the cultural baggage they carried. Following new criteria for admission to the United States, educated professionals—some of whom carried multiple degrees—numbered many among the new immigrants. Schooled in the British educational system, Jamaicans, Barbadians, Ghanaians, Nigerians, and other migrants from Anglophone Africa and the Caribbean enjoyed a high degree of English-language literacy. Indeed, among immigrants entering the United States at the end of the twentieth century, African arrivals stood at the apex in terms of educational attainment. In 1990, nearly nine of ten African immigrants held a high school diploma and more than half had graduated from college. Many had achieved a considerable measure of economic success, often as part of the global economy, like the petroleum engineers who moved between Lagos and Houston. Rather than being driven by acts of desperation to escape political repression or drought-born famines, these well-placed men and women arrived with knowledge, money, and connections. They desired only to transfer their credentials to the United States to obtain better jobs and higher pay as doctors, lawyers, engineers, and accountants.[15]

Not all were so fortunate. Refugees generally fled with little more than the clothes on their backs, traumatized by the nightmarish events that had driven them from their homes and the months, sometimes years, spent in refugee encampments. For example, Haitians came from the poorest country in the Western Hemisphere. Unlike their well-placed counterparts, many had no facility with English and faced linguistic isolation. Seeking to escape the endemic poverty that characterized the economies of their homelands and carrying no marketable skills, these displaced men and women found themselves consigned to work that Americans shunned. Most labored as domestics, gardeners, hospital orderlies, taxi drivers, and casual laborers.[16]

Yet, taken as a whole, the new arrivals did remarkably well. Working long hours, often at several jobs, they began to accumulate capital.

Drawing upon long-standing entrepreneurial traditions and some-times bankrolled by credit associations that reached back to their countries of origin, they took their places at flea markets and on street corners, selling a variety of "native crafts"—ebony carvings, colorful textiles, jewelry—mixed with faux Rolexes, all of which may have been manufactured in Korea or Taiwan. Some opened small grocer-ies, restaurants, and taverns, supplying their countrymen with famil-iar food and drink. As a result, although they faced much the same kind of racial discrimination as American-born blacks, immigrants enjoyed higher median incomes and lower rates of poverty. Even after remitting portions of their income to support families back home, their standard of living was a cut above that of nonimmigrant black families.[17]

Immigrants of African descent initially spread across the American landscape. While many new arrivals had clear destinations, others had little knowledge of American geography. Viewing the United States from Lagos or Brazil, Memphis looked much like Minneapolis, and newcomers settled in every corner of the United States. The American government contributed to the dispersion by shipping refu-gees to some unlikely destinations. Sudanese refugees were sent to Fargo, North Dakota, while Somalis were settled in Lewiston, Maine.[18]

But like earlier immigrants, newcomers did not always remain at their initial point of debarkation. For many, arrival in the United States was just another stop in a long migratory trail. Refugees from Sierra Leone and Liberia had earlier found shelter in Ghana, and Sudanese spent time in camps in Kenya. Others had been funneled through Europe and Australasia before they reached the United States. The long experience of Caribbean peoples in inter-island movement continued on the mainland in a different form.[19]

Over time, however, the newly arrived gravitated to the great Ameri-can metropoles. At the beginning of the twenty-first century, when

migrants equaled about 5 percent of the African American population, they generally composed more than 10 percent of black people
in the largest American cities. In many cities and suburbs, the count
was much higher. Immigrants numbered better than 15 percent of
the black population of the Washington metropolitan area and more
than one-third of the population of New York, where black immigrants and their children compose a near majority—and a projected
majority—of the city's black population.[20]

The unsettled geography of immigrant life soon fixed into a recognizable matrix whose coordinates were city and nationality. Proximity made Miami and other Gulf ports the natural destination for
migrants from the Caribbean, where Afro-Caribbeans composed
more than one-third of the population. Black Cubans settled in Little
Havana as a part of the larger Cuban migration, and an analogous
Little Haiti—where a main street was renamed Boulevard Toussaint
L'Ouverture—soon emerged. New York and Florida, which had
become a center for Caribbean life earlier in the twentieth century,
continued to draw more than their share of migrants from Jamaica,
Barbados, and other islands.[21] Their Haitian populations became the
largest in the nation. Africans also crowded into New York, finding
niches in various areas of the great metropolis. Ghanaians and Nigerians settled in the borough of Queens, Liberians in Staten Island,
and Dominicans in the north end of Manhattan. Likewise, Ethiopians
gravitated to the Washington metropolitan area, where their numbers
reached some 75,000 at the end of the twentieth century.[22]

Like soon attracted like, and not by mere happenstance, as the
familiar migrant chains connected newcomers to places where their
earlier arriving countrymen had settled. Those first arrivals provided
their kin, friends, and compatriots who followed with information,
cash, temporary quarters, and even employment, as well as a host of
other services that helped to integrate newcomers into the United
States—and brought in yet other families to sponsor and continue

the chain. Much as Cleveland had become Alabama North early in the twentieth century, so Providence, Rhode Island, became Liberia East, Flatbush-Canarsie in Brooklyn became Jamaica North, and a few blocks of Harlem became Little Senegal. Similar national concentrations could be found in other cities, as with the Sudanese in Minneapolis or the Brazilians in Boston.[23]

An infrastructure of community life soon emerged, much as it had in past migrations. Dotting immigrant neighborhoods were churches, schools, and fraternal and benevolent societies bound by familial ties and reinforced by networks that reached back to "hometown associations" in the various countries of origin. Celebrating rites of passage—the birth of a child, naming godparents, weddings, funerals—along with sporting events, theatrical performances, and lectures, these networks became important links in the chain that immigrants traveled. They often functioned as surrogate kin, providing guidance for the newly arrived, rallying points for the established, and places of political mobilization for all. They helped newcomers find employment and financed small enterprises. The restaurants and bars, along with a host of small shops that these associations helped fund, sold food and drink prepared in the familiar way; some braided hair according to custom and prepared burials that followed traditional funerary practice.[24]

The men and women who stood behind the counters of these small enterprises found advantage in maintaining the old ways in the new world. Ethnic solidarity proved to be good business, and some articulated a fierce nationalism. But ethnic entrepreneurs also found benefit in easing the path of new arrivals by acting as a bridge between their homelands and their new homes, serving as agents of Americanization. Most found no contradiction between the two roles.[25]

Community formation became the occasion for men and women to clarify the multiple identities they carried to the United States, or at least to sort them out. Mary C. Waters, a Harvard sociologist who

studies late-twentieth-century West Indian immigrants, tells of a clerk
of Barbadian origin who distinguished herself from an African American by asserting her Caribbean heritage, only to be reprimanded by
her Jamaican superior that she was not Caribbean but rather West
Indian, meaning Anglophone Caribbean. Yet, upon further investiga-
tion, Waters discovered that a mere 3 percent of the Jamaicans living
in New York described themselves as West Indian, while some 80
percent continued to call themselves Jamaicans. Waters concluded
that "it appears the identity adopted by the first generation is in part
a learned response to American categories and ways of defining people." Indeed, another immigrant told Waters that before she "came
here I used to be Jamaican. But now I am West Indian."[26]

As Waters's interview suggests, the process by which immigrants
reinvent themselves amid the fourth great migration does not differ
substantially from that of earlier arrivals, forced or free. Just as Igbos
and Hausas became Africans in the eighteenth century, so those
same ethnic groups made themselves into Nigerians at the end of the
twentieth. The nation-state—although new—often had a more powerful pull on the west side of the Atlantic than on the east, if only
because the American government recognizes nationality and not
ethnicity. A sense of how the migratory process has sharpened
national allegiances can be garnered by the calendar of some of the
fetes celebrated in Chicago. There, on April 20 Cameroonians mark
their nation's independence day; soon after, the DuSable Museum of
African American History hosts the Nigerian Festival, which is followed in late July by the Liberian Independence Day Parade, the celebrations of Angolan and Ghanaian independence (November 11 and
March 6), and finally by Jamhuri Day (December 12), when Kenyans
mark the British withdrawal from their native land.[27]

Nationality, however, does not always trump ethnicity. Yorubas—
who came from all parts of the Atlantic world—found that they had
more in common with each other than they did with their putative

215

countrymen. They established distinctive neighborhood enclaves, along with associations that reflected the transnational character of African ethnicity, as with the Egbe Omo Yoruba (National Association of Yoruba Descendants in North America) which drew its membership not only from west Africa but also from the Caribbean and portions of South America. Similar transnational, rather than national, entities emerged among Ewes from Benin, Ghana, and Togo, as well as the Jollas from Gambia and Senegal. Moreover, if Yorubas, Jollas, Ewes, and others reestablished their transnational ethnicity on the west side of the Atlantic, they were joined by others to create new forms of solidarity, like the African National Union, an association that claimed to speak for all Africans in the United States. The process whereby Igbos and Angolans, Mandes and Mandinkas had joined to establish African churches, schools, and burial societies at the end of the eighteenth century was repeated two hundred years later. In much the same way, the diverse peoples of the Caribbean not only celebrate Dominican or Jamaican independence but also march in local Caribbean parades.[28]

Such connections suggest that rather than become African Americans, immigrants of African descent manufactured new nationalities distinctive from that of native black Americans. Angolans, Kenyans, and Somalis became Africans, and Barbadians, Jamaicans, and Trinidadians became Caribbeans—not necessarily African Americans—as a result of their experience on the mainland.

Whether understood in transnational, national, or ethnic terms, the ability to create new ties or maintain old ones complicated the process of identity formation. Old allegiances have perhaps been strongest among political refugees, awaiting regime change before returning home. But attachments to the homeland affected nearly all newcomers, creating a farrago of multiple identities while birthing yet a new one.

As African and Afro-Caribbean people—along with the scattering of black people from other parts of the globe—forged new selves, they also discovered a common experience as immigrants of African descent in the United States. In centuries past, Africans and African Americans, Virginians and Mississippians, and Southerners and Northerners had little choice but to find common ground. Differences between Africans and creoles had disappeared quickly in the seventeenth and eighteenth centuries, just as slaves from the seaboard had been silently incorporated into the plantations of the interior in the nineteenth century and just as Northerners and Southerners eventually had joined together in the cities of the North in the twentieth century. The often intense conflict that accompanied the confrontation of distinctive cultures rarely lasted more than a generation, as African American society achieved remarkable unity. Africans became African Americans in mainland North America, slaves from the seaboard became Southerners in the black belt, and black Southerners became urbanites in the cities of the North. The places they created in eighteenth-century Virginia, nineteenth-century Alabama, or twentieth-century Chicago were the products of the intermixture of natives and newcomers.

The unity of past centuries proved more elusive for black men and women journeying in the fourth great migration. To be sure, from the time of their arrival in the United States—and, for some, even before—immigrants of African descent confronted the realities of American racism—a reality made visible by the global reach of American culture, tourism, and military interventions. Primed to expect the worst, black immigrants nonetheless were outraged at the harassment, denigration, and physical abuse many experienced. Primal moments—like the death of Amadou Diallo, a west African student and street merchant, at the hands of the New York City police—starkly revealed the dangers all black people, regardless of origins, faced in the United States.[29]

But most black immigrants needed no primer on race. Racial denigration was familiar, especially to those who had been subject to European colonial rule and, for some, whose country had experienced slavery. Yet the confrontation with white America was different from anything most had previously experienced. For the most part, the immigrants came from societies with overwhelmingly black majorities, and they dealt with race from a position of numerical—and generally political—superiority. Holding the reins of power had enabled some to obtain privileged places within the social hierarchy. The sting of second-class citizenship and derision heaped upon minorities had never been felt, and race never attained the central place in their lives. Having lived within a black majority—where ancestry or tribal affiliation, facial features, hair, and wealth were as much a determiner of status as skin color—immigrants arrived in a society where pigmentation was paramount.[30]

The standard American definition of race—the one-drop rule—also perplexed the new arrivals. So too did the absence of a middle group— a third caste generally described as "colored"—and the lack of privileges accorded people of mixed racial origins. The redrawing of the color line to create a two-caste system often alienated those who had been neighbors, friends, and even kin. A few discovered, for the first time, that they themselves were black. If immigrants were confused by the redefining of racial boundaries, so too were African Americans, who were both confounded and offended by the assumptions implicit in racial regimes where lineage and money could whiten.[31]

Differences created by the racial regimes were further befuddled by mutual ignorance. Although African Americans have long celebrated their connection with Africa—at least since Paul Cuffe began trading on the west coast of the continent in the 1790s—ties between African Americans and Africans had always been problematic. While black nationalists celebrated the link, others frankly admitted the "closest they've ever come to Africa is Busch Gardens." To these, the nature of slavery outside the bounds of the United States, the worldwide struggles against colonialism, and the origins of independence in the Caribbean or Africa constituted unknown territory. Some dismissed Africa as a primitive place bereft of civilization—a place where, in the satirical formulation of comic Eddie Murphy, people "ride around butt-naked on a zebra." Likewise, the Caribbean was merely a vacation spa. Others celebrated a mythological Africa, wrapping themselves in kente cloth and observing Kwanza, but with small appreciation of the continent itself. In the words of one Nigerian American, who found himself the target of racial slurs by native blacks, "just because African-Americans wear kente cloth does not mean they embrace everything that is African."[32]

Black immigrants, for their part, held a similar battery of stereotypes of black Americans. Gleaned in part from American movies, TV sitcoms, and music, such superficial fragments offered contradictory images of African Americans: on the one hand, as being hypersexed and superrich, and on the other hand, as being impoverished, impotent, and much abused.[33] Selecting from these conflicting portrayals, immigrants' conceptions of black Americans often had no more connection to reality than the African Americans' view of the immigrants.

Others saw the connection all too clearly. Given the choice of aligning with a minority burdened by the weight of discrimination or maintaining a separate identity, they tried to create an identity "which would separate them from the group they [were] closest to," stressing differences—be they linguistic, religious, cultural, or political—which distinguished them from African Americans. A sociologist of Haitian descent noted that the "Haitian flags on cars and in store windows have become not only symbols of ethnic pride but also a message to the white community that they expect to be treated differently because they are not African Americans." Haitians were not the only ones to wrap themselves in the flag to emphasize their difference from African Americans.[34]

The unforgiving character of the two-caste system that jumbled all black people together mitigated distrust and debunked stereotypes among people of African descent. But shared oppression no more created a shared politics in a twentieth-century city than it did in a nineteenth-century plantation or an eighteenth-century slave ship. Those who had long enjoyed the benefits of majority status had difficulty seeing an advantage in defending minority rights. "I don't want to be Black twice," asserted a Haitian immigrant. Some, while cognizant of the reality of American racism, quietly accepted it as part of a Faustian bargain in which economic opportunity and material prosperity were exchanged for silent assent.[35] Still others saw their national origins providing immunity from the problems that dogged black Americans. They had once been Ghanaians and Barbadians and relocation did not change that. In fact, the denigration of blackness in American society made it imperative to maintain the customs of the homeland. Although outraged by racial discrimination, they nonetheless turned a blind eye, conceiving themselves as sojourners whose future lay elsewhere or as a people apart.[36]

Behind these differences, according to one political scientist, stood a radically different understanding of the racism of white Americans. Whereas recent African and Caribbean immigrants tended to view racism as a barrier to be overcome, African Americans saw it more as systemic and so deeply entrenched that it is nearly impossible to breach.[37]

The latter views had little attraction for many—perhaps most—black immigrants. If such unspoken bargains that exchanged silence for economic advancement existed, they repudiated them. Newcomers instead found common cause with African Americans and embraced long-established African-American political traditions. Pushing to the forefront of the struggle for equality, they seized the banner of racial justice and demanded an end to inequality. African American heroes from Nat Turner to Martin Luther King, Jr., became their heroes and Black History Month their commemoration, as newcomers refit their own abolitionist and anticolonial politics to the circumstances of American life. "I would not be here had it not been for the black civil rights activists who cleared a pathway for blacks in America by standing up against racial and ethnic discrimination and inequality," declared one Ghanaian immigrant. African Americans, for their part, generally welcomed their black brothers and sisters to the fray. "There are old African Americans and new African Americans," declared one African American leader, "but we're all African Americans."[38]

But not all brothers and sisters became family. Some of the newcomers continue to think of themselves in terms of their former nationality. Asked why he and other Caribbean immigrants do not share the racial sensibility of American-born blacks, a Guyanese man responded, "We're immigrants. So we come here to uplift ourselves and go back home. We don't focus on that." Even among those whose long-term residence gives them more common ground with black natives, differences—rooted in circumstances and aspirations—remained. Language, dress, food, and music, along with attitudes toward family, gender conventions, religious practice, work ethic, and patterns of recreation—among other matters—separated them from African Americans. In a perceptive essay entitled "'Black Like Who?,'" a leading scholar of African American life found the largest division within black society was "between native- and foreign-born."[39]

Differences expressed themselves in a variety of ways, many of which resonated beyond a preference for basketball over soccer or for fufu over fries, or even in an exchange of mean-spirited schoolyard epithets. Practices like female circumcision or animal sacrifice offend many African Americans. Others have more material concerns, fearful that new arrivals would take their jobs, a suspicion compounded by the view—articulated by many white employers—that immigrants were more industrious and disciplined than nonimmigrants. The ability of some immigrants to transport their wealth, education, and connections from their homelands to the United States affirmed African American suspicions that the newcomers desired to elbow them aside. In the competition with newcomers, many natives saw themselves falling behind in the struggle for everything from sexual partners to education. When Harvard University gathered black students to celebrate its expanding black enrollment, university officials were surprised and a bit taken aback to discover that they were not celebrating the success of black students with long American lineages so much as they were that of Africans and West Indians with more recent immigrant roots.[40]

The sense of being outpaced stoked jealousies that led to the denial of a common heritage. New arrivals were seen as acting white, not really being black. The newcomers' desire to maintain ties with their countrymen—for example, their own churches and associations, endogenous marriages, culinary preferences, frequent returns to their homelands, and celebrations of their own holidays and heroes— suggested a sense of difference in the eyes of many African Americans. While they shared a similar complexion and African roots, they had little else in common. "A shared complexion does not equal a shared culture," observed Kofi Glover, a native of Ghana and a professor at the University of South Florida. Even the recognition of similar circumstances and an appreciation of common ancestry does not always draw natives and newcomers together. Differences, upon occasion, turn violent. Under the headline "Tensions between Africans and African Americans Surface Again," New York's *Amsterdam News* reported, "Some of the more than 4,400 Africans living in Central Harlem have been routinely targeted and singled out for discrimination and abuse, both verbal and physical. . . ." The abuse could be deadly. In the summer of 2006, following the murder of an East African man by an African American woman in Seattle, leaders from the African and African American communities aired their differences. "I think a lot has to do with the appearance of success [among recent African immigrants]," declared one longtime resident. "Some African Americans see themselves as having been left out, and people who have been in Kenya (and other African countries) don't understand the African American struggle." The differences festered, so that qualities African Americans celebrated in their own community, they condemned in the newcomers'. The solidarities of immigrant life were at times viewed as arrogance—a conceit embodied by their distinctive food, dress, accents, and institutions that distanced them from African American traditions. African leaders agreed: "These people, they don't like us; that is why they kill us."[41]

While violence is a rare occurrence, some newcomers returned African American condescension in kind, displaying their own brand of xenophobic intolerance. They boasted of their work ethic, comparing it as favorable to that of African Americans. Laboring at several jobs, attending school at night, and rising early the next day to work, they ridiculed the knots of unemployed men who occupied the street corners of black neighborhoods and the women who queued for food stamps. Advancing their children's education or assuring higher SAT scores with private tutors and other academic supplements, upward-striving immigrants looked askance at the large number of African American high school dropouts. Giving voice to traditional stereotypes of African American economic dependency and criminality that white Americans had long employed, they condemned unsuccessful African American neighbors in ways that infuriated natives.

The distance—physical and social—that new arrivals placed between themselves and African Americans was enlarged by the violence and disorder of the inner-city neighborhoods that they often shared. Newcomers feared not only for their lives and property, but also for their children, who they worried would embrace a culture foreign to their own. "We tend to raise our children differently," declared one Haitian immigrant. "African American kids do not respect their parents who let them talk to them any kind of way. They don't teach them the meaning of respect for adults." Rather than trust what they understood as the failures of inner-city school systems, some immigrants sent their children back home to be educated, believing schools in Bridgetown, Lagos, Port au Prince, and elsewhere would better inculcate their values.[42]

Yet these very same inner-city neighborhoods in which natives and newcomers awkwardly confronted one another also became sites where they began to create a new African American culture. As with earlier passages, the most visible manifestations of the transformation of black life could be found in the sounds emanating from the shared quarters. Much as the spirituals arose from the transcontinental transit from the seaboard to the black belt and jazz emerged amid the movement from south to north, so hip-hop grew amid the fourth great migration.

In the late 1970s, the impoverished African American community in the South Bronx seemed an unlikely spot to nurture a new musical form. But as Caribbean immigrants entered the old, established neighborhood, a new sound emerged. Hip-hop drew upon the mixing of mainland and island music traditions with shared rhetorical conventions of toasting (self-aggrandizing, rhymed praise poems), from the islands, and playing the dozens or capping (competitive exchanges of insults), from the mainland. It drew on a variety of expressions from diverse forms, such as break dancing (or b-boying and g-girling), graffiti art ("masterpieces" spray-painted on the sides of building and subway cars), and recorded and live music mixes, but it made its most powerful statement in the aggressive rhetorical style of MCing or rap.[43]

In the Bronx and later Harlem and Queens, the origins of hip-hop took root before audiences of young African Americans and Afro-Caribbeans, on the street and in clubs. Pioneers of the genre—

Jamaican-born Clive "DJ Kool Herc" Campbell, Bronx-born Afrika Bambaataa, and Barbados-born Grandmaster Flash—midwifed the new sound by fusing these musical and rhetorical forms at local dance halls and public outings. Drawing on the island tradition of mobile DJs and splicing together multiple recorded songs with drum machine sounds in electronic samplers (or sometimes playing two turntables simultaneously), they created a pulsating rhythm that looped around in repeated phrases and rhymed poetics. DJs broadcasted on massive speakers, or ghetto blasters—Kool Herc called his "Herculords"—with an emphasis on bass, making for an overwhelmingly loud sound.

The new music emerged quickly in neighborhoods in which people of African descent mixed. By the late 1970s, the Bronx would boast several hip-hop groups, among them the Funky Four Plus One and Grandmaster Flash and the Furious Five. Within a decade, entrepreneurs—many of them black—had discovered the popularity of the innovative music and its commercial possibilities. Before long, they began to construct a national and then an international market for hip-hop that extended far beyond New York City. New superstars like LL Cool J and groups like Public Enemy emerged, but they never lost touch with the early themes and sounds that had sparked the genre.

From the beginning, MCs, many of them immigrants from the Caribbean, drew on traditions of rhyming, a tradition they shared with other African Americans: "Kool Herc is in the house and he'll turn it out without a doubt." They also shared traditions of verbal dueling—the dozens or capping—that often exaggerated muscular strength and sexual prowess, frequently through the figure of an admired *baaad* man. But raps always identified with life in the inner city—including various urban sounds, like the wailing sirens and rattling trucks on urban streets—suggesting how movement was again giving way to place as the central theme of African American

life. Rap depicted in harsh, unforgiving terms the disorder and violence all too familiar to inner-city neighborhoods, where employment
was short and poverty widespread. It reflected a society in which
injustice could be seen as legitimizing the most antisocial behavior.
Often rappers did so with a sharp political edge, critiquing American
society. They also lionized the "coolness" of young black men who
had been denied access to meaningful work and the possibility of
supporting a family. Amid the disorder and decay, artists like Run-
D.M.C. celebrated blackness in songs like "Proud to Be Black." They
also identified an oppositional authenticity as the sine qua non of
black manhood. Building on such themes, some hip-hop artists
expressed more directly a radical egalitarianism, as with Brand Nubian's "One for All" and Public Enemy's "Fight the Power" and "It Takes
a Nation of Millions to Hold Us Back." But even this had limits. The
antiauthoritarian hypermasculinity was also by turns misogynistic,
depicting a world peopled by parasitic bitches and hos and trailing
off into nihilistic sexual fantasies.[44]

During the 1980s, hip-hop leaped across the country from New
York to California, often propelled by the new MTV and often taking
root in neighborhoods with mixed populations much like the Bronx.
New hip-hop artists like Ice-T, Dr. Dre, and Snoop Doggy Dogg celebrated South Central and Compton much as the first generation of
hip-hop artists had set their music in the Bronx and Harlem. Often
they competed with each other—sometimes to murderous effect—
emphasizing the superiority of the local brand of rap. As the East
Coast–West Coast rivalry dominated the early world of hip-hop, people
in other localities—Atlanta, Chicago, Houston, New Orleans, and
dozens of other places—joined the fray and developed their own
styles. Although the moguls of the corporate entertainment business
tried to curb the destructive violence that pervaded hip-hop, it continued to reflect the harsh realities of urban life, particularly with
N.W.A. (Niggaz With Attitude) and Public Enemy.

Place, it appeared, was ousting movement as the central theme of black life in the United States, as hip-hoppers told unvarnished stories of life in the hood, often using the language of the street.[45] Rap videos firmly rooted hip-hop—the spray-painted masterpieces and the break dancing as well as the music—in the inner city. They depicted urban street corners, playgrounds, rooftops, abandoned buildings, subway stations, giving an unmistakable sense of place. "I want my shit to be in my hood," declared one video director.[46]

But by the end of the twentieth century—perhaps even before—the cosmopolitan roots of hip-hop's South Bronx beginnings had expanded outward. Rapping and hip-hop more generally had become a global medium (along with its signature dress of hoodies, snooties, and oversized pants) that was as much at home in Accra and Cape Town as it was in Bridgetown and Salvador. It had taken on a life of its own, often influencing white suburban teenagers as well (the phenomenon of the so-called wiggers, or white niggers, was an example of white youth emulating blacks as portrayed in hip-hop imagery). The dynamic combination of natives and newcomers who had been hip-hop's founding fathers had faded, swallowed—sometimes literally—by the violence of inner-city black life about which they sang and the commodification of their music. New arrivals, with their ambitions for self-improvement, were often appalled at the lyrics, which spoke of and sometimes celebrated the meanness of the inner city they entered with grand hopes of remaking their lives. Ironically, the Afrocentrality embedded in hip-hop seemed to have little appeal to Africans, at least on the east side of the Atlantic. Rather than provide cohesion to black life, the new culture seemed to be a divisive force.

At the beginning of the twenty-first century, tensions between American-born and foreign-born blacks remained. Even the most routine interactions could reveal that distrust overwhelmed camaraderie. One authoritative survey of American-born blacks and West Indian and African (Ghanaian and Nigerian) immigrants concluded that while these groups shared appreciation of a common African heritage, "preconceived notions and myths about each other . . . allowed only a surface cordiality." These groups "remained suspicious that each wanted to get what was the other's just due."[47]

Such conflicts produced different strategies for addressing the omnipresent matter of race. While American-born blacks continued to press for equality, immigrants often dismissed the African American protest tradition as a self-defeating culture of complaint. Meanwhile, they looked inside their own nationally or ethnically defined communities and bolstered their ties to their homelands. Often they greeted what they saw as an African American preoccupation with "their rights" with a shrug or a curt "get over it." Asked how the newcomers' perspective differed from that of African Americans, one West Indian put the matter this way: "We are concerned about racism. But basically we don't walk around with a chip on our shoulders like African Americans, although . . . we experience a lot of racial prejudice. America owes African Americans something . . . opportunity. We feel less owed." Such views imply another, often unspoken, belief that black Americans have not taken advantage of the opportunities available if they worked hard and took responsibility for their families and for each other.[48]

Tensions between peoples with diverse African roots have continued to linger in the twenty-first century in part because immigrants have more options than earlier arrivals. Many immigrants continue to be more engaged with the politics of their old homeland rather than their new one. Others find no necessity to choose between them. The ease of international travel and communication, the possibilities of dual citizenship, and the autonomy of ethnic neighborhoods—refreshed and revitalized by new arrivals from the homeland—have allowed immigrants to maintain multiple identities. Immigrants thus can conceive of themselves, for example, as being both Nigerian and African American. Many newcomers see no conflict between membership in both their own national associations and the NAACP. On college campuses, the offices of the African American Student Association and the African Student Association stand side by side. Sometimes African Americans of all backgrounds stand together and sometimes they maintain their distance. Men and women who demonstrate against police brutality and racial profiling often maintain membership in different churches and insist their children marry within their group.[49]

The contrapuntal narrative—movement and place, fluidity and fixity, routes and roots—that has characterized black life throughout American history has not always followed the same course. But, at the beginning of the twenty-first century, and the fourth great migration, it would continue to shape African American life.

Epilogue

At the beginning of the twenty-first century, the latest—although doubtless not the last—of the great migrations continues to remake African American and American life. This massive transformation has affected every aspect of American society but perhaps none as much as the unlikely presidential candidacy of the son of a Kenyan goat herder. Barack Obama's triumphant election speaks directly to the changes set in motion with the legislation that President Lyndon Johnson signed some four decades earlier in the extraordinary year of 1965. The Civil Rights Act permitted African Americans to participate fully in the electoral arena from which they had been excluded nearly a century earlier. Equally significantly, the Immigration and Nationality Act allowed people of African descent from all over the world to enter a nation from which nearly all had been excluded for almost two centuries. The changes in politics and people created a new African America and a new America.

That much had been anticipated of the Civil Rights Act, whose origins could be found in centuries of struggle capped by a decade of intense, often violent conflict. Black leaders who gathered in the nation's capitol in the summer of 1965 and witnessed President Johnson sign the historic legislation affirmed its special significance. Armed with fresh guarantees of the franchise and refusing to be intimidated by legal challenges and extralegal violence, black men and women rushed to register to vote and to take their place on the hustings. As they did, they made swift and lasting changes to American politics.

The new politics changed everything. Embracing the Democratic Party, which had abandoned its historic defense of white supremacy to usher in black enfranchisement, African Americans cut their remaining ties to the party of Lincoln. Republicans did little to prevent the departure. Instead, they hurriedly shed the last remnants of their emancipatory inheritance. First under the guise of Richard Nixon's Southern Strategy, Republicans welcomed white Democrats and others who had opposed the Civil Rights revolution. In the years that followed, Republicans employed the politically charged issues of busing, welfare, and affirmative action to become the party of racial reaction. By 1980, it seemed only fitting that Ronald Reagan would announce his candidacy for the presidency in Philadelphia, Mississippi, the site of the murder of three civil rights workers. As Republicans used barely disguised racialist code words of "law and order" and "neighborhood schools," invented the myth of the black welfare queen, and publicized a recidivist Willie Horton to secure their political hegemony, Democrats became identified—often to their dismay—with programs favored by black Americans. By the end of the twentieth century, black voters had become the Democratic Party's most reliable constituency.[1]

Although centuries of movement had made and remade African and African American life, few Americans—certainly few black Americans—expected that the Immigration and Nationality Act would have a similar impact on African American life. While black leaders rejoiced at the passage of the Civil Rights Act, they paid little attention to immigration reform. In the decade following the passage of the new law, little happened to alter their response. Even as the number of black immigrants increased during the 1980s, African Americans viewed the new arrivals with a mixture of indifference and suspicion. By the end of the twentieth century, however, the changing demography of black life could no longer be ignored. The large-scale mixing of diverse peoples of African descent, some newly arrived and some deeply rooted in this country, once again began to remake the way African Americans saw themselves collectively. The old story of movement and rootedness was about to play itself out yet once again.

As hip-hop reverberated from boom boxes and then iPods, the presence of black immigrants began to have a more influential role in the politics and culture of African America. At first, newcomers focused on access to visas, the treatment of asylees, and other matters that revealed a greater preoccupation with their old homelands than their new one. However, in late 2006, with the beginning of the American presidential campaign, that changed dramatically. Suddenly, the immigrants' presence loomed large, as the newly arrived found a candidate who not only looked like them but shared many of their experiences.[2]

Barack Obama's father did not arrive in the United States under the new legislation, and his son was born prior to the historic reform of civil rights and immigration. However, Barack came of age in a society shaped by the changes initiated by those two laws. The interplay between them propelled him to a position that suggested how the fourth great migration had begun to redefine the lives of African Americans, and then American life, at the end of the twentieth century and the beginning of the twenty-first. New circumstances demanded a new narrative.

Like the children of immigrants in passages past, Barack Obama struggled to define a sense of self. In his autobiography, he reveals his complex genealogy, his peripatetic childhood, and the discovery that he "needed a race" as he mapped the multiple meanings of blackness between Jakarta and Nairobi until finding his own African American self on the South Side of Chicago.[3] As the interplay of movement and place that had made and remade African American life in the past again reshaped lives of black men and women, Obama—like others who shared his experience—became an exemplar of the remaking of African American society and its history.

In 1991, returning to Chicago with a Harvard law degree and ambitions aplenty, Obama gravitated to the Democratic Party, which recently elected a Democratic mayor and which dominated that city's African American politics much as it did the nation's at large. He played a small role in a voter registration drive during the 1992 election and began "constructing a political identity for himself." Four years later, drawing on his record as a community organizer, Obama won a Democratic seat in the Illinois state senate, where he gained a reputation as a political comer.

But as Obama attempted to expand his political reach, he found that his immigrant origins confounded his ambitions. In 2000, he challenged Bobby Rush, the Democratic incumbent representing South Side Chicago, for his seat in the House of Representatives. Obama identified Rush, a former Black Panther who had recently been defeated in the Democratic mayoral primary, with "a politics that is rooted in the past." Rush, who had spent his life in Chicago, happily conceded the point. He advertised his own place as a founder of the Illinois chapter of the Black Panther Party and dismissed Obama as an outsider with a strange lineage, a foreign upbringing, a peculiar name, and little knowledge of the African American experience. "Barack Obama went to Harvard and became an educated fool," Rush informed his constituents. "Barack is a person who read about the civil rights protests and thinks he knows all about it." Others were even more direct. "Barack is viewed in part to be the white man in blackface in our community," asserted one South Side politico. Many believed the charge to be self-evident. Rush crushed the newcomer, winning reelection by a two to one margin.[4]

By 2004, Obama had recovered from defeat, redoubled his ambitions, and declared his candidacy for the United States Senate. His black Republican opponent, Alan Keyes, drawing a lesson from Rush's victory, sought to undercut Obama's support within the black community by counterposing his family's roots in the slave South to Obama's peculiar lineage.[5] This time Obama was ready, demonstrating his rootedness not only by rehearsing his community service but also by his choice of recreation—pickup basketball.

Obama dispatched Keyes but not the concerns Keyes had raised about Obama's relationship to the historic African American experience. When Obama announced his presidential bid, the issue exploded on the national stage. Stanley Crouch, a combative African American music critic and syndicated columnist who sounded more like the nativist Henry Cabot Lodge of another era, reiterated Keyes's campaign screed—"lived the life of a black American"—in a manner that soon found its way to the front page of the *New York Times, Newsweek,* and other like venues. Is "Obama really black?" asked Crouch in a manner that anticipated his answer. "Other than color, Obama did not—does not—share a heritage with the majority of black Americans, who are descendants of plantation slaves. So when black Americans refer to Obama as 'one of us,'" Crouch concluded, "I do not know what they are talking about."[6]

The question of whether Obama was "black enough" soon reverberated across the Internet as bloggers of all persuasions seized the issue; simultaneously, the debate animated neighborhood barbershops and beauty parlors.[7] While some fixated on matters of Obama's mixed racial origins, class standing, and elite education, in his broadside Crouch kept the focus on the increasingly tangled relations between African Americans and the newly arrived people of African descent. As yet another commentator described it, "In such distinctions between black immigrants and African Americans lay buried a history of competitive intraracial tensions and cultural differences that have never been resolved."[8] Again, the tensions that once played out between Africans and creoles in the seventeenth and eighteenth centuries, between old-timers and newcomers in the nineteenth-century black belt, and between Old Settlers and the new middle class in the twentieth-century urban North were manifesting themselves, although this time for a national audience.

Debra Dickerson, a journalist whose work explores matters of African American identity, drew the lines even more sharply. "'Black,' in our political and social reality, means those descended from West African slaves. Voluntary immigrants of African descent (even those descended from West Indian slaves) are just that, voluntary immigrants of African descent with markedly different outlooks on the role of race in their lives and in politics. At a minimum, it can't be assumed," she insisted with mind-chopping logic, "that a Nigerian cabdriver and a third-generation Harlemite have more in common than the fact a cop won't bother to make the distinction. They're both 'black' as a matter of skin color and DNA, but only the Harlemite, for better or worse, is politically and culturally black, as we use the term."[9]

Parsing the differences between Nigerian cabdrivers and third-generation residents of Harlem was no idle matter, for, at base, Dickerson saw them as central to the very meaning of the African American experience and who would define it. "We know a great deal about black people," Dickerson observed in defining the intraracial struggle. "We know next to nothing about immigrants of African descent (woe be unto blacks when the latter groups find their voice and start saying all kinds of things we don't want said)."[10]

Much the same could be noted of immigrants of African descent from other parts of the world. Louis Chude-Sokei, a professor of literature at the University of California, whose mixed Nigerian and Jamaican origins suggest that he may have heard those voices of woe and hence understood the matter precisely as had Dickerson. "As the numbers of black immigrants and their progeny grow to challenge the numerical supremacy of the native black minority, can a challenge to African Americans' cultural dominance, racial assumptions and politics be far behind?"[11]

Obama eventually defused the controversy over whether he was black enough. Reiterating the traditional American measure of race, he pointed to the inexorable function of the one-drop rule. "When I leave this interview and go out on the street and attempt to hail a taxi," Obama told television interviewer Charlie Rose, "there is no question who I am."[12]

But Dickerson had already conceded that litmus test—"a cop won't bother to make the distinction." While the fealty of cabdrivers and policemen to the one-drop rule may have satisfied the "rank-and-file black voters"—"as long as Obama acts black and does us proud"—it did nothing to satisfy Dickerson and perhaps others, except to confirm that such men and women were "no less complicit in this shell game we're playing."[13]

The shell game—the shifting meaning of blackness under the cover of the persistence of race—had been played in mainland North America at least since John Rolfe purchased those "twenty Negars." It had hardly ended at the beginning of the twenty-first century. Obama's struggle "to raise myself to be a black man in America" spoke precisely to the reality that the millions of other black immigrants and children of immigrants had confronted and continue to confront. After graduating from Columbia University, Obama took his search for groundedness to Chicago, with its charismatic black mayor, and began a job as an organizer in a dilapidated Chicago housing development. Later he joined an African American church and married into a family with deep roots in the city and, beyond that, in the slave south. Obama had found his place; he was rooted, finding in Chicago "a vision of black life in all its possibilities, a vision that filled me with longing—a longing for place, and a fixed and definite history."[14]

Obama, in short, had moved beyond the blood quotient of the one-drop rule to the ideological terrain upon which race had always rested. But in convincing some that he was black enough, Obama had become too black for many white Americans. While the suspicions of some white Americans—along with his own electoral successes—affirmed Obama's racial credentials in the eyes of black Americans, his new position required a fuller, more public explication of race. He found the occasion in quelling the firestorm created by the angry racial musing of his pastor.

In Obama's speech on race in Philadelphia in March 2008, his tone was philosophical and his subject historical as he unraveled the American dilemma from the site where three centuries earlier the Founding Fathers had drafted their call for a more perfect Union. Obama emphasized that the Union created with the ratification of the Constitution had never been perfect but "a union that could be and should be perfected over time." Thus the nation, like himself, was made and remade.[15]

Beginning with the "nation's original sin of slavery," Obama traced the American struggle through the "successive generations . . . [of] protest and struggle, on the streets and in the courts, through a civil war and civil disobedience—and always at great risk—to narrow that gap between the promise of our ideals and the reality of their time." Obama thus retold the tale of the "long march of those who came before us, a march for a more just, more equal, more free, more caring and more prosperous America." It was a progressive tale, which conceded past errors but celebrated "the greatness and the goodness" of the American people.[16]

Obama's remarks on race were politically astute as well as historically informed. In placing the question of race within the familiar confines of the master narrative of African American history, he then found his own place in the story as the "son of a black man from Kenya and a white woman from Kansas . . . raised with the help of a white grandfather who survived a depression to serve in Patton's Army during World War II and a white grandmother who worked on a bomber assembly line at Fort Leavenworth while he was overseas. "I am married to a black American who carries within her the blood of slaves and slaveowners," Obama continued, "an inheritance we pass on to our two precious daughters."[17]

In reiterating the story spanning from slavery to freedom Barack Obama affirmed his place in the long course of African American history. He was at one with the Africans who had crossed the Atlantic in the Middle Passage, with Frederick Douglass, for whom a slave "was pegged down to one single spot," with the African Americans who had crossed the continent and whose children Booker T. Washington advised to "cast down your bucket," and with Martin Luther King, Jr., whose "arc of justice" always bent toward freedom.

But even as Obama retold the story of slavery to freedom, he too had lived the story of movement and place. The contrapuntal narrative—fluidity and fixity, routes and roots—began with the Middle Passage and continued through the massive migrations that propelled peoples of African descent across the continent, first from east to west and then from south to north, and finally the diaspora which brought Obama's father and millions of others to American soil.

Each of these titanic passages had created major discontinuities in the lives of black men and women. They broke families, impoverished peoples, despoiled communities, and produced worlds of oppression and exploitation that wore on self-worth and promoted the most heinous inhumanity. Yet these same migrations also promoted hope, opportunity, and life. They forged new families, strengthened peoples, and promoted mutuality and reciprocity and revealed the best of human qualities. They produced new expectations and institutions, at once altering the migrants' material world and moral sensibility and setting the ground for a creative cultural explosion. In remaking African American life blackness was redefined both for the enslaved, and later for the free. What had been true in the seventeenth century was also true in the twenty-first.

The same can be said of place, which, after all, was a product of movement. As a people often forced to be on the move, black men and women developed a firm attachment to place. They became, in succession, the archetypal agriculturalists, with a deep knowledge, appreciation, and love of the land, and then the quintessential urbanites, with a streetwise understanding of city life. A love of locality celebrated—by turns—Africa, the South, and the inner city, which became the stock in trade of a succession of black artists who wrote, painted, photographed, and sang about the particular places that were at the heart of the black experience. Frederick Douglass's postemancipation return to the eastern shore of Maryland and the Great House Farm, Booker T. Washington's visit to the mines of Malden in West Virginia, the reverse migration of thousands of immigrants to the rural South, and the swelling number of heritage tourists who pilgrim to the Door of No Return all reflect the hold of place on African American life.

The cumulative impact of the repeated interplay between movement and place has required continued innovation in black society: movement set loose the creative impulse and place gave it a platform to develop. Over the course of four centuries, cultural innovation—in language, cuisine, rhetoric, theology, music—became the signature of the African American experience. The repeated reinvention of self and society created patterns of expression that prized the originality of an Edisto Island spiritual, a Bessie Smith blues, a John Coltrane riff, or an LL Cool J rap. Looking backward while moving forward, black people created a society with a deep reverence for what was as well as an obsessive concern for what would become. Memories of what had been done to them as well as of what they had done for themselves helped to create a sense of peoplehood.

The transformation of peoples of African descent was about more than an exchange of bib overalls for a zoot suit, for with it came new meanings of blackness. The definition of race has changed even as the concept may seem impervious to alteration. Some of the new meanings had been foisted upon unwilling subjects by white slave masters, planter-merchants, xenophobic politicos, or well-meaning reformers. But in a more important sense, it was black people themselves who did much of the making, refusing to be the product of others, no matter what their power or intentions. The repeated reinvention of self created new identities, as newcomers became Americans.

As a representative of the most recent passage—the renewed diaspora of the twentieth and twenty-first centuries—Barack Obama embodies the collective experience of those who have journeyed, found new places, and constantly remade themselves—as well as African American life and, with it, the nation. Obama—like so many before him—articulated the master narrative of slavery to freedom. But, also like many before him, he has lived the narrative of movement and place. His experience—like theirs—suggests the utility of the new narrative.

The conjunction of the two great histories returns me to my memorable discussion with the group of black Americans for whom the Emancipation Proclamation was part of a great history—even a heroic history—but not *their* history. Like previous new arrivals, they are remaking African American life by combining their own histories with the histories they inherited in a new land. How and when it happens will be a new chapter in the story of African America.

Acknowledgments

More than most fields of study, history is artisanal work, often the solitary labor of a lone mechanic tapping away at a word processor. Fortunately, that work goes on within a larger community, and while I have spent much time roaming stacks by myself and even more facing the blank screen of my PowerBook, I have also enjoyed—and profited mightily from—the conviviality of my fellow historians, archivists, and librarians as well as the editors, publishers, and booksellers who compose the larger community of historical scholarship. While this book could have been written and perhaps published and distributed without them, it would be a lesser product and I would be much impoverished by their absence.

I would like to thank all of those who helped to grow this book from a fledging idea. My colleagues at the University of Maryland—most especially Elsa Barkley Brown, David Freund, Julie Greene, and Richard Price—listened to the ideas that form the basis of *The Making of African America* and provided the kind of nurturing intellectual environment in which they could grow. The Freedmen and Southern Society Project has been my intellectual home, even after I left home; a new member and an old hand—John McKerley and Susan O'Donovan, respectively—took a special interest in my project, for which I am most grateful. Professor O'Donovan, now of the University of Memphis, permitted me to quote from her own work on slave mobility. A grant from the University of Maryland's Graduate Research Board allowed me to launch this study, and a fellowship at the W. E. B.

DuBois Center for the Study of the African Diaspora at Harvard University provided quiet time to think through the ideas and begin to put them on paper. The Center's director, Henry Louis Gates, Jr., and my fellow fellows—Vincent Carretta, Prudence Cumberbatch, Derek Hydra, Marisa Parham, Jeffery Steward, Wole Soyinka, and Ermien van Pletzen—provided an intellectual perspective that reached from Cape Cod to Cape Coast to Cape Town. When the manuscript was complete, Skip Gates read key chapters with his usual discerning eye.

Others have also read parts of the manuscript and saved me from numerous errors of fact and judgment with the kind of encouragement that only friends can provide. I would like especially to thank Ronald Hoffman, Ted Maris-Wolf, and Sally Mason—good friends from the Omohundro Institute of Early American History and Culture—who shared their thoughts while we collectively contemplated the meaning of the Middle Passage during the institute's historic conference in the shadow of the great slave factory at El Mina. William Chafe and Gary Gerstle, along with David Freund and Julie Greene, helped me navigate what to me was the strange terrain of twentieth-century historiography. Finally, Eric Foner, Steven Hahn, Leslie Harris, and Marcus Rediker read the entire manuscript, offering guidance on the whole.

Early on in my research on migration and place, while sitting at one of Chris Vadala's jam sessions in the Clarice Smith Center for the Performing Arts, I—as much from naïveté as from ignorance—saw connections between African American migrations and African American music. Thereafter, I called upon two friends, Harvey Cohen and Bill Ferris, to help me enlarge those connections. Their deep knowledge of the development of black music allowed me to make connections I otherwise would have missed.

Among the most important members of the community of historians are those apprentices we have come to call students. There is no better testing ground for ideas than the classroom, where the tolerance for sloppy thinking and shallow thoughts is small indeed. I would like to thank my many students at the University of Maryland for their impatience as well as their patience as I tested untried ideas. In addition, several more advanced students have aided this study in a variety of practical ways, tracking down fugitive texts, checking endnotes, and proofreading yet incomplete texts. I owe a special debt of gratitude to Katrina Keane, Megan Coplen, and Kimberly Welch for their good cheer and keen eye.

Also of good cheer and keen eye, Wendy Wolf, my editor, oversaw the development of *The Making of African America*, herself making knowing corrections to keep the matters on course and on time. Her imprint has made a difference. So has the timely interventions of Sandra Dijkstra, agent and friend, who poked and prodded until I made critical changes which made this book more accessible and better.

Like much artisanal work, making history—at least my history—is done within the bounds of a household. Members of my extended household—now, thanks to Samantha, three generations deep—proved it was possible to balance the world and the world of ideas. Lisa and Bob, Richard and Kara, and now Samantha gave meaning to this whole enterprise. Martha, as always, made it not only possible, but also great fun.

John Hope Franklin and I began with shared interest and rather uneven knowledge of free people of color in the antebellum South, with the balance heavily in his favor. He encouraged my interest and expanded my knowledge, providing sage advice and an example that only a master craftsman could offer. Later, he became a dear friend as well as the archetype of what a scholar should be. He left this world as *The Making of African America* was in the final stages of completion. It is dedicated to him with respect, gratitude, and love. He is missed.

Notes

Prologue

1 Ira Berlin, "Emancipation and Its Meaning in American Life," *Reconstruction* 2 (1994), 41–44. For the National Public Radio interview, see *Talk of the Nation*, July 13, 1994, number 513640, National Public Radio Archives.

2 Jacqueline A. Goggin, *Carter G. Woodson: A Life in Black History* (Baton Rouge LA, 1993); William Fitzhugh Brundage, *Southern Past: A Clash of Race and Memory* (Cambridge MA, 2005), chap. 4.

3 A point made most forcefully by Melville J. Herskovits, *The Myth of the Negro Past* (New York, 1941).

4 "Governor McDuffie's Message" to the South Carolina legislature reprinted in the Boston *Liberator*, Dec. 12, 1835. Punctuation has been altered for readability.

5 Aristide R. Zolberg, *A Nation by Design: Immigration Policy in the Fashioning of America* (Cambridge MA, 2006), 334. Also John Higham, *Strangers in the Land: Patterns of American Nativism, 1860–1925* (New Brunswick NJ, 1955); Philip Gleason, "American Identity and Americanization" in Stephan Thernstrom, ed., *Harvard Encyclopedia of American Ethnic Groups* (Cambridge MA, 1980); quoted in Mary C. Waters and Reed Ueda with Helen B. Murrow, eds., *The New Americans: A Guide to Immigration since 1965* (Cambridge MA, 2007), 8. Congressman Emanuel Celler, a cosponsor of the legislation, declared "there will not be, comparatively, many Asians or Africans entering the country . . . since the people of Africa and Asia have very few relatives here, comparatively few could immigrate from those countries because they have no family ties to the U.S." *Congressional Record*, 89th Congress, 1st session, pp. 21, 758.

6 *Washington Post*, Oct. 4, 1965.

7 *New York Times*, Aug. 15, 2007, Nov. 29, 2007; David M. Reimers, *Other Immigrants: The Global Origins of the American People* (New York, 2005), chap. 9; April Gordon, "The New Diaspora—African Immigration to the United States," *Journal of Third World Studies* 15 (1998), 79–103.

8 Quoted in Waters and Ueda, eds., *The New Americans*, 8; Reimers, *Other Immigrants*, chap. 9.

9 With the close of the slave trade at the beginning of the nineteenth century, the proportion of black people of foreign birth in the United States began to decline. In 1910, it was less than four-tenths of 1 percent for the United States and some

one-tenth of 1 percent for the South. U.S. Census Bureau, *Negro Population: 1790–1915* (Washington DC, 1918), 61.

10   Stanley Lieberson, "Selective Black Migration from the South: A Historical View" in Frank D. Bean and W. Parker Frisbie, eds., *The Demography of Racial and Ethnic Groups* (New York, 1978), 122; Karl E. Taeuber, "The Negro Population in the United States" in John P. Davis, ed., *The American Negro Reference Book* (Englewood Cliffs NJ, 1966), 109.

11   U.S. Census Bureau, *Profile of the Foreign-Born Population in the United States: 2000* (Washington DC, 2001), 3. Many more people of African descent derived from the West Indies and other parts of the world, although they too made up only a small percentage of the post-1965 immigration.

12   U.S. Census Bureau, *Profile of the Foreign-Born Population in the United States: 2000* (Washington DC, 2001), 10; David Dixon, "Characteristics of the African Born in the United States" (January 2006) in Migration Information Source (www.migrationinformation.org); Reimers, *Other Immigrants*, chap. 9; Gordon, "The New Diaspora," 79–103; Yoku Shaw-Taylor and Steven Tuch, eds., *The Other African Americans: Contemporary African and Caribbean Immigrants in the United States* (Lanham MD, 2007). During the 1990s legal immigration from Ghana increased 380 percent and immigration from Nigeria increased 220 percent in New York City. Nancy Foner, ed., *New Immigrants in New York* (New York, 2001), 23.

13   U.S. Census Bureau, *Profile of the Foreign-Born Population in the United States: 2000* (Washington DC, 2001).

14   Waters and Ueda, eds., *The New Americans*, 4; Reuel Rogers, "'Black Like Who?': Afro-Caribbean Immigrants, African Americans, and the Politics of Group Identity" in Nancy Foner, ed., *Islands in the City: West Indian Migration to New York* (Berkeley CA, 2001), 164.

15   Rogers, "'Black Like Who?,'" 164; James R. Grossman, Ann Durkin Keating, Janice L. Reiff, eds., *The Encyclopedia of Chicago* (Chicago, 2004), 21, 281, 446, 476–77, 571–72; *New York Times*, Aug. 29, 2004.

16   Flore Zéphir, *Haitian Immigrants in Black America: A Sociological and Sociolinguistic Portrait* (Westport CT, 1996), 85–86.

17   *New York Times*, Aug. 29, 2004; Also see *Washington Post*, Feb. 24, 2002; *New York Amsterdam News*, Mar. 9, 2005.

18   *New York Times*, Aug. 29, 2004.

19   Washington *City Paper*, Nov. 5, 2004.

20   *Washington City Paper*, Nov. 5, 2004. For a more general discussion of the relationship between African Americans and Africans, see Violet M. Showers Johnson, "'What, Then, Is the African American?': African and Afro-Caribbean Identities in Black America," *Journal of American Ethnic History* 28 (2008), 77–103.

21   Franklin's *Slavery to Freedom* was first published in 1947. In 2007, a seventh edition, coauthored by Alfred A. Moss, Jr., appeared, and another edition, authored by Evelyn Higginbotham, is scheduled for publication in 2010.

22   No one has written more thoughtfully about the matter of "master narratives" than Nathan Huggins. See especially his "The Deforming Mirror of Truth: Slav-

ery and the Master Narrative of American History," *Radical History Review* 49 (1991), 25–48, and "The Afro-American, National Character, and Community: Toward a New Synthesis" in Brenda Smith Huggins, ed., *Revelations: American History, American Myths* (New York, 1995), 36–60, and "Integrating Afro-American History into American History" in Darlene Clark Hine, ed., *The State of Afro-American History: Past, Present, and Future* (Baton Rouge LA, 1986), 157–68.

23 Benedict Anderson, *Imagined Communities: Reflections on the Origins and Spread of Nationalism*, rev. ed. (London, 1991).

24 King's precise words were: "The moral arc of the universe bends at the elbow of justice."

25 Rogers, "'Black Like Who?,'" 178; quoted in *Newsweek*, July 16, 2007. For a powerful invocation of the differences between the African American and African perspective, see Saidiya V. Hartman, *Lose Your Mother: A Journey Along the Atlantic Slave Route* (New York, 2007).

26 Charlotte Sussman, "The Colonial Afterlife of Political Arithmetic: Swift, Demography, and Mobile Populations," *Cultural Critique* 56 (2004), 117.

27 A point made with respect to European migrations in John Bodnar, *The Transplanted: A History of Urban Immigration* (Bloomington IN, 1985).

Chapter One: Movement and Place in the African American Past

1 Colin A. Palmer, "The Middle Passage" in Beverly C. McMillan, ed., *Captive Passage: The Transatlantic Slave Trade and the Making of the Americas* (Newport News VA, 2002), 53; Maria Diedrich, Henry Louis Gates, Jr., and Carl Pedersen, eds., *Black Imagination and the Middle Passage* (New York, 1999); Palmer added that the Middle Passage "remains alive in the memories of the people of African descent, linking them across the geographic expanse of the diaspora."

2 The number of Africans sent across the Atlantic to slavery in the Americas has been subject to considerable debate. The latest and most authoritative estimate is 10.7 million, with some 3.6 percent arriving in the territories that eventually became part of the United States. David Eltis, "The U.S. Transatlantic Slave Trade, 1644–1867: An Assessment," *Civil War History* 54 (2008), 353.

3 Focusing on the four great migrations that frame the history of people of African descent in the United States does not reduce the significance of the dozens, perhaps hundreds, of lesser migrations. Historians have rightly marked some of these—the eighteenth-century movement from tidewater to piedmont, the early-nineteenth-century flight from Saint Domingue to the mainland of the United States (and the later one following the United States occupation of Haiti), the post–Civil War movement of black "carpetbaggers" from north to south, the late-nineteenth-century exodus from Mississippi to Kansas, and most especially the twentieth-century migrations from the Caribbean—as critical to any understanding of African American and American life. To the social transformation they wrought and the renaissances they initiated can be added similar transformations set in motion by smaller, generally ignored, migrations, as for example: the post-Revolutionary evacuation of the Northern countryside, the postemancipation

westward drift, or the post–Civil Rights return to the South. Focusing on the four great migrations of African and African American peoples—the rivers, not the rills—does nothing to diminish the importance of the lesser migrations; indeed the great migrations cannot be understood apart from these smaller ones. But trying to address all of these movements reduces the African American past to one great itinerancy—a sort of endless peregrination—and expunges the sense of place that so informed black life.

4 George P. Rawick, ed., *The American Slave: A Composite Autobiography*, 41 vols. (Westport CT, 1972–79), ser. 1, vol. 10, pt. 5, 226–227; *American Slave*, ser. 1, vol. 12, pt. 2, 119.

5 Henry Louis Gates, Jr., "New Negroes, Migration, and Cultural Exchange" in Elizabeth Hutton Turner, ed., *Jacob Lawrence: The Migration Series* (Washington DC, 1993), 17–21; Jutta Lorensen, "Between Image and Word, Color and Time: Jacob Lawrence's *The Migration Series*," *African American Review* 40 (2006), 572. Another black artist deeply touched by the movement north was Walter Ellison, whose 1935 *Train Station* also gave a sense of the central role of movement in African American life. Jamie W. Johnson, "Instructional Resources: Journeys Through Art: Tracing the Great Migration in Three American Paintings," *Art Education* 55 (2002), 25–31.

6 On African American literature and migration see Farah Jasmine Griffin, "*Who Set You Flowin'?": The African-American Migration Narrative* (New York, 1995) and Lawrence Rodgers, *Canaan Bound: The African American Great Migration Novel* (Chicago, 1997).

7 Langston Hughes, *The Big Sea: An Autobiography* (New York, 1940), 23.

8 Langston Hughes, *One-Way Ticket* (New York, 1949), 61–62; "Sweet Home Chicago," http://www.lyricsfreak.com/b/blues+brothers/sweet+home+chicago_20020736.html.

9 Among the more useful theoretical works on the significance of "place" is E. Relph, *Place and Placelessness* (London, 1976); David Harvey, *Justice, Nature, and the Geography of Difference* (Cambridge MA, 1996); Doreen Massey, *Space, Place, and Gender* (Minneapolis MN, 1994).

10 Paul Gilroy, *The Black Atlantic: Modernity and Double Consciousness* (Cambridge MA, 1993).

11 Quoted in Marcus Rediker, *The Slave Ship: A Human History* (New York, 2007), 305. For the role of fictive kin, see Sidney W. Mintz and Richard Price, *The Birth of African-American Culture: An Anthropological Perspective* (Boston, [1976] 1992), 62–79.

12 For insightful discussions of the "discourse and etiquette of place" within the context of the late-nineteenth-century South, see James R. Grossman, "'Amiable Peasantry' or 'Social Burden': Constructing a Place for Black Southerners" in Rick Halpern and Jonathan Morris, eds., *American Exceptionalism?: US Working-Class Formation in an International Context* (New York, 1997), 221–43, and Angel David Nieves and Leslie M. Alexander, *"We Shall Independent Be": African American Place Making and the Struggle to Claim Space in the United States* (Boulder CO, 2008).

13 Clifton Taulbert, *The Last Train North* quoted in Malaika Adero, ed., *Up South:*

Stories, Studies, and Letters of this Century's Black Migrations (New York, 1993), xii.

14　Quoted in Walter Johnson, "Introduction" in Johnson, ed., *The Chattel Principle: Internal Slave Trades in the Americas* (New Haven CT, 2005), 2.

15　Toni Morrison, "Rootedness: The Ancestor in African American Fiction" in Mari Evans, ed., *Black Women Writers: A Critical Evaluation* (Garden City NY, 1984), 339–45.

16　The point is made forcefully by Marc S. Rodriguez, "Placing Human Migration in Comparative Perspective" in Rodriguez and Anthony T. Grafton, eds., *Migration in History: Human Migration in Comparative Perspective* (Rochester NY, 2007), ix–x.

17　J. Lorand Matory, *Black Atlantic Religion: Tradition, Transnationalism, and Matriarchy in the Afro-Brazilian Candomblé* (Princeton NJ, 2005), 3.

18　Orlando Patterson, *Slavery and Social Death: A Comparative Study* (Cambridge MA, 1982).

19　Frederick Douglass, *Life and Times of Frederick Douglass* (New York, 1881), 97; *New York Times*, Nov. 28, 1863, quoted in Leon F. Litwack, *Been in the Storm So Long: The Aftermath of Slavery* (New York, 1979), 307.

20　Quoted in Ira Berlin et al., eds., "The Terrain of Freedom: The Struggle over the Meaning of Free Labor in the U.S. South," *History Workshop* 22 (1986), 127–28; Dylan C. Penningroth, *The Claims of Kinfolk: African American Property and Community in the Nineteenth-Century South* (Chapel Hill NC, 2003), 158; Julie Saville, *The Work of Reconstruction: From Slave to Wage Laborer in South Carolina, 1860–1870* (Cambridge UK, 1994), chap. 1; Julia Peterkin, *Roll, Jordan, Roll* (New York, 1933), 11.

21　All quoted in James C. Cobb, *Away Down South: A History of Southern Identity* (New York, 2005), 268; also Helen Taylor, *Circling Dixie: Contemporary Southern Culture through a Transatlantic Lens* (New Brunswick NJ, 2001), 173. "Home," reports Geneva Smitherman in her dictionary of African American colloquialisms (1994), is "a generic reference to any area south of the Mason-Dixon Line. . . . Thus, 'My Momma nem went home last month,' does not refer to the current home of the speaker, but to a place in the South where the speaker and her family are from." *Black Talk: Words and Phrases from the Hood to the Amen Corner* (Boston, 1994), 136. I would like to thank Elsa Barkley Brown for bringing this reference to my attention.

22　Gates, "New Negroes, Migration, and Cultural Exchange," 20.

23　Cobb, *Away Down South*, especially chap. 10; Powledge quoted on p. 264.

24　Adero, ed., *Up South: Stories*, 55.

25　Robert N. Brown and John Cromartie, "Black Homeplace Migration to the Yazoo-Mississippi Delta: Ambiguous Journeys, Uncertain Outcomes," *Southeastern Geographer* 46 (2006), 189-214. Quoted on 190–92.

26　Quoted in Cobb, *Away Down South*, 269.

27　Tony Burroughs, *Black Roots: A Beginner's Guide to Tracing the African American Family Tree* (New York, 2001).

28　Richard Wright, *Black Boy: A Record of Childhood and Youth* (New York, 1966), 284. Similar sentiments were voiced by the Harvard-educated historian Elizabeth

Arroyo, declaring that she felt "southern the same way an Irish American feels Irish. My roots are in the South, and southern worlds and ways are a part of me." See Cobb, *Away Down South*, 287. See also Lawrence W. Levine, *Black Culture and Black Consciousness: Afro-American Folk Thought from Slavery to Freedom* (New York, 1978), 364.

29 Piri Thomas, *Down These Mean Streets* (New York, 1967), 138. For a similar journey back to Africa, Saidiya V. Hartman, *Lose Your Mother: A Journey Along the Atlantic Slave Route* (New York, 2007). The general phenomenon is brilliantly addressed in James T. Campbell, *Middle Passages: African American Journeys to Africa, 1787–2005* (New York, 2006). I would like to thank Julie Greene for the reference to Piri Thomas's autobiography.

30 A point made with great concreteness by Anthony E. Kaye, *Joining Places: Slave Neighborhoods in the Old South* (Chapel Hill NC, 2007).

31 Morrison, "Rootedness," 343.

32 The black belt refers to the three hundred mainly contiguous counties that stretched across the South from South Carolina to Texas in which, by the mid-nineteenth century, black people composed the majority.

33 Shane White and Graham White, *Stylin': African American Expressive Culture from Its Beginnings to the Zoot Suit* (Ithaca NY, 1998), 37–62, 168–91.

34 Sterling Stuckey, *Slave Culture: Nationalist Theory and the Foundations of Black America* (New York, 1987), 3–5; Michael A. Gomez, *Exchanging Our Country Marks: The Transformation of African Identities in the Colonial and Antebellum South* (Chapel Hill NC, 1998), 209–13; Benjamin Quarles, "The Revolutionary War as a Black Declaration of Independence" in Ira Berlin and Ronald Hoffman, eds., *Slavery and Freedom in the Age of the American Revolution* (Charlottesville VA, 1983), 283–301; Eddie S. Glaude, Jr., *Exodus!: Religion, Race, and Nation in Early Nineteenth-Century Black America* (Chicago, 2000); Molefi Kete Asante, *An Afrocentric Manifesto: Toward an African Renaissance* (Cambridge MA, 2007).

35 Brilliantly demonstrated by Matory, *Black Atlantic Religion*, the phrase is drawn from p. 43.

36 Levine, *Black Culture and Black Consciousness*, 6; Alan Lomax, "Folk Song Style," *American Anthropologist* 61 (1959), 930; Ronald Radano, *Lying up a Nation: Race and Black Music* (Chicago, 2003), 96–102; LeRoi Jones, *Blues People: The Negro Music in White America* (New York, 1965), x. For Ralph Ellison, "the blues were a total way of life, and major expression of an attitude toward life," see *Shadow and Act* (New York, 1964), 78. The same might be said for the spirituals in an earlier age and hip-hop in a later one. Also see James M. Trotter, *Music and Some Highly Musical People* (Chicago, [1880] 1969).

37 Brown and Cromartie, "Black Homeplace Migration," 191. There is a long history of essentializing the musical nature of black people. Ronald Radano follows that strand of romantic thought in "Denoting Difference: The Writing of the Slave Spirituals," *Critical Inquiry* 22 (1996), 506–44.

38 Toni Morrison makes the same point about the sermon in "Rootedness"; quoted in B. B. King with David Ruiz, *Blues All Around Me: The Autobiography of B. B. King* (New York, 1996), 17.

39 J. H. Kwabena Nketia, *The Music of Africa* (New York, 1974); Dena J. Epstein and Rosita M. Sands, "Secular Folk Music" in Mellonee V. Burnim and Portia K. Maultsby, eds., *African American Music: An Introduction* (New York, 2006), 37–43; John M. Chernoff, *African Rhythm and African Sensibility: Aesthetics and Social Action in African Musical Idioms* (Chicago, 1979), chap. 4; Levine, *Black Culture and Black Consciousness*, 6–7.

40 Jefferson, *Notes on the State of Virginia*, 140; Shane White and Graham White, *The Sounds of Slavery* (Boston, 2005), xix; Levine, *Black Culture and Black Consciousness*, 186; Joe W. Trotter, "The African American Worker in Slavery and Freedom" in *The African American Experience: An Historiographical and Bibliographical Guide* (Westport CT, 2001), 364.

41 What John and Alan Lomax said about the origins of the Blues—the unknown moment "when a lonely Negro man plowing in some hot, silent river bottom" raised his voice—can be extended to the spirituals, jazz, and hip-hop. *American Ballads and Folks Songs* (New York, 1924), 191.

42 Oscar Handlin, *The Uprooted: The Epic Story of the Great Migrations that Made the American People* (Boston, 1952), 3.

43 Carl Russell Fish, "The Pilgrim and the Melting Pot," *Mississippi Valley Historical Review* 7 (1920), 187–205; Lerone Bennett, *Before the Mayflower: A History of Black America*, 4th ed. (Chicago, 1969); quoted in Reed Ueda, "Immigration in Global Perspective" in Mary C. Waters and Reed Ueda with Helen B. Murrow, eds., *The New Americans: A Guide to Immigration since 1965* (Cambridge MA, 2007), 27.

44 Steven Shulman, ed., *The Impact of Immigration on African Americans* (New Brunswick NJ, 2004), x; Allan H. Spear, *Black Chicago: The Making of a Negro Ghetto, 1890–1920* (Chicago, 1967), 228–29; Nell I. Painter, "Forward" in Trotter, ed., *Great Migration*, viii.

45 Jan Lucassen and Leo Lucassen, "Migrations, Migration History, History: Old Paradigms and New Perspectives" in Jan Lucassen and Leo Lucassen, eds., *Migration, Migration History, History* (Bern, 1997), 11–14.

46 Rediker, *The Slave Ship*, 106; Stephanie E. Smallwood, *Saltwater Slavery: A Middle Passage from Africa to American Diaspora* (Cambridge MA, 2007), 7–8.

47 Frank Thistlewaite, "Migration from Europe Overseas in the Nineteenth and Twentieth Centuries" in Rudolph J. Vecoli and Suzanne M. Sinke, eds., *A Century of European Migrations, 1830–1930* (Urbana IL, 1991); Mark Wyman, *Round Trip America: The Immigrants Return to Europe, 1880–1930* (Ithaca NY, 1993).

48 John Cromartie and Carol B. Stack, "Reinterpretation of Black Return and Non-return Migration to the South, 1975–1980," *Geographical Review* 79 (1989), 298.

49 Charles Tilly, "Transplanted Networks" in Virginia Yans-McLaughlin, ed., *Immigration Reconsidered: History, Sociology, and Politics* (New York, 1990), 83. However, David Eltis sees chain migrations created by "shipping patterns and credit arrangements," even where—in the case of the slave trade—the migrants lacked choice. David Eltis, "Free and Coerced Migration from the Old World to the New" in Eltis, ed., *Coerced and Free Migration* (Stanford CA, 2002), 27.

50 David R. Roediger, *The Wages of Whiteness*, rev. ed. (London, 1999); Matthew

Frye Jacobson, *Whiteness of a Different Color: European Immigrants and the Alchemy of Race* (Cambridge MA, 1998); Thomas Guglielmo, *White on Arrival: Italians, Race, Color, and Power in Chicago, 1890–1945* (New York, 2003).

51 Russell A. Kazal, "Revisiting Assimilation: The Rise, Fall, and Reappraisal of a Concept of American Ethnic History," *American Historical Review* 100 (1995), 437–71, quoted on p. 444. Also see Philip Kasinitz, *Caribbean New York: Black Immigrants and the Politics of Race* (Ithaca NY, 1992), 4–6.

52 Nathan Glazer and Daniel Patrick Moynihan, *Beyond the Melting Pot: The Negroes, Puerto Ricans, Jews, Italians, and Irish of New York City*, 2nd ed. (Cambridge MA, 1970); Michael Novak, *The Rise of the Unmeltable Ethnics: Politics and Culture in the Seventies* (New York, 1973).

53 Victoria Hattam connects race with heredity, body and blood, fixity, singularity, homogeneity, boundedness, and hierarchy, while ethnicity is identified with culture, language and religion, malleability, plurality, heterogeneity, openness, and equality. *In the Shadow of Race: Jews, Latinos, and Immigrant Politics in the United States* (Chicago, 2007), quoted on p. 2. Also see John Higham, "The Amplitude of Ethnic History: An American Story" in Nancy Foner and George M. Frederickson, eds., *Not Just Black and White: Historical and Contemporary Perspectives on Immigration, Race, and Ethnicity in the United States* (New York, 2004), 61–82. "[I]t sometimes seems as if the people who study immigration or race or ethnicity—or all these together—inhabit two different intellectual worlds." Stephen Cornell and Douglas Hartmann, "Conceptual Confusions and Divides: Race, Ethnicity, and the Study of Immigration," *ibid.*, p. 23.

54 Roediger, *The Wages of Whiteness*; also see note 47, above.

55 For a heroic attempt to do just this, see Dirk Hoerder, *Cultures in Contact: World Migrations in the Second Millennium* (Durham NC, 2002). The process remaking black society—"creolization"—is given a different name than the processes remaking of European American society—"transformation." Rarely are these two concepts addressed collectively, although the processes they describe are precisely the same. Few scholars maintain that African American nationality, like white ethnicity, can be—and have been—reinvented in the course of the American past.

56 "Historians probably view," writes David Eltis in a broad-ranging discussion of free and forced migrations, "most migrations as forced at some level as social and ecological conditions at the point of origins might be such that individuals have no choice but to leave." Eltis, "Introduction" and "Free and Coerced Migration from the Old World to the New" in Eltis, ed., *Coerced and Free Migration*, 5–6, 49–60.

57 Although the slave trade remains the largest forced migration in human history, the number of forced migrations seems to be increasing. See Reed Ueda, "Immigration in Global Historical Perspective" in Waters and Ueda, eds., *The New Americans*, 20.

58 Alan Kraut, *Huddled Masses: The Immigrant in American Society, 1880–1921* (Arlington Heights, IL, 1982), 57; Peter C. Marzio, ed., *A Nation of Nations: The People Who Came to America as Seen Through Objects and Documents Exhibited at the Smithsonian Institution* (New York, 1976), 431, 438.

Chapter Two: The Transatlantic Passage

1   In the era of the transatlantic slave trade, "national" identities had little meaning to most of the peoples of Africa. The African economies and societies promoted parochial identifications with village and family. Large states existed in some parts of the continent, but they had a weak hold on individual men and women. Joseph Miller, "Central Africa during the Era of the Slave Trade, 1490s to 1850s" in Linda M. Heywood, ed., *Central Africans and Cultural Transformations in the American Diaspora* (Cambridge UK, 2002), 35–39, 41–43, 48–49; James H. Sweet, *Recreating Africa: Culture, Kinship, and Religion in the African Portuguese World, 1441–1770* (Chapel Hill NC, 2003), 22–30; James Horn and Phillip D. Morgan, "Settlers and Slaves: European and African Migrations to Early Modern British America" in Elizabeth Mancke and Carole Shammas, eds., *The Creation of the British Atlantic World* (Baltimore MD, 2005), 40–41.

2   The confusion, sometimes purposeful, of the identity of captive Africans is manifest in the complaint made upon the arrival of a slave ship in Barbados: "Those . . . by whom you stild good Gold Coast negroes we here found not to be so, but of several nations and languages as Alampo the worst Negroes, Papas & some of unknown parts & a few right Gold Coast negroes amongst them." Quoted in Stephanie E. Smallwood, *Saltwater Slavery: A Middle Passage from Africa to American Diaspora* (Cambridge MA, 2007), 106. Also Herbert S. Klein, *The Atlantic Slave Trade* (Cambridge UK, 1999), 115. Klein emphasizes the ignorance of the European traders of the interior: "They only had the vaguest notions of the names of interior groups or their placement and relative importance."

3   For some historians of Africa even these national affiliations like Igbo were a product of contact with Europeans. Elizabeth Isichei, *A History of the Igbo People* (New York, 1976).

4   Rolfe quoted in Winthrop D. Jordan, *White over Black: American Attitudes Toward the Negro, 1550–1812* (Chapel Hill NC, 1968), 73; also see John Thornton, "The African Experience of the '20. and Odd Negroes' Arriving in Virginia in 1619," *William and Mary Quarterly* 55 (1998), 421–34. For the struggle over what black people were called and what they called themselves, see Patrick Rael, *Black Identity and Black Protest in the Antebellum North* (Chapel Hill NC, 2002), chap. 3, and more generally Randall Kennedy, *Nigger: The Strange Career of a Troublesome Word* (New York, 2002).

5   Quoted in Philip D. Morgan, *Slave Counterpoint: Black Culture in the Eighteenth-Century Chesapeake and Lowcountry* (Chapel Hill NC, 1998), 67, n. 55.

6   Miller, "Central Africa in the Era of the Slave Trade" in Heywood, ed., *Central Africans and Cultural Transformations*, 46–48; Sweet, *Recreating Africa*, 20–22.

7   Alexander X. Byrd, "Captives and Voyagers: Black Migrants Across the 18th Century World of Olaudah Equiano," unpublished doctoral dissertation, Duke University, 2001; Byrd, "Eboe, Country, Nation, and Gustavus Vassa's 'Interesting Narrative,'" *William and Mary Quarterly* 63 (2006), 123–148; David Northrup, "Igbo and Myth Igbo: Culture and Ethnicity in the Atlantic World: 1600–1850," *Slavery and Abolition* 21 (2000), 1–20; Kristin Mann, "Shifting Paradigms in the

Study of the African Diaspora and of Atlantic History and Culture," *Slavery and Abolition* 22 (2001), 3–21.

8 Orlando Patterson, *Slavery and Social Death: A Comparative Study* (Cambridge MA, 1982), 53–54; John Thornton, *African and Africans in the Making of the Atlantic World: 1400–1800* (Cambridge MA, 1998), 13; Kopytoff and Miers, "African 'Slavery' as an Institution of Marginality" in Kopytoff and Miers, eds., *Slavery in Africa*, 3–69; Claire Robertson and Martin A. Klein, eds., *Women and Slavery in Africa* (Madison WI, 1977).

9 Kopytoff and Miers, "African 'Slavery' as an Institution of Marginality" in Kopytoff and Miers, eds., *Slavery in Africa*, 26–27; Lovejoy, *Transformations in Slavery*, 136; Manning, *Slavery and African Life*, 28, 46–47, 118, 160.

10 The distinction between societies with slaves and slave societies is elaborated in Ira Berlin, *Many Thousands Gone: The First Two Centuries of Slavery in North America* (Cambridge MA, 1998), 9–13.

11 A. C. de C. M. Saunders, *A Social History of Black Slaves and Freedmen in Portugal, 1441–1555* (Cambridge UK, 1982), 60; Herbert S. Klein, *African Slavery in Latin America and the Caribbean* (New York, 1986), 13.

12 Philip D. Curtin, *The Rise and Fall of the Plantation Complex: Essays in Atlantic History*, 2nd ed. (Cambridge UK, 1998), chaps. 1–3; B. W. Higman, "The Sugar Revolution," *Economic History Review* 53 (2000), 213–36; Alberto Vieira, "Sugar Islands: The Sugar Economy of Madeira and the Canaries, 1450–1650" in Stuart Schwartz, ed., *Tropical Babylons: Sugar and the Making of the Atlantic World, 1450–1680* (Chapel Hill NC, 2004), 42–84.

13 Curtin, *Plantation Complex*, chaps. 4–6; Robin Blackburn, *The Making of New World Slavery: From the Baroque to the Modern, 1492–1800* (London, 1997), chaps. 3–10; quoted in Morgan Godwyn, *The Negro's and Indians Advocate* (London, 1680), 101.

14 Marcus Rediker, *The Slave Ship: A Human History* (New York, 2007), chap. 3; quoted in William Bosman, *New and Accurate Description of the Coast of Guinea, 1705: Divided into the Gold, the Slave, and the Ivory Coasts* (London, 1750), 364; Smallwood, *Saltwater Slavery*, 61.

15 Joseph Miller, "Mortality in the Atlantic Slave Trade: Statistic Evidence on Causality," *Journal of Interdisciplinary History* 2 (1981), 385–424 and Miller, *African Way of Death: Merchant Capitalism and the Angolan Slave Trade, 1730–1830* (Madison WI, 1988), 384–85; Lovejoy, *Transformations in Slavery*, 63–64; Klein, *Atlantic Slave Trade*, 155–57; quoted in Falconbridge, *An Account of the Slave Trade*, 19 and Klein, *Atlantic Slave Trade*, 156–157. Death became a central experience of the black people in the New World; see Vincent Brown, *The Reaper's Garden: Death and Power in the World of Atlantic Slavery* (Cambridge MA, 2007).

16 Smallwood, *Saltwater Slavery*, chap. 2, esp. 36–43; A. W. Lawrence, *Trade Castles and Forts on West Africa* (Palo Alto CA, 1964); Falconbridge, *Account of the Slave Trade*, 51–52.

17 Sylviane A. Diouf, ed., *Fighting the Slave Trade: West African Strategies* (Athens OH, 2003); Smallwood, *Saltwater Slavery*, chap. 2, especially 43–57; Eric Robert Taylor, *If We Must Die: Shipboard Insurrections in the Era of the Atlantic Slave Trade* (Baton Rouge LA, 2006). For an excellent discussion of insurrections, see Colin

Palmer, "The Slave Trade, African Slavers and the Demography of the Caribbean to 1750" in Franklin W. Knight, ed., *General History of the Caribbean*, 6 vols. (London, 1997), 3: 29–35.

18 W. Jeffrey Bolster, *Black Jacks: African American Seamen in the Age of Sail* (Cambridge MA, 1997), 50–51; Herbert S. Klein, *The Middle Passage: Comparative Studies in the Atlantic Slave Trade* (Princeton NJ, 1978), 58–59; Ty M. Reese, "The Drudgery of the Slave Trade: Labor at the Cape Coast Castle, 1750–1790" in Peter A. Coclanis, ed., *The Atlantic Economy during the Seventeenth and Eighteenth Centuries: Organization, Operation, Practice, and Personnel* (Columbia SC, 2005), 282–83; Stephanie E. Smallwood, "African Guardians, European Slave Ships, and the Changing Dynamics of Power in the Early Modern Atlantic," *William and Mary Quarterly* 64 (2007), 679–716; Rediker, *Slave Ship*, 152, 190–91, 194, 268–67. For Denmark Vesey's duty on his owner's slave ship, see Douglas R. Egerton, *He Shall Go Out Free: The Lives of Denmark Vesey* (Lanham MD, 2004), 13.

19 Rediker, *Slave Ship*, esp. chaps. 5–8; Klein, *The Transatlantic Slave Trade*, 159.

20 Klein, *The Transatlantic Slave Trade*, chap. 6; Herbert S. Klein and Stanley L. Engerman, "Long-Term Trends in African Mortality in the Transatlantic Slave Trade," *Slavery and Abolition* 18 (1997), 36–48; Herbert S. Klein, Stanley L. Engerman, Robin Haines, and Ralph Shlomowitz, "Transoceanic Mortality: The Slave Trade in Comparative Perspective," *William and Mary Quarterly* 58 (2001), 93–117; Kenneth F. Kiple and Brian T. Higgins, "Mortality Caused by Dehydration during the Middle Passage" in Joseph E. Inikori and Stanley L. Engerman, eds., *The Atlantic Slave Trade: Effects on Economies, Societies and Peoples in Africa, the Americas, and Europe* (Durham NC 1992), 321–37.

21 Olaudah Equiano, *The Interesting Narrative of the Life of Olaudah Equiano, or Gustavus Vassa, the African, Written by Himself* (London, 1789), reprinted in Vincent Carretta, ed., *The Interesting Narrative and Other Writings* (New York, 1995), 59; William D. Piersen, "White Cannibals, Black Martyrs: Fear, Depression, and Religious Faith as Causes of Suicide Among New Slaves," *Journal of Negro History* 62 (1977), 147–51; Rediker, *Slave Ship*, 108, 117, 266. See Brown, *The Reaper's Garden*, 136–144.

22 Rediker, *Slave Ship*, 9–10, 260, 306–7; Smallwood, *Saltwater Slaves*, chaps. 4–6; Elizabeth Donnan, ed., *Documents Illustrative of the History of the Slave Trade to America*, 4 vols. (Washington DC, 1930), 1: 442 (quoted), 438; 2, 352, 359, 557, 634; William Snelgrave, *A New Account of Some Ports of Guinea and the Slave Trade* (London, 1734), 163. By the same token, the slave ship was also the place where black people distinguished themselves from whites, as they understood their captors as the enemy. The watchword of ship rebellions was "Kill the whites." Quoted in David Eltis, *Rise of African Slavery in the Americas* (Cambridge UK, 2000), 226–27.

23 Quoted in Bosman, *New and Accurate Description of the Coast of Guinea*, 394; Snelgrave, *A New Account*, 163; John Atkins, *A Voyage to Guinea, Brazil and the West Indies in His Majesty's Ships, The 'Swallow' and 'Weymouth'* (London, 1735), 41; Mungo Park, *Travels in the Interior Districts of Africa* (London, 1799), 353–54.

24 Rediker, *Slave Ship*, 17–19, 120–21, 212–13, 289–91; quoted in John W. Blassingame, ed., *Slave Testimony: Two Centuries of Letters, Speeches, Interviews, and Autobiographies* (Baton Rouge LA, 1977), 227.

25 Colin A. Palmer, "The Middle Passage" in *Captive Passage: The Transatlantic Slave Trade and the Making of the Americas* (Newport News VA, 2002), 54; Klein and Engerman, "Long-Term Trends in African Mortality in the Transatlantic Slave Trade," 36–48; Klein, Engerman, Haines, and Shlomowitz, "Transoceanic Mortality," 93–117. Estimates 40 percent of the captives died in crossing the Atlantic during the sixteenth century, 15 percent during the seventeenth century, and 5 to 10 percent in later years. Many more died while waiting for transit and in the journey across Africa; the total number who were enslaved may have been as high as twenty million.

26 Klein, *The Transatlantic Slave Trade*, 94–95, 130–160; Genevieve Fabre, "The Slave Ship Dance" in Maria Diedrich, Henry Louis Gates, Jr., and Carl Pedersen, eds., *Black Imagination and the Middle Passage* (New York, 1999); Palmer, "The Middle Passage," 60–65; quoted in Equiano, *The Interesting Narrative*, 56.

27 Donnan, ed., *Documents Illustrative of the History of the Slave Trade*, 1: 289–90, 2: 460; Piersen, "White Cannibals, Black Martyrs," 155; J. M. Postma, *The Dutch in the Atlantic Slave Trade, 1600–1815* (Cambridge UK, 1990), 241; Rediker, *Slave Ship*, 17–19, 120–21; 212–14, 289–91.

28 James A. Rawley, *The Transatlantic Slave Trade: A History* (New York, 1981), 296; Rediker, *Slave Ship*, 128, 142–146, 151–52, 179, 203–4, 215–16, 241–44, 265–66; quoted in Donnan, ed., *Documents Illustrative of the History of the Slave Trade*, 1:463.

29 Smallwood, "African Guardians," 679–716; Rediker, *Slave Ship*, 229, 349; Eltis, *Rise of African Slavery*, 226–29; Klein, *African Slavery in Latin American*, 76–77; also see castle slaves in Johannes Postma and Victor Enthoven, *Riches from Atlantic Commerce: Dutch Transatlantic Trade and Shipping, 1585–1817* (Boston, 2003), 71–73; Miller, *African Way of Death*, 409–10.

30 Donnan, ed., *Documents Illustrative of the History of the Slave Trade*, 2: 357, 486; Rediker, *Slave Ship*, 149–50; Bernard Martin and Mark Spurrell, eds., *The Journal of a Slave Trader (John Newton), 1750–1754* (London, 1962), 72.

31 Quoted in Eltis, *Rise of African Slavery*, 229–30; Rediker, *Slave Ship*, 271–76, 297–98; Smallwood, *Saltwater Slavery*, 103–9, quoted on 103.

32 Quoted in Rediker, *Slave Ship*, 101, 270–276; Snelgrave, *A New Account*, 49.

33 Ibid.

34 Taylor, *If We Must Die*; Rediker, *Slave Ship*, 259–62, 279–81; David Richardson, "Shipboard Revolts, African Authority, and the Atlantic Slave Trade," *William and Mary Quarterly* 58 (2001), 69–92; Klein, *The Transatlantic Slave Trade*, 159; Michael Craton, *Testing the Chains: Resistance to Slavery in the British West Indies* (Ithaca NY, 1982), 24.

35 Quoted in Rediker, *Slave Ship*, 282, 284.

36 Ira Berlin, *Many Thousands Gone: The First Two Centuries of Slavery in North America* (Cambridge MA, 1998), pt. 1; Linda M. Heywood and John K. Thornton, *Central Africans, Atlantic Creoles, and the Foundation of the Americas, 1585–1660* (Cambridge UK, 2007).

37 Berlin, *Many Thousands Gone*, pt. 2.

38 Alan Kulikoff, *Tobacco and Slaves: The Development of Southern Cultures in the Chesapeake 1680–1800* (Chapel Hill NC, 1986), 37–42, 65, 319–20; Kulikoff, "A 'Prolifick' People: Black Population Growth in the Chesapeake Colonies, 1700–1790," *Southern Studies* 16 (1977), 391–96, 403–5; and Kulikoff, "The Origins of Afro-American Society in Tidewater Maryland and Virginia, 1700 to 1790," *William and Mary Quarterly* 35 (1978), 229–31; Russell R. Menard, "The Maryland Slave Population, 1658 to 1730: A Demographic Profile of Blacks in Four Counties, *William and Mary Quarterly* 32 (1975), 30–32.

39 Kulikoff, *Tobacco and Slaves*, 37–42, 65, 319–24; Kulikoff, "A 'Prolifick' People," 391–96, 403–5; Kulikoff, "Origins of Afro-American," 229–31; Menard, "From Servants to Slaves," *Southern Studies* 16 (1977), 366–69; Darrett B. Rutman and Anita H. Rutman, *A Place in Time: Middlesex County, Virginia, 1650–1750* (New York, 1984), 72; quoted in Marion Tinling, ed., *The Correspondence of the Three William Byrds of Westover, Virginia, 1684–1776*, 2 vols. (Charlottesville VA, 1977), 2: 487.

40 Kulikoff, *Tobacco and Slaves*, 336–39, chap. 9, esp. 359–80; Kulikoff, "The Beginnings of the Afro-American Family in Maryland" in Aubrey C. Land et al., eds., *Law, Society, and Politics in Early Maryland* (Baltimore MD, 1977), 177–96; Morgan, *Slave Counterpoint*, 82.

41 Morgan, *Slave Counterpoint*, 58; Peter Wood, *Black Majority: Negroes in Colonial South Carolina from 1670 through the Stono Rebellion* (New York, 1974), xiv.

42 Peter A. Coclanis, *The Shadow of a Dream: Economic Life and Death in the South Carolina Low Country, 1670–1920* (New York, 1988), 64–65, 80–81; Peter H. Wood, "'More Like a Negro Country': Demographic Patterns in Colonial South Carolina, 1700–1740" in Stanley L. Engerman and Eugene D. Genovese, eds., *Race and Slavery in the Western Hemisphere: Quantitative Studies* (Princeton NJ, 1975), 131–45; Wood, *Black Majority*, 13–91; Daniel C. Littlefield, *Rice and Slaves: Ethnicity and the Slave Trade in Colonial South Carolina* (Baton Rouge LA, 1981); Russell R. Menard, "Slave Demography in the Lowcountry, 1670–1740: From Frontier Society to Plantation," *South Carolina Historical Magazine* 96 (1995), 291–302; Betty Wood, *Slavery in Colonial Georgia, 1730–1775* (Athens GA, 1984), 91–98; James A. McMillan, *The Final Victims: Foreign Slave Trade to North America, 1783–1810* (Columbia SC, 2004).

43 Jennifer L. Morgan, "Slavery and the Slave Trade" in Nancy A. Hewitt, ed., *A Companion to American Women's History* (Oxford UK, 2002), 20–24; Morgan, *Slave Counterpoint*, 68–75, quoted on 71; Rediker, *The Slave Ship*, 101; David Eltis and Stanley L. Engerman, "Was the Slave Trade Dominated by Men?" *Journal of Interdisciplinary History* 23 (1992), 237–57.

44 David Eltis, Paul E. Lovejoy, and Davis Richardson, "Slave-Trading Ports: Toward an Atlantic Wide Perspective, 1676–1821" in Robin Law and Silke Stickrodt, eds., *Ports of the Slave Trade (Bights of Benin and Biafra). Papers from the Centre for Commonwealth Studies, University of Stirling, June 1998* (Stirling UK, 1999), 12–34; David Eltis, "Free and Coerced Migration from the Old World to the New" in Eltis, ed., *Coerced and Free Migration* (Palo Alto CA, 2002), 49–50; Rediker, *Slave Ship*, chap. 3; Horn and Morgan, "Settlers and Slaves," 38–39; David

Northrup, *Trade without Rulers: Pre-Colonial Economic Development in South-Eastern Nigeria* (Oxford UK, 1978), 65–80; James F. Searing, *West African Slavery and Atlantic Commerce: The Senegal River Valley, 1700–1860* (Cambridge UK, 1993); Boubacar Barry, *Senegambia and the Atlantic Slave Trade* (Cambridge UK, 1998); Miller, *African Way of Death*; Falconbridge, *An Account of the Slave*, 12.

45 Diouf, ed., *Fighting the Slave Trade*; Taylor, *If We Must Die*. The high number of shipboard insurrections by Africans taken from the Senegambia coast may have led slave traders to look elsewhere for slaves, despite the proximity of Senegambia to Europe.

46 Littlefield, *Rice and Slaves*, 8-11; Coclanis, *Shadow of a Dream*, 60, 243–44, n. 44; W. Robert Higgins, "Charleston Terminus and Entrepot of the Colonial Slave Trade" in Martin L. Kilson and Robert Rotberg, eds., *The African Diaspora: Interpretative Essays* (Cambridge MA, 1976), 118–27; Philip Hamer et al., eds., *Papers of Henry Laurens*, 16 vols. (Columbia SC, 1968–2003), 1: 275, 294–95 (quoted), 331; 2: 179–82, 186, 357, 400–2, 423, 437; 4: 192–93.

47 The case for the Igbo preeminence in the Chesapeake region is made most vigorously by Douglas B. Chambers, "'He is an African But Speaks Plain': Historical Creolization in Eighteenth-Century Virginia" in Alusine Jalloh and Stephen Maizlish, eds., *Africa and the African Diaspora* (College Station TX, 1996), 100–33 and "'My Own Nation': Igbo Exiles in the Diaspora," *Slavery and Abolition* 18 (1997), 73–97. Also Lorena S. Walsh, "The Differential Cultural Impact of Free and Coerced Migration to Colonial America" in David Eltis, ed., *Coerced and Free Migration: Global Perspectives* (Palo Alto CA, 2002), 129–35; Gwendolyn Midlo Hall, *Slavery and African Ethnicities in the Americas: Restoring the Links* (Chapel Hill NC, 2005). Even if the Igbos dominated the region, there remains a question of exactly who the Igbos were. David Northrup points to the complex social divisions within Igbo culture in "Igbo and the Igbo Myth," 1–20. For the collapse of African nationality into the term "New Negro," see Michael Mullin, *Africa in America: Slave Acculturation and Resistance in the American South and the British Caribbean, 1736–1831* (Urbana IL, 1992), 3.

48 Linda M. Heywood, "Introduction" in Heywood, ed., *Central Africans and Cultural Transformations in the American Diaspora*, 12; Heywood and Thornton, *Central Africans, Atlantic Creoles, and the Foundations of the Americas, 1585–1660*, chaps. 2–5; Hall, *Slavery and African Ethnicity in the Americas*.

49 Philip D. Morgan, "The Cultural Implications of the Atlantic Slave Trade: African Regional Origins, American Destinations and New World Developments," *Slavery and Abolition* 18 (1997), 122–45; Morgan, "Trends in the Study of Early American Slavery of Potential Interest to Archaeologists" presented at the Digital Archaeological Archive of Chesapeake's Slavery Steering Committee Workshop, International Center for Jefferson Studies, Charlottesville VA, Oct. 6, 2000; Rediker, *Slave Ship*, 212–13; Klein, *Atlantic Slave Trade*, 155–56.

50 Klein, *Atlantic Slave Trade*, 90–93, 104, 122–24; quoted in Rediker, *Slave Ship*, 279.

51 Smallwood, *Saltwater Slavery*, 65–66 and chap. 3; Klein, *Transatlantic Slave Trade*, 90–91. According to one leading student of the slave trade, "there is no recorded instance of a slave vessel sailing direct from Africa to a port on the North Ameri-

can mainland." David Eltis, "The U.S. Transatlantic Slave Trade, 1644–1867: An Assessment," *Civil War History* 54 (2008), 354.

52 Quoted in David Hackett Fischer and James C. Kelly, *Away, I'm Bound Away: Virginia and the Westward Movement* (Richmond VA, 1993), 60–68, quoted on 62.

53 Charles Tilly, "Transplanted Networks" in Virginia Yans-McLaughlin, ed., *Immigration Reconsidered: History, Sociology, and Politics* (New York, 1990), 83–84; Douglass Massey et al., "Theories of International Migration: A Review and Appraisal," *Population and Development Review* 19 (1993), 448–62.

54 Carter to Robert Jones, Oct. 10, 1727 [misdated 1717], Oct. 24, 1729, quoted in Lorena Walsh, "A 'Place in Time' Regained: A Fuller History of Colonial Chesapeake Slavery through Group Biography" in Larry E. Hudson, Jr., ed., *Working Toward Freedom: Slave Society and Domestic Economy in the American South* (Rochester NY, 1994), 14; Lorena S. Walsh, *From Calabar to Carter's Grove: A History of a Virginia Slave Community* (Charlottesville VA, 1997), 34.

55 Gerald W. Mullin, *Flight and Rebellion: Slave Resistance in Eighteenth-Century Virginia* (New York, 1972), chap. 2; Kulikoff, *Tobacco and Slaves*, 317–35; Morgan, *Slave Counterpoint*, 444–45.

56 Quoted in Equiano, *The Interesting Narrative*, 62 and in Billy Smith and Richard Wojtowicz, comps., *Blacks Who Stole Themselves: Advertisements for Runaways in the Pennsylvania Gazette, 1728–1790* (Philadelphia, 1989), 56–57. Also Hugh Jones, *The Present State of Virginia*, Richard Morton, ed. (Chapel Hill NC, [1774] 1956), 75–76.

57 Lathan A. Windley, comp., *Runaway Slave Advertisements: A Documentary History from the 1730s to 1790*, 4 vols. (Westport CT, 1983), 3: 468; W. Abbot and Dorothy Twohig, eds., *The Papers of George Washington: Colonial Series*, 10 vols. (Charlottesville VA, 1983–1985), 7: 65–66; Morgan, *Slave Counterpoint*, 444–51. Over time members of various African ethnic or nations groups cooperated: see *ibid.*, 448.

58 Walsh, "The Differential Cultural Impact." Also see Morgan, *Slave Counterpoint*, 20–21, 524–30.

59 Morgan, *Slave Counterpoint*, 560–80; Philip D. Morgan and Michael L. Nicholls, "Slaves in Piedmont Virginia, 1720-1790," *William and Mary Quarterly* 46 (1989), 211–289; see also *Charleston South Carolina and American General Gazette*, Aug. 21, 1776; *Charleston City Gazette*, Aug. 17, 1790, Aug 21, 1776.

60 Steven Deyle makes the case that slave sales increased in frequency after the Revolution: Deyle, *Carry Me Back: The Domestic Slave Trade in American Life* (New York, 2005), 54. In the first half of the eighteenth century, the number of runaway advertisements that mention a previous owner is less than 10 percent; this increased to 28 percent in the 1790s.

61 Mullin, *Flight and Rebellion*, 87–88, 124–29; Kulikoff, *Tobacco and Slaves*, 339–41; Herbert Gutman, *The Black Family in Slavery and Freedom, 1750–1925* (New York, 1976), 347; Kathleen M. Brown, *Good Wives, Nasty Wenches and Anxious Patriarchs: Gender, Race, and Power in Colonial Virginia* (Chapel Hill NC, 1996), 357–61; Sarah S. Hughes, "Slaves for Hire: The Allocations of Black Labor in Elizabeth City County, Virginia, 1782 to 1800," *William and Mary Quarterly* 35 (1978),

260–86; Jonathan D. Martin, *Divided Mastery: Slave Hiring in the American South* (Cambridge MA, 2004).

62 John J. McCusker and Russell R. Menard, *The Economy of British America, 1607–1789* (Chapel Hill NC, 1985), 123–33; Carville Earle and Ronald Hoffman, "Staple Crops and Urban Development in the Eighteenth Century," *Perspectives in American History* 10 (1976), 7–78; Walsh, "Slaves and Tobacco in the Chesapeake," 179–186; Morgan, *Slave Counterpoint*, 523.

63 Jean Butenhoff Lee, "The Problem of Slave Community in the Eighteenth-Century Chesapeake," *William and Mary Quarterly* 43 (1986), 357; quoted in Morgan, *Slave Counterpoint*, chap. 9, quoted on 532 and also see 539–40. On the rootedness of eighteenth-century slaves, see Morgan, *ibid.*, 519–30; Edwin Morris Betts, ed., *Thomas Jefferson's Farm Book* (Princeton NJ, 1953), 19.

64 Kulikoff, *Tobacco and Slaves*, chap. 9, and *The Beginnings of the Afro-American Family*, 177–96; Gutman, *Black Family*, 75–78; Morgan, *Slave Counterpoint*, chap. 9.

65 Quoted in *South-Carolina Gazette* (Timothy) 1, Feb. 7, 1759 in Windley, comp., *Runaway Slave Advertisements*, 3: 170.

66 Phillips P. Moulton, ed., *Journal and Major Essays of John Woolman* (New York, 1971), 65; Morgan, *Slave Counterpoint*, 544–46; Gutman, *Black Family*, esp. chaps. 2–6; Mary Beth Norton, Herbert G. Gutman, and Ira Berlin, "The Afro-American Family in the Age of Revolution" in Ira Berlin and Ronald Hoffman, eds., *Slavery and Freedom in the Age of Revolution* (Charlottesville VA, 1983), 181; Rhys Isaac, *Landon Carter's Uneasy Kingdom: Revolution and Rebellion on a Virginia Plantation* (New York, 2004), chap. 13.

67 Ira Berlin and Philip D. Morgan, eds., *Cultivation and Culture: Labor and the Shaping of Slave Life in the Americas* (Charlottesville VA, 1993), chaps. 5–7, 10; Morgan, *Slave Counterpoint*, 246–49, 376, 574–79, 601–9; Shane White and Graham White, *Stylin': African American Expressive Culture from its Beginnings to the Zoot Suit* (Ithaca NY, 1998), chaps. 1–2; L. Baumgarten, "'Clothes for the People': Slave Clothing in Early Virginia," *Journal of Early Southern Decorative Arts* 14 (1998), 26–70; Barbara J. Heath, "Buttons, Beads, Buckles: Contextualizing Adornment Within the Boundaries of Slavery" in Maria Franklin and Garrett Fesler, eds., *Historical Archeology, Identity Formation, and the Interpretation of Ethnicity* (Williamsburg VA, 1999), 47–71.

68 Quoted in John Oldmixon, *The British Empire in America*, 2 vols. (London, 1708), 2: 121–22; Orlando Patterson, *The Sociology of Slavery: An Analysis of the Origins, Development, and Structure of Negro Slave Society in Jamaica* (Rutherford NJ, 1967), 146; Dana J. Epstein, *Sinful Tunes and Spirituals: Black Folk Music to the Civil War* (Urbana IL, 1977), 84; quoted in Charles Ball, *Slavery in the United States: A Narrative of the Life and Adventures of Charles Ball* (Lewistown PA, 1837), 23; Michael A. Gomez, *Exchanging Our Country Marks: The Transformation of African Identities in the Colonial and Antebellum South* (Chapel Hill NC, 1998), 189–91. Gomez notes that such antagonism existed into the nineteenth and perhaps into the twentieth century (at least in the minds of some scholars).

69 Kulikoff, *Tobacco and Slaves*, chaps. 8–9; quoted in Gomez, *Exchanging Our Country Marks*, 191.

70 Epstein, *Sinful Tunes and Spirituals*, chaps. 2–3; Epstein with Rosita M. Sands, "Secular Folk Music" in Mellonee V. Burnim and Portia K. Maultsby, eds., *African American Music: An Introduction* (New York, 2006), 35–50; Eileen Southern, *The Music of Black Americans: A History* (New York, 1971), chaps. 2–3; quoted in Shane White and Graham White, *The Sounds of Slavery: Discovering African American History Through Songs, Sermons, and Speech* (Boston, 2005), 8.

71 S. Max Edelson, "Affiliation without Affinity: Skilled Slaves in Eighteenth-Century South Carolina" in Jack P. Greene, Rosemary Brana-Shute, and Randy J. Sparks, eds., *Money, Trade, and Power: The Evolution of South Carolina's Plantation Society* (Columbia SC, 2001), 221–59; Morgan, *Slave Counterpoint*, 131, 136, 212–15, 225–36, 246, 545–46; Mullin, *Flight and Rebellion*, chap. 3; Joyce E. Chaplin, *An Anxious Pursuit: Agricultural Innovation and Modernity in the Lower South, 1730–1815* (Chapel Hill NC, 1993), 270–74.

72 Morgan, *Slave Counterpoint*, 425; Sylvia R. Frey, "'The Year of Jubilee is Come': Black Christianity in the Plantation South in Post Revolution America" in Ronald Hoffman and Peter J. Albert, eds., *Religion in a Revolutionary Age* (Charlottesville VA, 1994), 94–124 and Sylvia R. Frey, *Water from the Rock: Black Resistance in a Revolutionary Age* (Princeton NJ, 1991), chap. 8; Russell E. Rickey, "From Quarterly to Camp Meeting: A Reconsideration of Early American Methodism," *Methodist History* 23 (1985), 199–213, especially 205–6; Christine Leigh Heyrman, *Southern Cross: The Beginnings of the Bible Belt* (New York, 1997), 217–18.

73 Quoted in Roger Bruns, ed., *Am I Not a Man and a Brother: The Antislavery Crusade of Revolutionary America, 1688–1788* (New York, 1977), 428; Herbert Aptheker, ed., *A Documentary History of the Negro People in the United States*, 2 vols. (New York, 1951), 1: 8–9.

74 Arthur Zilversmit, *The First Emancipation: The Abolition of Slavery in the North* (Chicago, 1967), chaps. 5–8; Gary B. Nash and Jean R. Soderlund, *Freedom by Degrees: Emancipation in Pennsylvania and Its Aftermath* (New York, 1991); Shane White, *Somewhat More Independent: The End of Slavery in New York City, 1770–1810* (Athens GA, 1991); Leslie M. Harris, *In the Shadow of Slavery: African Americans in New York City, 1626–1863* (Chicago, 2003), chap. 2.

75 Ira Berlin, *Slaves Without Masters: The Free Negro in the Antebellum South* (New York, 1974), chap.1, esp., 46–47.

76 Berlin, *Slaves Without Masters*, 51–53; Gary B. Nash, *Forging Freedom: The Formation of Philadelphia's Black Community, 1720–1840* (Cambridge MA, 1988), 79–88, 99; Morgan, *Slave Counterpoint*, 451–52; Darrett B. Rutman and Anita H. Rutman, *A Place in Time: Explicatus* (New York, 1984), 100.

77 Berlin, *Slaves Without Masters*, chap. 3.

78 Frey and Wood, *Come Shouting to Zion*, chaps. 4–6; Eddie S. Glaude, Jr., *Exodus!: Religion, Race, and Nation in Early Nineteenth-Century Black America* (Chicago, 2000); Benjamin Quarles, "The Revolutionary War as a Black Declaration of Independence," in Berlin and Hoffman, eds., *Slavery and Freedom in the Age of the American Revolution*, 283–305.

79 For the "Union Association," see William H. Robinson, ed., *The Proceedings of the Free, African Union Society and the African Benevolent Newport, Rhode Island, 1780–1824* (Providence RI, 1976), x–xi. Later, when many of the blacks migrated

to Sierra Leone, partisan divisions were between the two largest religious factions, Methodists and Baptists. James W. Walker, *The Black Loyalists: The Search for a Promised Land in Nova Scotia and Sierra Leone, 1783–1870* (New York, 1976), 180.

80 Robinson, ed., *Proceedings of the Free, African Union*, x–xi; White, *Somewhat More Independent*, 166–71; Nash, *Forging Freedom*, 75–76. One of the first matters of business of Philadelphia's Free African Society, founded in 1787, was to establish "a regular mode of procedure with respect to . . . marriages." William Douglass, *Annals of the First African Church in the United States of America* (Philadelphia, 1862), 34–42.

81 Allen, *A Collection of Spiritual Songs* quoted in Dorothy Porter, ed., *Early Negro Writing, 1760–1837* (Boston, 1971), 571; Southern, *Music of Black Americans*, 84–93; Southern, ed., *Readings in Black American Music* (New York, 1971), 52–61; "Hymnals of the Black Church," *Journal of Interdenominational Theological Seminary* 14 (1987). For the dispute over the social purposes of Allen's Hymnal, see Kenneth L. Waters, Sr., "Liturgy, Spirituality, and Polemic in the Hymnody of Richard Allen," *The North Star* 2 (1999).

82 John F. Watson, "Methodist Error" in Southern, ed., *Readings in Black* American Music, 2nd. ed. (New York, 1983), 62–64; Mellonee V. Burnim, "Religious Music" in Burnim and Maultsby, eds., *African American Music*, 51–61.

83 Frey, *Water from the Rock*, chap. 6; Cassandra Pybus, *Epic Journeys of Freedom: Runaway Slaves of the American Revolution and their Global Quest for Liberty* (Boston, 2006); Simon Schama, *Rough Crossings: Britain, Slaves, and the American Revolution* (New York, 1907); Walker, *Black Loyalists*, chap. 1, esp. p. 12; Ellen G. Wilson, *The Loyal Black* (New York, 1976), chaps. 2–3; Graham R. Hodges, ed., *The Black Loyalist Directory: African Americans in Exile after the American Revolution* (New York, 1996); Walker, *The Black Loyalists; The Book of Negroes*.

84 John W. Davis, "George Liele and Andrew Bryan, Pioneer Negro Preachers," *Journal of Negro History* 3 (1918), 119–27; Pybus, *Epic Journeys*; Sidney Kaplan, *The Black Presence in the Era of the American Revolution* (Washington, DC, 1973); James T. Campbell, *Middle Passages: African American Journeys to Africa, 1787–2005* (New York, 2006), 29–30.

85 James Sidbury, *Becoming African in America: Race and Nation in the Early Black Atlantic* (New York, 2007); Michael A. Gomez, *Exchanging Our Country Marks: The Transformation of African Identities in the Colonial and Antebellum South* (Chapel Hill NC, 1998).

86 Walker, *The Black Loyalists*, chap. 9, especially 207.

87 Quoted in Christopher Fyfe, *A History of Sierra Leone* (London, 1962), 308. Sierra Leone, as its leading historian notes, was shaped early by the "social distinctions and peculiarities brought from North America." Also see Walker, *The Black Loyalists*, chap. 9, esp. 195.

88 Aptheker, ed., *A Documentary History of the Negro People*, 1: 7–8.

89 Quoted in Walker, *Black Loyalists*, 339, 204–5.

90 Walker, *Black Loyalists*, esp. 251–252.

91 James Forten, *Letters from a Man of Colour, on a late Bill before the Senate of Pennsylvania* (Philadelphia, 1813), 13.

Chapter Three: The Passage to the Interior

1 Michael Tadman, *Speculators and Slaves: Masters, Traders, and Slaves in the Old South* (Madison WI, 1996); Walter Johnson, *Soul by Soul: Life Inside the Antebellum Slave Market* (Cambridge MA, 1999); Robert H. Gudmestad, *A Troublesome Commerce: The Transportation of the Interstate Slave Trade* (Baton Rouge LA, 2003); Steven Deyle, *Carry Me Back: The Domestic Slave Trade in American Life* (New York, 2005); Edward E. Baptist, "'Stol and Fitched Here': Enslaved Migration, Ex-Slave Narratives, and Vernacular History" in Edward E. Baptist and Stephanie M. H. Camp, eds., *New Studies in the History of American Slavery* (Athens GA, 2006), 243–74 guide the discussion of the second great migration.

2 Tadman, *Speculators and Slaves*, chap. 1; Tadman, "The Interregional Slave Trade in the History and Myth-Making of the U.S. South" in Walter Johnson, ed., *The Chattel Principle: Internal Slave Trades in the Americas* (New Haven CT, 2004), 123; Gudmestad, *A Troublesome Commerce*, 8; also see Edward E. Baptist, *Creating an Old South: Middle Florida's Plantation Frontier before the Civil War* (Chapel Hill NC, 2002), 65–66.

3 On Georgia men, see Steven Deyle, *Carry Me Back*, chap. 2 and especially p. 63; Gudmestad, *A Troublesome Commerce*, 73.

4 Deyle, *Carry Me Back*, 90; Gudmestad, *A Troublesome Commerce*, 62–63, 73–74, 99–100, 154–60; Carol Wilson, *Freedom at Risk: The Kidnapping of Free Blacks in America, 1780–1865* (Lexington KY, 1994), chap. 1; Gary B. Nash and Jean R. Soderlund, *Freedom By Degrees: Emancipation in Pennsylvania and Its Aftermath* (New York, 1991), 195–99.

5 Like the number of slaves who crossed the Atlantic in the first Middle Passage, the number of slaves transported to the Southern interior is also contested. Robert Fogel and Stanley L. Engerman, *Time on the Cross* (Boston, 1974), 47, estimate it at 835,000 between 1790 and 1860. Herbert G. Gutman and Richard Sutch, "The Slave Family: Protected Agent of Capitalist Masters or Victim of the Slave Trade?" in Paul A. David et al., eds., *Reckoning with Slavery: A Critical Study in the Quantitative History of American Negro Slavery* (New York, 1976), 99, put the total at "more than a million"; Tadman, *Speculators and Slaves*, chap. 2 and 237–47, estimates that interregional movement averaged some 200,000 slaves each decade between 1820 and 1860 and that the total for the period between 1790 and 1820 was at least 200,000. Also see Peter McClelland and Richard Zeckhauser, *Demographic Dimensions of the New Republic: American Interregional Migration, Vital Statistics and Manumissions, 1800–1860* (New York, 1982), 159–64.

6 Tadman, *Speculators and Slaves*, 12; Richard H. Steckel, "The African American Population of the United States" in Michael R. Haines and Richard H. Steckel, eds., *A Population History of North America* (Cambridge UK, 2000), 437–53.

7 Deyle, *Carry Me Back*, 144–45, 166–73; Thomas D. Russell, "Sale Day in Antebellum South Carolina: Slavery, Law, Economy, and Court-Supervised Sales," unpublished doctoral dissertation, Stanford University, 1993; Russell, "A New Image of the Slave Auction: An Empirical Look at the Role of Law in Slave Sales and a Conceptual Reevaluation of Slave Property," *Cardozo Law Review* 18 (1996), 493–523.

8   Wilma A. Dunaway, *The African-American Family in Slavery and Emancipation* (Cambridge UK, 2003), 20, 42–45; quoted in *Baltimore American*, Feb. 21, 1860; Max L. Grivno, "'There Slavery Cannot Dwell': Agriculture and Labor in Northern Maryland, 1790–1860," unpublished Doctoral Dissertation, University of Maryland, 2007; T. Stephen Whitman, *The Price of Freedom: Slavery and Manumission in Baltimore and Early National Maryland* (Lexington KY, 1997), chaps. 1, 4.

9   Quoted in Nicholas B. Wainwright, ed., *A Philadelphia Perspective: The Diary of Sidney George Fisher Covering the Years 1834–1871* (Philadelphia, 1967), 188–89; George P. Rawick, comp., *The American Slave: A Composite Autobiography*, 41 vols. (Westport CT, 1972–79) ser. 1, vol. 6, 72; Gudmestad, *Troublesome Commerce*, 44–45. See slaves sold for impertinence and sauciness. Deyle, *Carry Me Back*, 469; Noreen T. Jones, *Born a Child of Freedom, Yet a Slave: Mechanisms of Control and Strategies of Resistance in Antebellum South Carolina* (Middleton CT, 1990), 3, 174–75.

10 Deyle, *Carry Me Back*, 100–108.

11 Gudmestad, *A Troublesome Commerce*, 20–21.

12 Baptist, *Creating an Old South*, 69–70; Tadman, *Speculators and Slaves*, 25–31; McClelland and Zeckhauser, *Demographic Dimensions*, 8; Jonathan P. B. Pritchett and Herman Freudenberger, "A Peculiar Sample: The Selection of Slaves for the New Orleans Market," *Journal of Economic History* 52 (1992), 110; Steven Miller, "Plantation Labor Organization and Slave Life" in Ira Berlin and Philip D. Morgan, eds., *Cultivation and Culture: Labor and the Shaping of Slave Life in the Americas* (Charlottesville VA, 1993), 157. Computed from the published U.S. census: *Census for 1820* (Washington DC, 1821); *Fifth Census . . . 1830* (Washington DC, 1832); *Sixth Census . . . 1840* (Washington DC, 1841); *Seventh Census of the United States 1850* (Washington DC, 1853); *Population of the United States in 1860* (Washington DC, 1862).

13 Computed from the published U.S. census: *Census for 1820*; Brenda E. Stevenson, *Life in Black and White: Family and Community in the Slave South* (New York, 1996), 177–78; Gudmestad, *A Troublesome Commerce*, 10–11.

14 David L. Lightner, "The Interstate Slave Trade in Antislavery Politics," *Civil War History* 36 (1990), 119–36; Tadman, *Speculators and Slaves*, 180–84, 212–216. On slave breeding, see Richard Sutch, "The Breeding of Slaves for Sale and the Westward Expansion of Slavery, 1830–1860" in Stanley Engerman and Eugene D. Genovese, eds., *Race and Slavery in the Western Hemisphere: Quantitative Studies* (Princeton NJ, 1975), 173–210; Robert W. Fogel and Stanley L. Engerman, "The Slave Breeding Thesis" in Fogel and Engerman, eds., *Without Consent or Contract: The Rise and Fall of American Slavery: Technical Papers*, 2 vols. (New York, 1992), 2: 455–72.

15 Tadman, *Speculators and Slaves*, 25–31; McClelland and Zeckhauser, *Demographic Dimensions*, 8; Pritchett and Freudenberger, "A Peculiar Sample: The Selection of Slaves for the New Orleans Market," 110; Miller, "Plantation Labor Organization and Slave Life," 157. Computed from the published U.S. census; see note 12, above. On the sexual balance, see Baptist, *Creating the Old South*, 69–70.

16 Tadman, *Speculators and Slaves*, 211–12; Tadman, "The Interregional Slave Trade"

in Johnson, ed., *The Chattel Principle*, 117–142; Herbert G. Gutman, *The Black Family in Slavery and Freedom, 1750–1925* (New York, 1976), 145–48; Cheryll Ann Cody, "Sale and Separation: Four Crises for Enslaved Women on the Ball Plantation, 1764–1854" in Larry Hudson, Jr., *Working Toward Freedom: Slave Society and the Domestic Economy of the American South* (Rochester NY, 1994), 119–42.

17 Ira Berlin, *Generations of Captivity: A History of African-American Slaves* (Cambridge MA, 2003), 170–71.

18 Baptist, *Creating an Old South*, 63–65. Susan O'Donovan's recent work makes evident the transience of the slave population, not only through sale but also through the system of hire and self-hire and in the nature of the slave's work, which allowed—even required—that they move from place to place. "Trunk Lines, Land Lines, and Local Exchanges: Operationalizing the Grapevine Telegraph," courtesy of the author.

19 John Hope Franklin and Loren Schweninger, *Runaway Slaves: Rebels on the Plantation* (New York, 1999), 225, 398; Rawick, comp., *American Slave*, ser. 2, vol. 16, pt. 1: 116; Charles Ball, *Fifty Years in Chains, or, The Life of an American Slave* (New York, 1859), 130–2.

20 Ball, *Fifty Years in Chains*, chaps. 1–3, quoted on 141–42.

21 Rawick, comp., *American Slave*, supp., ser. 1, vol. 5: 284–85, 320–21; Dunaway, *The African-American Family*, 33–36; Gudmestad, *A Troublesome Commerce*, 93–84, 100–101; Tadman, *Speculators and Slaves*, 68–70, 237–38, 298–300. After more than a century of decline, the slave mortality rate began increasing in the second and third decades of the nineteenth century. Robert William Fogel, *Without Consent or Contract: The Rise and Fall of American Slavery* (New York, 1989), 127–28, 142–48.

22 Tadman, "The Interregional Slave Trade," 126.

23 Deyle, *Carry Me Back*, 111, 187, chap. 4, esp. 231, 240; William Wells Brown, *Narrative of William W. Brown, a Fugitive Slave* (Boston, 1847), chap. 6.

24 Edward E. Baptist, "'Cuffy,' 'Fancy Maids,' and 'One-Eyed Men': Rape, Commodification, and the Domestic Slave Trade in the United States," *American Historical Review* 106 (2001), 1–55; quoted in John Brown, *Slave Life in Georgia: A Narrative of the Life, Sufferings, and Escape of John Brown, A Fugitive Slave*, F. N. Boney, ed. (Savannah GA, 1972), 95; Deyle, *Carry Me Back*, 126–27; Tadman, *Speculators and Slaves*, 125–27; Johnson, *Soul by Soul*, 113–115, 154–55.

25 Jesse Torrey, Jr., *A Portraiture of Domestic Slavery in the United States*, 2nd ed. (Ballston Spa MD, 1818), 55–56, 61, 67; Rawick, comp., *American Slave*, supp., ser. 2, vol. 7B: 24–64; Brown, *Narrative of William W. Brown*, 45; Ball, *Fifty Years in Chains*, 30; E. S. Abdy, *Journal of a Residence and Tour in the United States*, 3 vols. (London, 1835), 2: 179–80; Carl David Arfwedson, *The United States and Canada in 1832, 1833, and 1834*, 2 vols. (London, 1834), 2: 429. One Arkansas planter found her slaves were deeply depressed and "so dissatisfied that they lost all ambition for almost anything" quoted in Donald P. McNeilly, *Old South Frontier: Cotton Plantations and the Formation of Arkansas Society* (Fayetteville AR, 2000), 51; Abraham Lincoln, *Collected Works of Abraham Lincoln*, Roy P. Basler, ed., 9 vols. (New Brunswick NJ, 1953–1955), 1: 259–61.

26 Anthony E. Kaye, *Joining Places: Slave Neighborhoods in the Old South* (Chapel Hill NC, 2007), 65.

27 Deyle, *Carry Me Back*, 253–69; Phillip Troutman, "Grapevine in the Slave Market: African American Geopolitical Literacy and the 1841 *Creole* Revolt" in Johnson, ed. *The Chattel Principle*, 203–233; Edward D. Jervey and C. Harold Huber, "The *Creole* Affair," *Journal of Negro History* 65 (1980), 196–211; Howard Jones, "The Peculiar Institution and National Honor: The Case of the *Creole* Slave Revolt," *Civil War History* 21 (1975), 28-50; J. Winston Coleman, *Slavery Times in Kentucky* (Chapel Hill NC, 1940), 173–75; Charles S. Sydnor, *Slavery in Mississippi* (New York, 1933), 149–50; George William Featherstonhaugh, *Excursions through the Slave States* (New York, 1844), 37; Gudmestad, *Troublesome Commerce*, chap. 6.

28 Quoted in Ball, *Fifty Years in Chains*, 48–49.

29 Baptist, *Creating an Old South*, 78–79.

30 Mrs. George P. Coleman, ed., *Virginia Silhouettes* (Richmond VA, 1934), Oct. 24, 1842; Rawick, comp., *American Slave*, supp., ser. 2, vol. 1A: 319; ser. 2, vol. 1: 14, 354–55; ser. 1, vol. 12: 335; Ulrich B. Phillips, *Life and Labor in the Old South* (Boston, 1929), 212; Stevenson, *Life in Black and White*, 179; James Williams, *Narrative of James Williams, an American Slave* (Boston, 1838), 32–33; Nehemiah Adams, *A South-side View of Slavery* (Boston, 1854), 73; Charles Lyell, *A Second Visit to the United States of North America*, 2 vols. (New York, 1849), 1: 209–10. Also see Blassingame, ed., *Slave Testimony*, 13–14.

31 Rawick, comp., *American Slave*, vol. 18, 156–57, 288; also ser. 1, vol., 7, 302.

32 Daina Ramey Berry, "'We'm Fus' Rate Bargain': Value, Labor, and Price in a Georgia Slave Community" in Johnson, ed., *The Chattel Principle*, 54–55; Ira Berlin, Marc Favreau, and Steven F. Miller, eds., *Remembering Slavery: African Americans Talk About their Personal Experiences of Slavery and Emancipation* (New York, 1998), 149–51.

33 Coleman, ed., *Virginia Silhouettes*, Oct. 24, 1842; Blassingame, ed., *Slave Testimony*, 96–97.

34 Todd H. Barnett, "Virginians Moving West: The Early Evolution of Slavery in the Bluegrass," *Filson Club Historical Quarterly* 73 (1999), 221–23, 239–43.

35 Blassingame, ed., *Slave Testimony*, 22–23; Robert S. Starobin, ed., *Blacks in Bondage: Letters of American Slaves* (New York, 1974), 58; Rawick, comp., *American Slave*, ser. 1, vol. 6: 72–73; ser. 2, vol. 15: 248–49; Hawkins Wilson to the Chief of the Freedmen's Bureau at Richmond, 11 May 1867, enclosing Hawkins Wilson to Sister Jane, Letters Received, ser. 3892, Bowling Green VA Assistant Commissioner, RG 105, National Archives.

36 Mary Furguson, Dec. 18, 1936, Born in Slavery Collection, Library of Congress (http://memory.loc.gov/).

37 Quoted in Michael Mullin, ed., *American Negro Slavery: A Documentary History* (Columbia SC, 1976), 214–16; Joan E. Cashin, *A Family Venture: Men and Women on the Southern Frontier* (New York, 1991), 70 (quoted), 74, 116; Starobin, ed., *Blacks in Bondage*, 57.

38 Starobin, ed., *Blacks in Bondage*, 57.

39 Quoted in Charles L. Perdue, Jr., Thomas E. Barden, and Robert K. Phillips, eds.,

Weevils in the Wheat: Interviews with Virginia Ex-slaves (Charlottesville VA, 1976), 206.

40 O'Donovan, "Trunk Lines, Land Lines, and Local Exchanges," 21.

41 Richard H. Steckel, "The African American Population of the United States, 1790–1920" in Haines and Steckel, eds., *Population History of North America* (Cambridge UK, 2000); also see Richard Follett, "Heat, Sex, and Sugar: Pregnancy and Childbearing in the Slave Quarters," *Journal of Interdisciplinary History* 28 (2003), 510–539.

42 Cashin, *A Family Venture*, 72; T. Lindsay Baker and Julie P. Baker, eds., *The WPA Oklahoma Narratives* (Norman OK, 1996), 82; Rawick, comp., *American Slave*, vol. 4, pt. 2: 115, also supp., ser. 2, vol. 5A: 1762–63; McNeilly, *Old South Frontier*, 31.

43 Kaye, *Joining Places*, chap. 3; Campbell, "As 'A Kind of Freeman'?" and Roderick A. McDonald, "Independent Economic Production by Slaves on Antebellum Louisiana Sugar Plantations" in Berlin and Morgan, eds., *Cultivation and Culture*, 243–74, 275–302; Charles S. Sydnor, *A Gentleman of the Old Natchez Region, Benjamin L. C. Wailes* (Westport CT, [1938] 1970), 101–104; Christopher Morris, *Becoming Southern: The Evolution of a Way of Life, Warren County and Vicksburg, Mississippi, 1770–1860* (New York, 1995), 75–76; Ball, *Fifty Years in Chains*, 131–33, quoted on 131, 147–48.

44 Gutman, *The Black Family*; Ann Patton Malone, *Sweet Chariot: Slave Family and Household Structure in Nineteenth-century Louisiana* (Chapel Hill NC, 1992). Sally Anne Chambers, who grew up in Louisiana, recalled how slaves turned to the business of family on Saturdays and Sundays: "De women do dey own washing den. De menfolks tend to de gardens round dey own house. Dey raise some cotton and sell it to massa and git li'l money dat way." Rawick, comp., *American Slave*, ser. 1, vol. 4, pt. 1–2, 215.

45 Gutman, *Black Family*; Baptist, *Creating the Old South*, 81–82.

46 Gutman, *Black Family*, chaps. 2, 5; Cheryll Ann Cody, "Naming, Kinship, and Estate Dispersal: Notes on Slave Family Life on a South Carolina Plantation, 1786 to 1833," *William and Mary Quarterly* 39 (1982), 192–211; Morris, *Becoming Southern*, 68–83.

47 Steven Hahn, *A Nation Under Our Feet: Black Political Struggle in the Rural South, from Slavery to the Great Migration* (Cambridge MA, 2003), 36.

48 Albert J. Rabateau, *Slave Religion: The "Invisible Institution" in the Antebellum South* (New York, 1978); Sylvia R. Frey and Betty Wood, *Come Shouting to Zion: African American Protestantism in the American South and British Caribbean to 1830* (Chapel Hill NC, 1998), chaps. 4–5; Eddie S. Glaude, Jr., *Exodus!: Religion, Race, and Nation in Early Nineteenth-Century Black America* (Chicago, 2000); Berlin, *Generations of Captivity*, 203–6.

49 In the early nineteenth century, African Americans touched by the "Second Awakening" attended camp meetings and, given the level of illiteracy, doubtless sang without hymnals. Also many songs were composed on the spot and elaborated in the field or in religious gatherings. They were called "spiritual songs" and the term "sperichil" appeared for the first time in 1867 in William Francis Allen,

Charles P. Ware, and Lucy McKim Garrison, *Slave Songs of the United States* (New York, [1867] 1951); also see Thomas Wentworth Higginson, "Negro Spirituals," *Atlantic Monthly* 19 (1867), 685–94; Sterling Stuckey, *Slave Culture: Nationalist Theory and the Foundations of Black America* (New York, 1987), chap. 1; Lawrence W. Levine, *Black Culture and Black Consciousness: Afro-American Folk thought from Slavery to Freedom* (New York, 1977), 17, 19–30, 59, 159–70; Gilbert Chase, *America's Music: From the Pilgrims to the Present*, 3rd ed. (Urbana IL, 1987), chap. 4, quote on 215. Dena J. Epstein, *Sinful Tunes and Spirituals: Black Folk Music to the Civil War* (Urbana IL, 1977); Eileen Southern, *The Music of Black Americans* (New York, 1971), chaps. 6–7.

50 A good selection of the spirituals can be found on the Internet. See for example www.hymnlyrics.org (although no dates of attribution are provided).

51 James Oakes, *The Ruling Race: A History of American Slaveholders* (New York, 1982), 77; Donald Schaefer, "A Statistical Profile of Frontier and New South Migration: 1850–1860," *Agricultural History* 59 (1986), 563–578; Gavin Wright, *Old South, New South: Revolutions in the Southern Economy since the Civil War* (New York, 1986), 25. Analysis of the records of the Freedman's Bank and Trust Company, courtesy of Susan O'Donovan, "Mapping Freedom's Terrain: The Political and Productive Landscape of Wilmington, North Carolina," 16.

52 Leon F. Litwack, *Been in the Storm So Long: The Aftermath of Slavery* (New York, 1979); Eric Foner, *Reconstruction: America's Unfinished Revolution, 1863–1877* (New York, 1988), esp. chap. 3; Ira Berlin et al., eds., *Freedom: A Documentary History of Emancipation* [hereafter cited as *Freedom*], 5 vols. (Cambridge UK and Chapel Hill NC, 1983–), ser. 3, vol. 1, esp., chap. 5.

53 W. E. B. DuBois, *Black Reconstruction in America: An Essay toward the History of the Part Black Folk Played in the Attempt to Reconstruct Democracy in America, 1860–1880* (New York, 1935), chaps. 1–5; Foner, *Reconstruction*, chaps. 1–3; Litwack, *Been in the Storm So Long*, chaps. 1–4; *Freedom*, quoted in ser. 2, 615–16; ser. 1, vol. 1: 23–27.

54 Foner, *Reconstruction*, chap. 5; *Freedom*, ser. 3, vol. 1.

55 U.S. Census Bureau, *Historical Statistics of the United States, Colonial Times to 1970* (Washington DC, 1975), I: part 2, p. 22.

56 *Freedom*, ser. 3, vol. 1: 23–24, and docs. 6, 15–22, 23 (quoted), 36, 67, 132, 162.

57 William Cohen, *At Freedom's Edge: Black Mobility and the White Southern Quest for Racial Control, 1861–1915* (Baton Rouge LA, 1991), 28–38; Theodore B. Wilson, *The Black Codes of the South* (Tuscaloosa AL, 1965), chap. 5; *Freedom*, ser. 3, vol. 1, 29–30, 81–84, also docs. 28, 33, 37, 43–45.

58 Gerald D. Jaynes, "Blacks in the Economy from Reconstruction to World War I" in William R. Scott and William G. Slade, eds., *Upon These Shores: Themes in the African American Experience to the Present* (New York, 2000), 168. Between 1860 and 1910, the south Atlantic states' share of African Americans declined from 46 to 42 percent, while the southwestern states increased from 15 to 20 percent. U.S. Census Bureau, *Negro Population of the United States, 1790–1915* (Washington DC, 1918), table 13; James R. Grossman, *Land of Hope: Chicago, Black Southerners, and the Great Migration* (Chicago, 1989), 22–23. The northward movement

of black Southerners was also small and selective: Elizabeth H. Pleck, *Black Migration and Poverty: Boston, 1865–1900* (New York, 1979), 89.

59 U.S. Census Bureau, *Negro Population, 1790–1915* (Washington DC, 1918), 65; Steckel, "African American Population of the United States" in Haines and Steckel, eds., *Population History of North America*, 465; Simon Kuznets, ed., *Population Redistribution and Economic Growth in the United States, 1870–1950*, 3 vols. (Philadelphia, 1957–1964), 3: 90; Edward L. Ayers, *Promise of the New South: Life after Reconstruction* (New York, 1992), chap. 3, pp. 68–72; Cohen, *At Freedom's Edge*, chap. 9, p. 254; Edwin S. Redkey, *Black Nationalist and Back-to-Africa Movements, 1890–1910* (New Haven CT, 1969), 57; James T. Campbell, *Middle Passages: African American Journeys to Africa, 1787–2005* (New York, 2006), chaps. 3–4, esp. p. 103; Thomas C. Cox, *Blacks in Topeka, Kansas, 1865–1915: A Social History* (Baton Rouge LA, 1982); Hahn, *A Nation Under our Feet.*

60 Kuznets, ed., *Population Redistribution and Economic Growth*, 3: 90; Cohen, *At Freedom's Edge*, 295–296.

61 *Negro Population*, 64; Karl E. Taeuber, "The Negro Population in the United States" in John P. Davis, ed., *The American Negro Reference Book* (Englewood Cliffs NJ, 1966), 107; Thomas J. Woofter, *Negro Migration: Changes in Rural Organization and the Population of the Cotton Belt* (New York, 1969), 134; O'Donovan, "Mapping Freedmen's Terrain," 16.

62 *Historical Statistics of the United States*, 22.

63 David Barrow, "A Georgia Plantation," *Scribner Monthly* 21 (1881), 830–36; D. W. Meinig, *The Shaping of America*, 4 vols. (New Haven CT, 1986–2004), 3: 190–95; Charles S. Aiken, "New Settlement Patterns of Rural Blacks in the American South," *Geographical Review* 75 (1985), 383–404; Milton B. Newton, Jr., "Settlement Patterns as Artifacts of Social Structure" in Miles Richardson, ed., *The Human Mirror: Material and Spatial Images of Man* (Baton Rouge LA, 1974), 339–61; Joel Williamson, *After Slavery: The Negro in South Carolina During Reconstruction, 1861–1877* (Chapel Hill NC, 1965), 278.

64 Dylan C. Penningroth, *The Claims of Kinfolk: African American Property and Community in the Nineteenth-Century South* (Chapel Hill NC, 2003), 158; Julie Seville, *The Work of Reconstruction: From Slave to Wage Worker in South Carolina, 1860–1870* (Cambridge UK, 1994), chap. 1.

65 Quoted in *Freedom*, ser. 3, vol. 1: 25, 46–52 and chap. 9; Frederick Law Olmsted, *The Cotton Kingdom: A Traveler's Observations on Cotton and Slavery*, Arthur M. Schlesinger, Sr., ed. (New York, 1984), 81; Ira Berlin et al., eds., "The Terrain of Freedom: The Struggle over the Meaning of Free Labor in the U.S. South," *History Workshop* 22 (1986), 127–28.

66 Quoted in Charles Joyner, *Down by the Riverside: A South Carolina Slave Community* (Urbana IL, 1984), 42–43; *Freedom*, ser. 3, vol. 1: chap. 3–4; Foner, *Reconstruction*, 102–110, 153–170; Claude F. Oubre, *Forty Acres and a Mule: The Freedmen's Bureau and Black Land Ownership* (Baton Rouge LA, 1978); quoted in Major [James Roy] to Bvt. Lieut. Col. W. L. Berger, 9 Dec. 1865, filed with Major James P. Roy to Bvt. Lieut. Col. W. L. M. Burger, 1 Feb. 1866, Letters Received, Dept. of SC, RG 393, Pt. 1 [C-1385], National Archives. Bracketed number refers

to the files at the Freedmen and Southern Society Project at the University of Maryland.

67 *Freedom*, ser. 3, vol. 1, chaps. 3–4. The outlines of the new labor system appeared even before the war was over in the occupied South; see *Freedom*, ser. 1, vol. 1, chaps. 1–3; *Freedom*, ser. 1, vol. 2; Louis S. Gerteis, *From Contraband to Freedman: Federal Policy toward Southern Blacks, 1861–1865* (Westport CT, 1973); Foner, *Reconstruction*, 78–84; Litwack, *Been in the Storm So Long*, chaps. 4–6.

68 *Freedom*, ser. 3, vol. 1, chaps. 1–5, 7–8; Litwack, *Been in the Storm So Long*, 4–8; Gerald David Jaynes, *Branches Without Roots: Genesis of the Black Workingclass in the American South, 1862–1882* (New York, 1986), chaps. 2–4; Roger L. Ransom and Richard Sutch, *One Kind of Freedom: The Economic Consequences of Emancipation* (New York, 1977), chaps. 3–4; Thavolia Glymph, "Freedpeople and Ex-Masters Shaping a New Order in the Post-Bellum South, 1865–1868" in Glymph and John J. Kushma, eds., *Essays on the Postbellum South Economy* (College Station TX, 1985), 48–72.

69 Harold D. Woodman, *New South, New Law: The Legal Foundations of Credit and Labor Relations in the Postbellum Agricultural South* (Baton Rouge LA, 1995); Jaynes, *Branches Without Roots*, chap. 10.

70 Quoted in Eric Foner, *Nothing but Freedom: Emancipation and its Legacy* (Baton Rouge LA, 1983), 61; Harold D. Woodman, "Post-Civil War Southern Agricultural and the Law," *Agricultural History* 53 (1979), 319–37; Leon F. Litwack, *Trouble in Mind: Black Southerners in the Age of Jim Crow* (New York, 1999), chap. 3.

71 Litwack, *Trouble in Mind*, esp. chap. 4.

72 Litwack, *Trouble in Mind*, esp. chaps. 5–6; Edward L. Ayers, *Vengeance and Justice: Crime and Punishment in the Nineteenth-Century American South* (New York, 1984), chap. 6; Alexander C. Lichtenstein, *Twice the Work of Free Labor: The Political Economy of Convict Labor in the New South* (London, 1996); Pete Daniel *The Shadow of Slavery: Peonage in the South, 1901–1969* (Urbana IL, 1972); Martha A. Myers, *Race, Labor, and Punishment in the New South* (Athens OH, 1998).

73 Litwack, *Trouble in Mind*, 128; C. Vann Woodward, *The Origins of the New South* (Baton Rouge LA, 1971), 205–6; Neil Fligstein, *Going North: Migration of Blacks and Whites from the South, 1900–1950* (New York, 1950), 131; Joe William Trotter, Jr., *The African American Experience* (Boston, 2001), 303. Quoted in Grossman, *Land of Hope*, 109.

74 Quoted in Jay R. Mandle, *The Roots of Black Poverty: The Southern Plantation Economy after the Civil War* (Durham NC, 1978), 20.

75 Charles S. Johnson, *Shadow of the Plantation* (Chicago, 1934), 11; Wright, *Old South, New South*, 65, 98; Mandle, *The Roots of Black Poverty*, 20; Thomas J. Woofter, *Negro Problems in Cities* (Garden City NY, 1928), 88–89, 105.

76 Wright, *Old South, New South*, 119–20.

77 James R. Grossman, "A Chance to Make Good, 1900–1929" in Robin D. G. Kelley and Earl Lewis, eds., *To Make Our World Anew: A History of African Americans* (New York, 2000), 358.

78 C. Eric Lincoln and Lawrence H. Mamiya, *The Black Church in the African American Experience* (Durham NC, 1994), chap. 5.

79   For the linkage between the blues and the commitment to migration in search of freedom that would transform the African landscape, see Waldo F. Martin, "The Sounds of Blackness: African-American Music" in William R. Scott and William G. Shade, eds., *Upon These Shores: Themes in the African American Experience* (New York, 2000), 260–61; Levine, *Black Culture and Black Consciousness*, 202–97; William Barlow, *"Looking Up at Down": The Emergence of Blues Culture* (Philadelphia, 1989), chaps. 1–2; Jeff Todd Tilton, *Early Down-home Blues: A Musical and Cultural Analysis* (Urbana IL, 1975); David Evans, "Blues: Chronological Overview" and Susan Oehler, "The Blues in Transcultural Context" both in Mellonee V. Burnim and Portia K. Maultsby, eds., *African American Music: An Introduction* (New York, 2006), 97–126; Chase, *America's Music*, chap. 27.

80   Levine, *Black Culture and Black Consciousness*, esp. 221–22; Barlow, "Looking Up at Down," chaps. 1–4; LeRoi Jones, *Blues People: The Negro Experience in White America and the Music that Developed From It* (New York, 1968), chap. 1; William Ferris, Jr., *Blues from the Delta* (London, 1970), 11–55.

81   http://www.geocities.com/BourbonStreet/delta/2541/blflewis.htm.

82   Steckel, "The African American Population of the United States" in Haines and Steckel, eds., *Population History of North America*, 464; Wright, *Old South, New South*, 98, 200–5.

83   Leslie H. Fishel, Jr., "The Negro in Northern Politics, 1870-1900," *Mississippi Valley Historical Review* 42 (1955), 466–89; Desmund King and Stephen Tuck, "De-Centering the South: America's Nationwide White Supremacist Order After Reconstruction," *Past and Present* 194 (2007), 213–53; Joe William Trotter, Jr., "Blacks in the Urban North: The 'Underclass Question' in Historical Perspective" in Michael B. Katz, ed., *The "Underclass" Debate: Views from History* (Princeton NJ, 1993), 59–60; Edward Meeker and James Kau, "Racial Discrimination and Occupational Attainment at the Turn of the Century," *Explorations in Economic History* 14 (1977), 250–76; Pleck, *Black Migration and Poverty*, 128, 134–36; quoted in Joe William Trotter, Jr., *Black Milwaukee: The Making of an Industrial Proletariat, 1915–1945* (Urbana IL, 1985), 30–31.

84   Johnson, *Shadow of the Plantation* quoted in Litwack, *Been in the Storm So Long*, 169.

85   Booker T. Washington, *Up From Slavery: An Autobiography* (New York, 1897), 219; also see Washington, "The Rural Negro and the South," *Proceedings of the National Conference of Charities and Corrections* 41 (1914), 123; Louis R. Harlan, *Booker T. Washington: The Making of a Black Leader, 1856–1901* (New York, 1972), 213–19; Grossman, *Land of Hope*, 81–82; Cohen, *Freedom's Edge*, 249. Even after black people began to move north in large numbers, the presumption of their attachment to the South remained. In 1923, *Atlantic Monthly* summarized the conventional wisdom: "The Negro race was found almost entirely within the Southern states, and it was always assumed that it would probably remain there" in E. T. H. Shaffer, "A New South—The Negro Migration," *Atlantic Monthly* 132 (Sept. 1923), 403.

86   Guido Van Rijn, "Coolidge's Blue: African American Blues on Prohibition, Migration, Unemployment, and Jim Crow" in Robert Springer, ed., *Nobody Knows Where The Blues Come From: Lyrics and History* (Jackson MS, 2006), 151–63.

Chapter Four: The Passage to the North

1 U.S. Census Bureau, *Historical Statistics of the United States, Colonial Times to 1970* (Washington DC, 1975), 22; Richard Easterlin, "The Population of the United States since 1920" in Michael R. Haines and Richard H. Steckel, eds., *A Population History of North America* (Cambridge UK, 2000), 642; J. Trent Alexander, "Demographic Patterns of the Great Migration (1915–1940)" and "Demographic Patterns of the Great Black Migration (1940–1970)" both in Steven A. Reich, ed., *Encyclopedia of the Great Black Migration*, 2 vols. (Westport CT, 2006), 1: 236–43.

2 My understanding of the third passage includes what has been called the "Great Migration"—the movement northward that accompanied World War I and extends through the Great Depression, World War II, and beyond, or roughly the years between 1910 and 1970, at which point the movement of black people between North and South reversed course.

3 Carole Marks, *Farewell—We're Good and Gone: The Great Black Migration* (Bloomington IN, 1989), 1; George A. Davis and O. Fred Donaldson, *Blacks in the United States: A Geographic Perspective* (Boston, 1975), 34–37; Hope Eldridge and Dorothy Swaine Thomas, *Population Redistribution and Economic Growth, 1870–1950* (Philadelphia, 1964), 90; James N. Gregory, *The Southern Diaspora: How the Great Migrations of Black and White Southerners Transformed America* (Chapel Hill NC, 2005), 14; Thomas J. Woofter, *Negro Migration: Changes in Rural Organization and the Population of the Cotton Belt* (New York, 1920), 134. The counties which compose the Alabama black belt are: Autauga, Bullock, Dallas, Greene, Hale, Lowndes, Macon, Marengo, Montgomery, Perry, Russell, Sumter, and Wilcox.

4 Blaine Brownell and David Goldfield, *Urban America: From Downtown to No Town* (Boston, 1979), 259–63; Joe W. Trotter, Jr., ed., *The Great Migration in Historical Perspective: New Dimensions of Race, Class, and Gender* (Bloomington IN, 1991), 482; James R. Grossman, *Land of Hope: Chicago, Black Southerners, and the Great Migration* (Chicago, 1989), 48; *Historical Statistics of the United States*, pt. 1: 95. Because of the differences in origins, size, and direction between migrations that accompanied the first and second world wars, some historians and demographers have treated them as distinct events. See, for example, Alexander, "Demographic Patterns of the Great Black Migration (1915–1940)" and "Demographic Patterns of the Great Black Migration (1940–1970)" both in Reich, ed., *Encyclopedia of the Great Black Migration*, 1: 236–43.

5 Rex R. Campbell, Daniel M. Johnson, and Gary J. Strangler, "Return Migration of Black People to the South," *Rural Sociology* 39 (1974), 514–28; Reynolds Farley and Walter R. Allen, *The Color Line and the Quality of Life in America* (New York, 1989), 117–28; John Cromartie and Carol B. Stack, "Reinterpretation of Black Return and Nonreturn Migration to the South, 1975–1980," *Geographical Review* 79 (1989), 300; Carol Stack, *Call to Home: African Americans Reclaim the Rural South* (New York, 1996); Michael A. Stoll, "African Americans and the Color Line" in Reynolds Farley and John Hagga, eds., *The American People: Census 2000* (New York, 2005), 402–3; Gregory, *Southern Diaspora*, 39–40; Gregory, "The Southern Diaspora and the Urban Dispossessed: Demonstrating the Cen-

sus Public Use Microdata Samples," *Journal of American History* 82 (1995), 130.

6 The six million total is a net migration rate and does not include those who migrated to the North and returned to the South. Many black Southerners migrated North, but returned to the South—thus participating in the northward migration.

7 Davis and Donaldson, *Blacks in the United States,* 30–31; Gregory, *Southern Diaspora,* 17–18; Steckel, "The African American Population of the United States" in Haines and Steckel, eds., *A Population History of North America,* 465; Reynolds Farley, *Growth of the Black Population: A Study of Demographic Trends* (Chicago, 1970), 50.

8 Brownell and Goldfield, *Urban America,* 260; Karl E. Taeuber "The Negro Population in the United States" in John P. Davis, ed., *The American Negro Reference Book* (Englewood Cliffs NJ, 1966), 116–34; Farley and Allen, *The Color Line and the Quality of Life in America,* 103–4; Gregory, "The Southern Diaspora and the Urban Dispossessed," 117; Howard Dodson and Sylviane A. Diouf, *In Motion: The African-American Migration Experience* (Washington DC, 2004), 136; Peter Gottlieb, *Making Their Own Way: Southern Blacks' Migration to Pittsburgh, 1916–1930* (Urbana IL, 1987), 1.

9 Brownell and Goldfield, *Urban America,* 260; Frank Hobbs and Nicole Stoops, *Demographic Trends in the Twentieth Century* (Washington DC, 2002), 260.

10 In analyzing the cause of the Great Migration, scholars have given different weight to the various pushes and pulls which set it in motion; my account is drawn from the following: Grossman, *Land of Hope;* Gregory, *Southern Diaspora;* Marks, *Farewell;* Florette Henri, *Black Migration: Movement North, 1900–1920* (Garden City NY, 1975); Neil Fligstein, *Going North: Migration of Blacks and Whites from the South, 1900–1950* (New York, 1981); Gottlieb, *Making Their Own Way;* Kimberley L. Phillips, *AlabamaNorth: African-American Migrants, Community, and Working-Class Activism in Cleveland, 1915–45* (Urbana IL, 1999); Trotter, ed., *The Great Migration in Historical Perspective.*

11 Phillips, *AlabamaNorth,* 57; Roi Ottley, *The Lonely Warrior: The Life and Times of Robert S. Abbott* (Chicago, 1955).

12 Davis and Donaldson, *Blacks in the United States,* 35; Gavin Wright, *Old South, New South: Revolutions in the Southern Economy since the Civil War* (New York, 1986), 95–96, 203–5.

13 Grossman, *Land of Hope,* 30; quoted in E. Franklin Frazier, *The Negro Family in the United States* (Chicago, 1966), 210, and R. H. Leavell, "The Negro Migration from Mississippi" in Leavell et al., *Negro Migration in 1916–17* (Washington DC, 1919), 17. Also see Marks, *Farewell,* chap. 3.

14 Wright, *Old South, New South,* 203–5; Marks, *Farewell,* chap. 3; quoted in Leavell, "The Negro Migration from Mississippi," 17, and Marks, "In Search of the Promised Land: Black Migration and Urbanization, 1900–1940" in William R. Scott and William G. Slade, eds., *Upon These Shores: Themes in the African American Experience, 1600 to the Present* (New York, 2000), 188.

15 William M. Tuttle, Jr., *Race Riot: Chicago in the Red Summer of 1919* (New York, 1970), 74–107; Grossman, *Land of Hope,* chap. 2; Phillips, *AlabamaNorth,* 53.

16 Wright, *Old South, New South*, chap. 7, esp. 231–33; Pete Daniel, *Breaking the Land: The Transformation of Cotton, Tobacco, and Rice Cultures since 1880* (Urbana IL, 1985); *Historical Statistics of the United States*, pt. 1, 109–153.

17 Wright, *Old South, New South*, 223–34.

18 Daniel, *Breaking the Land*, chaps. 2–4; Gilbert C. Fite, *Cotton Fields No More: Southern Agriculture, 1865–1980* (Lexington KY, 1984), chaps. 8–9; Neil Fligstein, "The Transformation of Southern Agriculture and the Migration of Blacks and Whites, 1930–1950," *International Migration Review* 17 (1983), 273; Craig W. Heinicke, "African American Migration and the Mechanized Cotton Harvesting, 1950–1960," *Explorations in Economic History* 31 (1994), 501–20; *Historical Statistics of the United States*, pt. 1, 109–153; Grossman, *Land of Hope*, 48; Brownell and Goldfield, *Urban America*, chaps. 10–11.

19 Edward L. Ayers, *The Promise of the New South: Life After Reconstruction* (New York, 1993), chap. 6; Neil R. McMillen, *Dark Journey: Black Mississippians in the Age of Jim Crow* (Urbana IL, 1989); Leon F. Litwack, *Trouble in Mind: Black Southerners in the Age of Jim Crow* (New York, 1998); Grossman, *Land of Hope*, 16–19; quoted in Kusmer, *A Ghetto Takes Shape*, 225.

20 Quoted in Theodore Rosengarten, *All God's Dangers: The Life of Nate Shaw* (New York, 1974), 27.

21 Ira de A. Reid, "Special Problems of Negro Migration During the War" in *Milbank Memorial Fund Quarterly, Postwar Problems of Migration* (New York, 1947), 155; Gregory, *Southern Diaspora*, 37; quoted in Grossman, *Land of Hope*, 3.

22 Peter Gottlieb, "Rethinking the Great Migration: A Perspective from Pittsburgh" in Trotter, ed., *The Great Migration*, 74. For a similar development in Flint, Michigan, see Gregory, *Southern Diaspora*, 29. Also Trotter, eds., *The Great Migration*, 482.

23 Gregory, *Southern Diaspora*, 365, n. 27; Jacqueline Jones, *Labor of Love, Labor of Sorrow: Black Women, Work, and the Family from Slavery to the Present* (New York, 1985), 153–60; Darlene Clark Hine, "Black Migration to the Urban Midwest: The Gender Dimension, 1915–1945" in Trotter, ed., *The Great Migration*, 127–46; Leslie Brown, "African American Women and Migration" in S. Jay Kleinberg, Eileen Boris, and Vicki L. Ruiz, eds., *The Practice of U.S. Women's History: Narrative, Intersections, and Dialogues* (New Brunswick NJ, 2007), 204; Beverly A. Bunch-Lyons, *Contested Terrain: African American Women Migrate from the South to Cincinnati, 1900–1950* (New York, 2002), 23–42; quoted in Elizabeth Rauh Bethel, *Promiseland: A Century of Life in a Negro Community* (Philadelphia, 1981), 122.

24 Taeuber "The Negro Population in the United States" in Davis, ed., *American Negro Reference Book*, 112–113; Wright, *Old South, New South*, 96–97; Clyde V. Kiser, *Sea Island to City: A Study of St. Helena Islanders in Harlem and Other Urban Centers* (New York, 1967), 117, 131, 144; Kusmer, *A Ghetto Takes Shape*, 39, 149.

25 Marks, *Farewell*, 34–48; C. Horace Hamilton, "Educational Selectivity of Net Migration from the South," *Social Forces* 38 (1959), 33–42; Stewart E. Tolnay, "Educational Selection in the Migration of Southern Blacks, 1880–1990," *Social Forces* 77 (1998), 487–514; Gregory, *Southern Diaspora*, 28, 30–33; Wright, *Old*

South, New South, 246–55; Elizabeth H. Pleck, *Black Migration and Poverty: Boston, 1865–1900* (New York, 1979), chap. 3. On literacy of the first immigrants and decline over time see Stanley Lieberson, "Selective Black Migration from the South: A Historical View" in Frank D. Bean and W. Parker Frisbie, eds., *The Demography of Racial and Ethnic Groups* (New York, 1978), 122. For the migration of musicians, see Burton W. Peretti, *The Creation of Jazz: Music, Race, and Culture in Urban America* (Urbana IL, 1992), 43–45.

26 Malaika Adero, ed., *Up South: Stories, Studies, and Letters of this Century's African-American Migrations* (New York, 1993), xvii; also Dwayne E. Walls, *The Chicken Bone Special* (New York, 1970).

27 Grossman, *Land of Hope*, 112–13; quoted from Armstrong, *Satchmo: My Life in New Orleans* (New York, 1954), 229–30.

28 Henri, *Black Migration*, 66; Marks, *Farewell*, 36–37; Abraham Epstein, *The Negro Migrant in Pittsburgh* (New York, [1918] 1969), 35.

29 Grossman, *Land of Hope*, 2, 109–111; quoted in Richard Wright, *Black Boy* (Chicago, 1947), 181.

30 Abraham Epstein, *The Negro Migrant in Pittsburgh* (New York, [1918] 1969), 27.

31 Marks, *Farewell*, chap. 2, esp. 20–21; Gottlieb, *Making Their Own Way*, 49–55; Phillips, *AlabamaNorth*, 54–55. For an explication of the theory of chain migrations, see John McDonald and Leatrice McDonald, "Chain Migration, Ethnic Neighborhood Formation, and Social Networks," *Milbank Memorial Fund Quarterly* 42 (1964), 82–97, and for how migrating pioneers make movement more accessible and cheaper for those who follow, see Douglas Massey, "Why Does Immigration Occur?" in Charles Hirschman, Philip Kasinitz, and Josh DeWind, eds., *The Handbook of International Migration: The American Experience* (New York, 1999), 45.

32 Grossman, *Land of Hope*, chap. 3; also see Henri, *Black Migration*, chap. 2.

33 Grossman, *Land of Hope*, chap. 3; Cromartie and Stack, "Reinterpretation of Black Return and Non Return Migration," 299–309.

34 Phillips, *AlabamaNorth*, 62-63; Kusmer, *A Ghetto Takes Shape*, 39–41, 160–62.

35 For a discussion of so-called stage or step migration, see J. Trent Alexander, "The Great Migration in Comparative Perspective: Interpreting the Urban Origins of Southern Black Migrants to Depression-Era Pittsburgh," *Social Science History* 22 (1998), 349–37; Taeuber, "The Negro Population in the United States" in Davis, ed., *American Negro Reference Book*, 129–130; and for repeated migration, see Julie DaVanzo, "Repeat Migration in the United States: Who Moves Back and Who Moves On?," *Review of Economics and Statistics* 65 (1983), 552–59; Wright, *Black Boy*, 221; Leslie Brown, "African American Women and Migration," 204.

36 Emmett J. Scott, *Negro Migration during the War* (New York, 1969), 106, 134; quoted in Dotson and Diouf, *In Motion*, 120; Henry Louis Gates, Jr., "New Negroes, Migration, and Cultural Exchange" in Elizabeth Hutton Turner, ed., *Jacob Lawrence: The Migration Series* (Washington DC, 1993), 17–21; Gottlieb, *Making Their Own Way*, 3–45; Gerald D. Jaynes, "Blacks in the Economy from Reconstruction to World War I" in Scott and Slade, eds., *Upon These Shores*, 185. DuBois had noted the same phenomenon early in the twentieth century. Michael

B. Katz and Thomas J. Sugrue, *W. E. B. DuBois, Race, and the City: The Philadelphia Negro and Its Legacy* (Philadelphia, 1998), 76.

37 Gottlieb, *Making Their Own Way*, 29–31; Kiser, *Sea Island to City*, 154; Walls, *The Chicken Bone Special*.

38 Emitt J. Scott, ed., "Letters from Negro Migrants of 1916–1918," *Journal of Negro History* 4 (1919), 334.

39 Otis Hicks, Greyhound Blues, http://www.geocities.com/BourbonStreet/delta/2541/bllslim.htm#Greyhound466.

40 Grossman, *Land of Hope*, 113–115; quoted in Richard Wright, *American Hunger* (New York, 1977), 307.

41 Grossman, *Land of Hope*, 113–17.

42 Walter Licht, *Getting Work: Philadelphia, 1840–1950* (Cambridge MA, 1992), 32–33; Allan H. Spear, *Black Chicago: The Making of a Negro Ghetto, 1890–1920* (Chicago, 1967), 29; Kusmer, *Ghetto Takes Shape*, chap. 4; Warren C. Whatley and Gavin Wright, "Race, Human Capital, and Labour Markets in American History" in George Grantham and Mary MacKinnon, eds., *Labour Market Evolutions: The Economic History of Market Integration, Wage Flexibility, and Employment Relation* (New York, 1994), 280–81; David M. Katzman, *Before the Ghetto: Black Detroit in the Nineteenth Century* (Urbana IL 1973), 217–22; Pleck, *Black Migration*, chap. 2; Joe William Trotter, Jr., *The African American Experience* (Boston, 2001), 311; quoted in W. E. B. DuBois, *The Philadelphia Negro* (Philadelphia, 1899), 323.

43 August Meier, "Negro Class Structure and Ideology in the Age of Booker T. Washington," *Phylon* 23 (1962), 258–66; Meier, *Negro Thought in America, 1880–1915: Racial Ideologies in the Age of Booker T. Washington* (Ann Arbor MI, 1963), esp. chap. 9; DuBois, *The Philadelphia Negro*, 310–21, 340–51; Kusmer, *Ghetto Takes Shape*, chaps. 1, 5; Spear, *Black Chicago*, chap. 3; Marcy S. Sacks, *Before Harlem: The Black Experience in New York City before World War I* (Philadelphia, 2006); Katzman, *Before the Ghetto*, chaps. 4–6; Bart Landry, *The New Black Middle Class* (Berkeley CA, 1987), 19–20.

44 Kusmer, *Ghetto Takes Shape*, 26–28, 75–78, 99–103, 114–40, 165–70, 236–43; Katzman, *Before the Ghetto*, chaps. 4–6; Licht, *Getting Work*, 32–33; St. Clair Drake and Horace R. Cayton, *Black Metropolis: A Study of Negro Life in a Northern City* (New York, 1945), chap. 9; Trotter, *The African American Experience*, 310; quoted in Spear, *Black Chicago*, 168 and Bayard Still, ed., *Urban America: A History with Documents* (Boston, 1974), 279.

45 Meier, "Negro Class Structure and Ideology in the Age of Booker T. Washington," 258–66; Sacks, *Before Harlem*, 26–28; Sacks, "Re-creating Black New York at Century's End" in Ira Berlin and Leslie M. Harris, eds., *Slavery in New York* (New York, 2005), 325–50; Katzman, *Before the Ghetto*; Kusmer, *Ghetto Takes Shape*, chaps. 5–6.

46 Spear, *Black Chicago*, chaps. 9–10, quoted in p. 168; Drake and Cayton, *Black Metropolis*, 73–76; Sacks, *Before Harlem*, 68–71; Kusmer, *Ghetto Takes Shape*, chaps. 10–11 and note 51, below.

47 William H. Harris, *The Harder We Run: Black Workers Since the Civil War* (New York, 1982), 61–66; Kusmer, *A Ghetto Takes Shape*, chap. 9, especially 191, 199–

222; Spear, *Black Chicago*; 150–151; Licht, *Getting Work*, 45, 141; David M. Katzman, *Seven Days a Week: Women and Domestic Service in Industrializing America* (New York, 1978), 204–19; Elizabeth Clark-Lewis, *Living In, Living Out: African American Domestics in Washington, D.C., 1910–1940* (Washington DC, 1994); Trotter, *African American Experience*, 388; Brown, "African American Women and Migration," 205.

48 August Meier and Elliot Rudwick, *Black Detroit and the Rise of the UAW* (New York, 1979); Elizabeth Cohen, *Making a New Deal: Industrial Workers in Chicago, 1919–1939* (Cambridge UK, 1990), 18–19, 165–67, 205–7; Tuttle, *Race Riot*, 108–58; William A. Sundstrom, "The Color Line: Racial Norms and Discrimination in Urban Labor Markets," *Journal of Economic History* 54 (1994), 382–96.

49 Gerald David Jaynes and Robin M. Williams, Jr., eds., *A Common Destiny: Blacks and American Society* (Washington DC, 1989), 271 and chap. 6; Jones, *Labor of Love, Labor of Sorrow*, 160–82; Katherine J. Curtis White, "Women in the Great Migration: Economic Activity of Black and White Southern-Born Female Migrants in 1920, 1940, and 1970," *Social Science History* 29 (2005), esp. 427; Maurine W. Greenwald, *Women, War and Work: The Impact of World War I on Women Workers* (Westport CT, 1980), 20, 22–23.

50 Kusmer, *Ghetto Takes Shape*, 166; Stanley Lieberson, *Ethnic Patterns in American Cities* (New York, 1963), 122–29; Karl E. Taeuber and Alma F. Taeuber, "The Negro as an Immigrant Group: Recent Trends in Racial and Ethnic Segregation in Chicago," *American Journal of Sociology* 69 (1964), 374–82.

51 Quoted in Kusmer, *Ghetto Takes Shape*, 163.

52 Drake and Cayton, *Black Metropolis*, chaps. 14, 19–22; David Levering Lewis, *When Harlem Was in Vogue* (New York, 1981); Kusmer, *Ghetto Takes Shape*, 91–156; Adam Green, *Selling the Race: Culture, Community, and Black Chicago, 1940–1955* (Chicago, 2007).

53 Quoted in Alain Locke, ed., *The New Negro: An Interpretation* (New York, 1925), ix; Nancy J. Weiss, *Farewell to the Party of Lincoln: Black Politics in the Age of FDR* (Princeton NJ, 1983); Harold Gosnell, *Negro Politicians: The Rise of Negro Politics in Chicago* (Chicago, 1935); Jeanne Theoharis and Komozi Woodard, eds., *Freedom North: Black Freedom Outside the South, 1940–1980* (New York, 2003); Patricia Sullivan, *Days of Hope: Race and Democracy in the New Deal Era* (Chapel Hill NC, 1996), 105; Thomas J. Sugrue, *Sweet Land of Liberty: The Forgotten Struggle for Civil Rights in the North* (New York, 2008), chap. 4.

54 Sugrue, *Sweet Land of Liberty*, chaps. 4–6, esp. 44–58, 73–79, 177; Jervis Anderson, *A. Philip Randolph: A Biographical Portrait* (Berkeley CA, 1973), 240–60; John Morton Blum, *V Was for Victory: Politics and American Culture during World War II* (New York, 1976), 208–18; Kennedy, *Freedom from Fear*, 764–68, quoted in 767.

55 Thomas J. Sugrue, *The Origins of the Urban Crisis: Race and Inequality in Postwar Detroit* (Princeton NJ, 1996), 26–27; Meier and Rudwick, *Black Detroit and the Rise of the UAW*, chaps. 1 and 3; William J. Collins, "African American Economic Mobility in the 1940s: A Portrait from the Palmer Survey," *Journal of Economic History* 60 (2000), 756–81 and "Race, Roosevelt, and Wartime Production: Fair Employment in World War II," *American Economic Review* 91 (2001), 272–86,

esp. 272; Sundstrom, "The Color Line: Racial Norms and Discrimination," 382–96; Karen Anderson, *Wartime Women: Sex Roles, Family Relations and the Status of Women During World War II* (Westport CT, 1981), 36–42; Louis Ruchames, *Race, Jobs, and Politics: The Story of the FEPC* (New York, 1953).

56 Landry, *The New Black Middle Class*, 54–55; Claudia D. Goldin, *Understanding the Gender Gap: An Economic History of American Women* (New York, 1990), 145–47, 163; Farley and Allen, *The Color Line and the Quality of Life in America*, 256, 264–65; quoted in Myrdal, *An American Dilemma: The Negro Problem and Modern Democracy* (New York, 1944), 306.

57 Gregory, *Southern Diaspora*, 96, 97–99, see note 30, above; James T. Patterson, *Grand Expectations: The United States, 1945–1974* (New York, 1996), 19, 382; David M. Kennedy, *Freedom from Fear: The American People in Depression and War, 1929–1945* (New York, 2005), 764–65; Katzman, *Seven Days a Week*, 65–78; Joe William Trotter, Jr., "Blacks in the Urban North: The 'Underclass Question' in Historical Perspective" in Michael B. Katz, ed., *The "Underclass" Debate: Views from History* (Princeton, NJ, 1993), 55–84; Sharon Harley, "'Working for nothing but for a living': Black Women in the Underground Economy" in Harley, ed., *Sister Circle: Black Women and Work* (New Brunswick NJ, 2002), 6–9; Brown, "African American Women and Migration," 212; Greenwald, *Women, War and Work*, 22–27, 41–43, 114–115.

58 Landry, *New Black Middle Class*, 74; Farley and Allen, *The Color Line and the Quality of Life in America*, 263–82; Benjamin P. Bowser, *The Black Middle Class: Social Mobility and Vulnerability* (Boulder CO, 2007), 71–72. For the importance of public service employment, see Michael B. Katz, Mark J. Stern, and Jamie J. Fader, "The New African American Inequality," *Journal of American History* 92 (2005), 87–88.

59 Cohen, *Making a New Deal*, 147–58; Abram L. Harris, *The Negro as a Capitalist: A Study of Banking and Businesses among American Negroes* (Philadelphia, 1936); Landry, *New Black Middle Class*, chap. 2–3; Bowser, *Black Middle Class*, 71–74.

60 Drake and Cayton, *Black Metropolis*, 412–29; Grossman, *Land of Hope*, chap. 5; Phillips, *AlabamaNorth*, 168–79; Spear, *Black Chicago*, 91–97, 174–79. Nick Salvatore traces the connections in his fine biography of C. L. Franklin, *Singing in a Strange Land: C. L. Franklin, the Black Church, and the Transformation of America* (Boston, 2005).

61 Arnold R. Hirsch, *Making the Second Ghetto: Race and Housing in Chicago, 1940–1960* (Chicago, 1998), 28; David M. P. Freund, *Colored Property: State Politics and White Racial Politics in Suburban America* Chicago, 2007), esp. chaps. 1–5; David M. P. Freund, "Marketing the Free Market: State Intervention and Politics of Prosperity in Metropolitan America" in Kevin M. Kruse and Thomas J. Sugrue, eds., *The New Suburban History* (Chicago, 2006), 16; Douglas S. Massey and Nancy Denton, *American Apartheid: Segregation and the Making of the Underclass* (Cambridge MA, 1993), chaps. 3–5; John F. Bauman, *Public Housing, Race, and Renewal: Urban Planning in Philadelphia, 1920–1974* (Philadelphia, 1987).

62 Adam Fairclough, *Better Day Coming: Blacks and Equality, 1890–2000* (New York, 2001), chaps. 9–10; William C. Berman, *The Politics of Civil Rights in the Truman*

Administration (Columbus OH, 1970); Richard M. Dalfiume, *Desegregation of the U.S. Armed Forces: Fighting on Two Fronts, 1939–1953* (Columbia MO, 1969).

63 Farley and Allen, *The Color Line and the Quality of Life in America*, 263–82; Landry, *New Black Middle Class*, chaps. 2–3; Bowser, *Black Middle Class*, 71–74; Cohen, *Making a New Deal*, 147–58; Harris, *The Negro as a Capitalist*; Thomas J. Durant, Jr., and Joyce S. Louden, "The Black Middle Class in America: Historical and Contemporary Perspectives," *Phylon* 47 (1986), 253–62.

64 Farley and Allen, *The Color Line and the Quality of Life in America*, chaps. 9–10; Landry, *New Black Middle Class*, chap. 2, esp. 196–97; Sharon M. Collins, *Black Corporate Executives: The Making and Breaking of a Black Middle Class* (Philadelphia, 1997), 3–4; William H. Chafe, *The Unfinished Journey: America Since World War II*, 6th ed. (New York, 2007), 431; Robin D. G. Kelley, "Into the Fire: 1970 to the Present" in Kelley and Earl Lewis, eds., *To Make our World Anew: A History of African Americans* (New York, 2000), 565–71. The occupational index of dissimilarity between black men and white men fell from 37 to 31 and that between black women and white women from 43 to 28. It would fall even more dramatically during the 1970s. Farley and Allen, *The Color Line and the Quality of Life in America*, 265.

65 Chafe, *The Unfinished Journey*, 423–26, 456, 466–67; William Julius Wilson, *The Truly Disadvantaged: The Inner City, the Underclass, and Public Policy* (Chicago, 1987) and *When Work Disappears: The World of the New Urban Poor* (New York, 1996), chaps. 1–5, appendix A; Massey and Denton, *American Apartheid*, chaps. 5–7; Christopher Jencks and Susan E. Mayer, "Residential Segregation, Job Proximity, and Black Job Opportunities" in Lawrence E. Lynn and Michael G. H. McGreary, eds., *Inner-City Poverty in the United States* (Washington DC, 1990), 187–222; Collins, *Making and Breaking of a Black Middle Class*, 5–6; also see Katz, ed., *The "Underclass" Debate* and Katz, Stern, and Fader, "The New African American Inequality," 96.

66 In 1960, some 15 percent of black men over eighteen years of age were not participating in the labor force. That percentage would increase over the course of the twentieth century. Katz, Stern, and Fader, "The New African American Inequality," 80–85, fig. 1, p. 82; John Blair and Rudy Fichtenbaum, "Changing Black Employment Patterns" in George C. Galster and Edward W. Hill, eds., *The Metropolis in Black and White: Place, Power, and Polarization* (New Brunswick NJ, 1992), 72–92; Wilson, *Truly Disadvantaged*; Sugrue, *Origins of the Urban Crisis*, chap. 5; Chafe, *The Unfinished Journey*, 424; Loïc J. D. Wacquant and William J. Wilson, "The Cost of Racial and Class Exclusion in the Inner City," *Annals of the American Academy of Political and Social Sciences* 501 (1989), 8–25; Kelly, "Into the Fire" in Kelly and Lewis, eds., *To Make Our World Anew*, 562; William A. Darity, Jr., and Samuel L. Meyers, Jr., "The Impact of Labor Market Prospects on Incarceration Rates" in Robert Cherry and William M. Rodgers, III, eds., *Prosperity for All? The Economic Boom and African Americans* (New York, 2000), 279–307.

67 Hirsch, *Making the Second Ghetto*, 24–28; Sugrue, *The Origins of the Urban Crisis*, chaps. 2, 7; Patterson, *Grand Expectations*, 336–37, 382; Elijah Anderson, *Streetwise: Race, Class, and Change in an Urban Community* (Chicago, 1990), 56–76;

Wilson, *Truly Disadvantaged*, 3–19; Kelly, "Into the Fire" in Kelly and Lewis, eds., *To Make Our World Anew*, 570–73. For the debate about the changing nature of inner-city African American life, see Nicholas Lemann, *The Promised Land: The Great Migration and How it Changed America* (New York, 1991); Rhonda Y. Williams, *The Politics of Public Housing: Black Women's Struggles Against Urban Inequality* (New York, 2004); Sudhir A. Venkatesh, *American Project: The Rise and Fall of a Modern Ghetto* (Cambridge MA, 2000).

68 Andrew Wiese, *Places of their Own: African American Suburbanization in the Twentieth Century* (Chicago, 2004); Harold Rose, *Black Suburbanization: Access to Improved Quality of Life or Maintenance of the Status Quo?* (Cambridge, MA, 1976); Karl Taeuber, "The Negro Population in the United States" in Davis, ed., *American Negro Reference Book*, 130–34; John Logan, "The New Ethnic Enclaves in America's Suburbs," 2001, Lewis Mumford Center for Comparative Urban and Regional Research, www.s4.brown.edu/cen2000/suburban/SuburbanReport. The travail of the black middle class is outlined in Joe R. Feagin and Melvin P. Sikes, *Living With Racism: The Black-Middle Class Experience* (Boston, 1994).

69 Chafe, *Unfinished Journey*, 419–25; David M. Grant, Melvin L. Oliver, and Angela D. James, "African Americans: Social and Economic Bifurcation" in Roger Waldinger and Mehdi Bozorgmehr, eds., *Ethnic Los Angeles* (New York, 1996), 379–411.

70 Robin D. G. Kelley, *Yo' Mama's Disfunktional!: Fighting the Culture Wars in Urban America* (Boston, 1997); Peniel E. Joseph, *Waiting 'Til the Midnight Hour: A Narrative History of Black Power in America* (New York, 2006).

71 Mellonee V. Burnim, "Religious Music" in Burnim and Maultsby, eds., *African American Music*, 61–73; Michael Harris, *Rise of Gospel Blues: The Music of Thomas Andrew Dorsey in the Urban Church* (New York, 1992); Bernice Johnson Reagon, ed., *We'll Understand It Better By and By: Pioneering African American Gospel Composers* (Washington DC, 1992); Lawrence W. Levine, *Black Culture and Black Consciousness: Afro-American Folk Thought from Slavery to Freedom* (New York, 1978), 174–89. A thoughtful meditation on the parsing of African American culture by class divisions can be found in Evelyn Brooks Higginbotham, "Rethinking Vernacular Culture: Black Religious and Race Records in the 1920s and 1930s" in Wahneema Lubiana, ed., *The House That Race Built: Black American, U.S. Terrain* (New York, 1997), 157–77.

72 David Evans, "Blues: A Chronological Overview" and Oehler, "The Blues in Transcultural Contexts" both in Burnim and Maultsby, eds., *African American Music*, 79–126; William Barlow, *"Looking Up at Down": The Emergence of Blues Culture* (Philadelphia, 1989); Levine, *Black Culture and Black Consciousness*, 202–97. For the rise of the blues women, see Daphne Duval Harrison, *Black Pearls: Blues Queens of the 1920s* (New Brunswick NJ, 1988).

73 Charles Keil, *Urban Blues* (Chicago, 1966); Evans, "Blues: A Chronological Overview" in Burnim and Maultsby, eds., *African American Music*, 79–126; Barlow, *"Looking Up at Down,"* chaps. 5–9.

74 Peter Guralnick, *Dream Boogie: The Triumph of Sam Cooke* (New York, 2005), 315–450; Brian Ward, *Just My Soul Responding: Rhythm and Blues, Black Conscious-*

ness, and Race Relations (Berkeley CA, 1998), chap. 4; Portia K. Maultsby, "Rhythm and Blues" and "Soul" and Bernice Johnson Reagon, "Civil Rights Movement" all in Burnim and Maultsby, eds., *African American Music*, 245–91, 598–624.

75 Michael Taft, *Talkin' to Myself: Blues Lyrics, 1921–1942* (New York, 2005).

76 Ingrid Monson, "Jazz, Chronological Overview" and Travis A. Jackson "Interpreting Jazz" both in Burnim and Maultsby, eds., *African American Music*, 145–184; Gilbert Chase, *America's Music: From the Pilgrims to the Present*, 3rd ed. (Urbana IL, 1987), chap. 28; Peretti, *The Creation of Jazz*; Paul F. Berliner, *Thinking in Jazz: The Infinite Art of Improvisation* (Chicago, 1994).

Chapter Five: Global Passages

1 David M. Reimers, *Other Immigrants: The Global Origins of the American People* (New York, 2005), esp. chap. 9; Karl E. Taeuber "The Negro Population in the United States" in John P. Davis, ed., *The American Negro Reference Book* (Englewood Cliffs NJ, 1966), 109; Philip Kasinitz, *Caribbean New York: Black Immigrants and the Politics of Race* (Ithaca NY, 1992), chap. 1; Marilyn Halters, *Between Race and Ethnicity: Cape Verdean American Immigrants, 1860–1965* (Chicago, 1993); quoted in Stanley Lieberson, "Selective Black Migration from the South: A Historical View" in Frank D. Bean and W. Parker Frisbiecorn, eds., *The Demography of Racial and Ethnic Groups* (New York, 1978), 122.

2 Aristide R. Zolberg, *A Nation By Design: Immigration Policy in the Fashioning of America* (Cambridge MA, 2006), 370–75. The 1965 Immigration and Nationality Act established a 20,000 person per nation limit for the nations of the Eastern Hemisphere and with a total hemispheric allotment of 170,000 and a hemispheric limit for the Western Hemisphere of 120,000.

3 Zolberg, *A Nation By Design*, 326–33; Reimers, *Other Immigrants*, chap. 9, esp. 238; Dirk Hoerder, *Cultures in Contact: World Migrations in the Second Millennium* (Durham NC, 2002), 513–14.

4 Marilyn Halter, "Africa: West" in Mary C. Waters and Reed Ueda, eds., *The New Americans: A Guide to Immigration since 1965* (Cambridge MA, 2007), 283–84; Abdi Kusow, "Africa: East" in *ibid.*, 297–98. Halter, "Africa: West" in Waters and Ueda, eds., *The New Americans*, 283, suggests an undercount of immigrants in the United States. For the census category of "Hispanics—origins, of all races," see Hoerder, *Cultures in Contact*, 525. In 2000, 11 percent of the foreign-born population from Latin America was black and some 3 percent was both Hispanic and black.

5 Mary C. Waters and Reed Ueda, "Introduction" in Waters and Ueda, eds., *The New Americans*, 5; John R. Logan and Glenn Deane, "Black Diversity in Metropolitan America," Lewis Munford Center for Comparative Urban and Regional Research, Aug. 15, 2003, 12; http://w3.uchastings.edu/wingate/PDF/Black_Diversity_final.pdf.

6 Waters and Ueda, "Introduction" in Waters and Ueda, eds., *The New Americans*, 5.

7 Hoerder, *Cultures in Contact*, 528; Sarah Collinson, *Beyond Borders: Western Euro-*

pean Migration Policy Towards the 21st Century (London, 1993), 36–37; April Gordon, "The New Diaspora—African Immigration to the United States," *Journal of Third World Studies* 15 (1998), 84–85.

8 U.S. Department of Justice, *Statistical Yearbook of the Immigration and Naturalization Service* (Washington DC, 1991, 1995); Reimers, *Other Immigrants*, 232–33, 250–60; Kasinitz, *Caribbean New York*, 19–31; Milton Vickerman, *Crosscurrents: West Indian Immigrants and Race* (New York, 1999), 64; Calvin B. Holder, "West Indies: Antigua, Bahamas, Barbados, Grenada, Guadeloupe, Guyana, Martinique, St. Kitts, Trinidad" in Waters and Ueda, eds., *The New Americans*, 675; Flore Zéphir, *The Haitian Americans* (Westport CT, 2004), chap. 4; Howard Dotson and Sylviane A. Diouf, *In Motion: The African-American Migration Experience* (New York, 2004), 176–83.

9 U.S. Census Bureau, *Profile of the Foreign-Born Population in the United States: 2000* (Washington DC, 2001), 10; David Dixon, "Characteristics of the African Born in the United States" (January 2006); Elizabeth Grieco, "The African Foreign Born in the United States" (September 2004), and Jill Wilson, "African-born Residents of the United States" (August 2000), all in Migration Information Source (www.migrationinformation.org); Violet M. Showers Johnson, "'What, Then, Is the African American?' African and Afro-Caribbean Identities in Black America," *Journal of American Ethnic History* 28 (2008), 82–83; Reimers, *Other Immigrants*, 232–33, 242; Halter, "Africa: West" and Kusow, "Africa: East" in Waters and Ueda, eds., *The New Americans*, 283, 296; John A. Arthur, *The African Diaspora in the United States and Europe: The Ghanaian Experience* (Burlington VT, 2008), 2–4. In 1960, about 35,000 Africans had registered in the United States. U.S. Census Bureau, *Profile of the Foreign-Born Population in the United States: 2000* (Washington DC, 2001), 10. Approximately 71,000 Ethiopians, 68,000 Ghanaians, 44,000 Kenyans, 43,000 Liberians, and 37,000 Somalis resided in the United States in 2000.

10 Dotson and Diouf, *In Motion*, 200. Similar undercounts of black immigrants from the Caribbean, especially Haitians: see Flore Zéphir, *Haitian Immigrants in Black America: A Sociological and Sociolinguistic Portrait* (Westport CT, 1996), 8, and Zéphir, *Haitian Americans*, chap. 4; Anthony V. Catanese, *Haitian: Migration and Diaspora* (Boulder CO, 1999), 87; John Logan, "Who Are the Other African-Americans? Contemporary African and Caribbean Immigrants in the United States" in Yoku Shaw-Taylor and Steven Tuch, eds., *The Other African Americans: Contemporary African and Caribbean Immigrants in the United States* (Lanham MD, 2007), 49–53.

11 Kofi K. Apraku, *African Émigrés in the United States: A Missing Link in Africa's Social and Economic Development* (New York, 1991), chaps. 1, 4–5. That sojourners composed a large portion of the fourth passage does not distinguish them from previous generations of European immigrants, some 30 percent of whom also returned home. See Frank Thistlewaite, "Migration from Europe Overseas in the Nineteenth and Twentieth Centuries" in Rudolph J. Vecoli and Suzanne M. Sinke, *A Century of European Migrations, 1830–1930* (Urbana IL, 1991) and Mark Wyman, *Round Trip America: The Immigrants Return to Europe, 1880–1930* (Ithaca NY, 1993).

12 Paul Stoller, *Money Has No Smell: The Africanization of New York* (Chicago, 2002); Arthur, *African Diaspora*, especially chaps. 3, 9; Reimers, *Other Immigrants*, 234–35; quoted in Francois Pierre-Louis, Jr., *Haitians in New York City: Transnationalism and Hometown Associations* (Gainesville FL, 2006), 1; also Michael J. Piore, *Birds of Passage: Migrant Labor in Industrial Societies* (Cambridge UK, 1979), 65.

13 U.S. Census Bureau, *Profile of the Foreign-Born Population in the United States: 2000* (Washington DC, 2001), 27; Dixon, "Characteristics of the African Born in the United States."

14 Reimers, *Other Immigrants*, chap. 9; Arthur, *African Diaspora*, 75–76; Halter, "Africa: West" and Kusow, "Africa: East" in Waters and Ueda, eds., *The New Americans*, 284–86 and 296; Agyemang Attah-Poku, *The Socio-Cultural Adjustment: The Role of Ghanaian Immigrant Associations in America* (Brookview VT, 1996) chap. 3.

15 U.S. Census Bureau, *Profile of the Foreign-Born Population in the United States: 2000* (Washington DC, 2001), 37, 41; Reimers, *Other Immigrants*, 235–36, 246–47; F. Nii-Amoo Dodoo, "Assimilation Differences among Africans in America," *Social Forces* 76 (1997), 527–46; Dixon, "Characteristics of the African Born in the United States"; Kusow, "Africa: East" and Holder, "West Indies" in Waters and Ueda, eds., *The New Americans*, 296–302 and 676, 682–85; Apraku, *African Émigrés*, chap. 1.

16 Reimers, *Other Immigrants*, 237–38; Kusow, "Africa: East" and Lisa Konczal and Alex Stepick, "Haiti" in Waters and Ueda, eds., *The New Americans*, 301–2 and 445–57.

17 U.S. Census Bureau, *Profile of the Foreign-Born Population in the United States: 2000* (Washington DC, 2001), 47; Vickerman, *Crosscurrents*, chap. 2, esp. 67–75; Kristin F. Butcher, "Black Immigrants in the United States: A Comparison with Native Blacks and Other Immigrants," *Industrial Relations Review* 47 (1994), 265–84; F. Nii-Amoo Dodoo and Baffour K. Takyi, "Africans in the Diaspora: Black-White Earnings Differences among America's Africans," *Ethnic and Racial Studies*, 25 (2002); Dixon, "Characteristics of the African Born in the United States"; Halter, "Africa: West" and Kusow, "Africa: East" in Waters and Ueda, eds., *The New Americans*, 291–93 and 299–300. For an excellent discussion of immigrant entrepreneurial activities in one city, see Marilyn Halter, ed., *New Migrants in the Marketplace: Boston's Ethnic Entrepreneurs* (Amherst MA, 1995), esp. chaps. 4, 8. Mary C. Waters traces the long debate over the comparative success of Afro-West Indian immigrants and African American natives from the work of Ira de A. Reid (*The Negro Immigrant: His Background Characteristics and Social Adjustment, 1899–1937* [New York, 1939]) early in the twentieth century through Thomas Sowell ("Three Black Histories" in Sowell, *Essays and Data on American Ethnic Groups* [Washington DC, 1978]), Dennis Forsythe ("Black Immigrants and the American Ethos: Theories and Observations" in Roy S. Bryce-Laporte and Delores M. Mortimer, eds., *Caribbean Immigrants in the United States* [Washington DC, 1976], 55–62), Stephen Steinberg (*The Ethnic Myth: Race, Ethnicity, and Class in America* [Boston, 1989]), Suzanne Model ("Caribbean Immigrants: A Black Successful Story," *International Migration Review* 25 [1991],

248–76), and Jennifer L. Hochschild (*Facing Up to the American Dream: Race, Class, and the Soul of the Nation* [Princeton NJ, 1995]), and adds her own analysis in Waters, *Black Identities: West Indian Immigrants Dreams and American Realities* (Cambridge MA, 1999), chap. 4. Also see Vickerman, *Crosscurrents*, 74–75.

18 Wilson, "African-born Residents of the United States," Aug. 1, 2000, Migration Information Source (www.migrationinformantion.org); Baffour K. Takyi and Kwame Safo Boate, "Location and Settlement Patterns of African Immigrants in the U.S.: Demographic and Spatial Context" in Kwadwo Konadu-Agyemang, Baffour K. Takyi, and John Arthur, eds., *The New African Diaspora in North America* (Lanham MD, 2006), 50–68. Also William Finnegan, "New in Town: The Somalis of Lewiston," *The New Yorker*, Dec. 11, 2006, 46–58.

19 Waters, *Black Identities*, 22–23; Jon D. Holtzman, *Nuer Journeys, Nuer Lives: Sudanese Refugees in Minnesota*, 2nd ed. (Boston, 2007), chap. 2.

20 In 2000, 95 percent of Africans lived in metropolitan areas, with almost half living in ten cities, with the New York and Washington metropolitan areas having the largest agglomerations of Africans. U.S. Census Bureau, *Profile of the Foreign-Born Population in the United States: 2000* (Washington DC, 2001), 16–18; Wilson, "African-born Residents of the United States," Aug. 1, 2000, Migration Information Source (www.migrationinformantion.org); Halter, "Africa: West" in Waters and Ueda, eds., *The New Americans*, 291–93, 299–300; Logan and Deane, "Black Diversity in Metropolitan American," 1. For the immigrant population, see Reuel Rogers, "'Black Like Who?': Afro-Caribbean Immigrants, African Americans, and the Politics of Group Identity" in Nancy Foner, ed., *Islands in the City: West Indian Migration to New York* (Berkeley CA, 2001), 163–64; Reimers, *Other Immigrants*, 246–48.

21 Calvin B. Holder, "West Indies" in Waters and Eeda, eds., *The New Americans*, 291–93, 299–300, 675–86.

22 Reimers, *Other Immigrants*, 243–44; Logan and Deane, "Black Diversity in Metropolitan America," 4.

23 Arthur, *African Diaspora*, 51–55; New York City Department of Planning, "Newest New Yorkers: Immigrant New York in the New Millennium" (2004), www .nyc.gov/html/dcp/html/census/nny.shtml; Marieme O. Daff, "Little Senegal: African in Harlem, Malcolm X Boulevard, America's Dakar" (www.africultures .com/anglais/articles_anglais/44senegal.htm); Jon D. Holtzman, *Nuer Journeys, Nuer Lives: Sudanese Refugees in Minnesota*, 2nd ed. (Boston, 2008).

24 Arthur, *African Diaspora*, chap. 6; Agyemang Attah-Poku, *The Socio-Cultural Adjustment Question: The Role of Ghanaian Immigrant Associations in America* (Brookview VT, 1996), chaps. 4–6. For a discussion of "hometown associations," see Pierre-Louis, *Haitians in New York City*.

25 Reimers, *Other Immigrants*, 245–46, 252–54.

26 Mary Waters, *Black Identities*, quoted on 47–48 and 57. For a sociological explication of this same phenomena, see Vickerman, *Crosscurrents*, 9–12.

27 James R. Grossman, Ann Durkin Keating, and Janice L. Reiff, eds., *The Encyclopedia of Chicago* (Chicago, 2004), 21, 281, 446, 476, 771, 775.

28 Hoerder, *Cultures in Contact*, 551; Johnson, "'What, Then, Is the African American?'" 84–87.

29 Arthur, *African Diaspora*, chaps. 5–6. On Diallo, see various articles online in the *New York Times* (www.nytimes.com).

30 Reimers, *Other Immigrants*, 253–54; Rogers, "'Black Like Who?,'" 182–83; Vickerman, *Crosscurrents*, chap. 2.

31 Milton Vickerman, "Tweaking a Monolith: The West Indian Immigrant Encounter with 'Blackness,'" in Foner, ed., *Islands in the City*, 237–56.

32 James T. Campbell, *Middle Passages: African American Journeys to Africa, 1787–2005* (New York, 2006); Penny Von Eschen, *Satchmo Blows Up the World: Jazz Ambassadors Play the Cold War* (Cambridge MA, 2004); Robin D. G. Kelley, "'But a Local Phase of a World Problem': Black History's Global Vision, 1883–1950," *Journal of American History* 86 (1999), 1045–77; Zachary Williams et al., "A History of Black Immigration in the United States" in Rachael Ida Buff, ed., *Immigrant Rights in the Shadow of Citizenship* (New York, 2008), 171; quoted in *Tampa Tribune*, 15 May 1998.

33 Arthur, *African Diaspora*, chap. 5; Holtzman, *Nuer Journeys*, 117–19.

34 Rogers, "'Black Like Who?'"; Louis, *Haitians in New York City*, 21–23, 117–34; quoted in Zéphir, *Haitian Immigrants in Black America*, 53; Rogers, "'Black Like Who?,'" 165–67, 174–76.

35 Expressing a sense of privilege that residence in the United States provided, a Ghanaian immigrant observed, "I could not afford a car, television, or even a one-bedroom to lay my head at night when I was in Ghana. I drive a good used car, able to educate my children, and I have some money left to remit home. I do made much but even in this status, I earn more than what over 70 per cent of Ghanaians at home earn," Arthur, *African Diaspora*, 78; quoted in Zéphir, *Haitian Immigrants*, 70, and *Haitian Immigrants in Black America*, 127.

36 Mary C. Waters, "Ethnic and Racial Groups in the USA: Conflict and Cooperation" in Kumar Rupesinghe and Valley Tishkov, eds., *Ethnicity and Power in the Contemporary World* (London, 1996); Vickerman, *Crosscurrents*, chap. 4.

37 Rogers, "'Black Like Who?,'" 178, 186–87.

38 Milton Vickerman, "Tweaking a Monolith: The West Indian Immigrant Encounter with 'Blackness,'" in Foner, ed., *Islands in the City*, 237–56; "Jamaicans: Balancing Race and Ethnicity" in Foner, ed., *The New Immigrants in New York*; Zéphir, *Haitian Immigrants*, 86-94; quoted in Arthur, *African Diaspora*, 72–73, and the *Seattle Post-Intelligencer*, July 20, 2006.

39 Quoted in Rogers, "'Black Like Who?,'" 178, 163. Rogers was referring to Afro-Caribbeans in New York City but his remarks can easily be extended to the United States at large. Also see Zéphir, *Haitian Immigrants*, chap. 4; Johnson, "'What, Then, Is the African American?,'" 77–103.

40 Tracie Reddick, "Africans vs. African-Americans: A Shared Complexion Does Not Guarantee Racial Solidarity," www.library.yale.edu/~fboateng/akata.htm; Johnson, "'What, Then, Is the African American?,' 94–95; *Harvard Crimson*, Mar. 9, 2007; *Journal of Blacks in Higher Education*, www.jbhe.com/news_views/56_race_sensitive_not_helping.html; for other conflicts over resources, see Rogers, "'Black Like Who?'" Although subject to considerable debate, economists have generally agreed that, at least in the short term, immigration, although not specifically black immigration, "has harm[ed] the earnings and employment

of African Americans": Steven Shulman, ed., *The Impact of Immigration on African Americans* (New Brunswick NJ, 2004), quoted on xii.

41 *Ibid.*; and quoted in *New York Amsterdam News*, Feb. 3–9, 2005; Tracie Reddick, "Africans vs. African-Americans: A Shared Complexion Does Not Guarantee Racial Solidarity," *Seattle Post-Intelligencer*, July 20, 2006.

42 Logan and Deane, "Black Diversity in Metropolitan America," 4–13; Rogers, "'Black Like Who?'"; Kusow, "Africa: East" in Waters and Ueda, eds., *The New Americans*, 291–93, 299–300; Zéphir, *The Haitian Americans*, 129–30; Arthur, *African Diaspora*, 79; Lynette Clemetson, "For Schooling, A Reverse Emigration to Africa," *New York Times*, Sept. 4, 2003; Zéphir, *Haitian Immigrants*, 74–76, quoted in 71.

43 Trica Rose, *Black Noise: Rap Music and Black Culture in Contemporary America* (Hanover NH, 1994), chap. 1–2; Dawn M. Norfleet, "Hip-Hop and Rap" in Mellonee V. Burnim and Portia K. Maultsby, eds., *African American Music: An Introduction* (New York, 2006), 353–57; Nelson George, *Hip-Hop America* (New York, 1998); Jeff Chang, *Can't Stop, Won't Stop: A History of the Hip-Hop Generation* (New York, 2005); Kelley, "Into the Fire," 583–90; Fernando Orejueda, "Hip Hop" in William Ferris and Glenn Hinson, eds., *Encyclopedia of Southern Culture*, forthcoming. I would like to thank Bill Ferris for sharing this reference.

44 Rose, *Black Noise*; Norfleet, "Hip-Hop and Rap" in Burnim and Maultsby, eds., *African American Music*, 57-68; Nelson George, *Hip-Hop America* (New York, 1998); Chang, *Can't Stop, Won't Stop: A History of the Hip-Hop Generation*; Kelley, "Into the Fire," 583–90.

45 Rose, *Black Noise*; Norfleet, "Hip-Hop and Rap" in Burnim and Maultsby, eds., *African American Music*, 68–71; Nelson George, *Hip-Hop America* (New York, 1998); Chang, *Can't Stop, Won't Stop: A History of the Hip-Hop Generation*; Kelley, "Into the Fire," 583–90; Orejueda "Hip Hop" in Ferris and Hinson, eds., *Encyclopedia of Southern Culture*, forthcoming. The antisocial tradition runs deep in African American culture; see especially the story of Stagger Lee, which became a standard of nervous blues musicians. Cecil Brown, *Stagolee Shot Billy* (Cambridge MA, 2003).

46 Rose, *Black Noise*, 10–11.

47 Jennifer V. Jackson and Mary E. Cothran, "Black Versus Black: The Relationship Among African, African American and African Caribbean Persons," *Journal of Black Studies* 33 (2003), 576–604.

48 Rogers, "'Black Like Who?,'" 171–79, quoted on 178; Arthur, *African Diaspora*, chap. 5, esp. 69–71; Philip Kasinitz, *Caribbean New York: Black Immigrants and the Politics of Race* (Ithaca NY, 1992); Zéphir, *Haitian Immigrants*, 78–82. Another student of West Indian immigrants in the United States notes that West Indians are "profoundly uncomfortable dealing with race, because, despite a history of colonialism, their societies socialize them to ignore it"; Vickerman, *Crosscurrents*, ix.

49 Rogers, "Black Like Who?" on people sharing multiple identities, 166–67.

Epilogue

1 Thomas B. Edsall and Mary D. Edsall, *Chain Reaction: The Impact of Race, Rights, and Taxes on American Politics* (New York, 1991); Dan T. Carter, *The Politics of Rage: George Wallace, the Origins of the New Conservatism, and the Transformation of American Politics* (New York, 1995); Mary C. Brennan, *Turning Right in the Sixties: The Conservative Capture of the GOP* (Chapel Hill NC, 1995).

2 For newly arrived Africans' support of Barack Obama, see the *Washington Post*, July 6, 2008.

3 Barack Obama, *Dreams from My Father: A Story of Race and Inheritance*, 2nd ed. (New York, 2004), 27.

4 *New York Times*, May 11, 2008; David Mendell, *Obama: From Promise to Power* (New York, 2007), chap. 9, quoted on 131; Ryan Lizza, "Making It: How Chicago Shaped Obama," *The New Yorker*, July 21, 2008; quoted in David Remnick, "The Joshua Generation: Race and the Campaign of Barack Obama," *The New Yorker*, Nov. 17, 2008.

5 *New York Times*, Aug. 29, 2004.

6 *New York Times*, Feb. 2 and 11, 2007; also see *New York Times*, Jan. 25, 2007; *Newsweek*, July 16, 2007; for Crouch's statement, New York *Daily News*, Nov. 2, 2006.

7 For the barbershop banter on Obama, see Darryl Pinckney, "Dreams from Obama," *New York Review of Books* 55 (Mar. 6, 2008), 41–46.

8 Louis Chude-Sokei, "Redefining 'Black': Obama's Candidacy Spotlights the Divide between Native Black Culture and African Immigrants," *Los Angeles Times*, Feb. 18, 2007.

9 Debra J. Dickerson, "Colorblind: Barack Obama Would Be the Great Black Hope in the Next Presidential Race—If He Were Actually Black," Jan. 22, 2007, *Salon* (www.salon.com/opinion/feature/2007/01/22/obama/); also Debra Dickerson interviewed by Stephen Colbert, *The Colbert Report*, Feb. 8, 2007. http://www .colbertnation.com/the-colbert-report-videos/81955/february-08-2007/debra -dickerson?videoId=81955.

10 Dickerson, "Colorblind," *Salon*, Jan. 22, 2007.

11 Louis Chude-Sokei, "Redefining 'Black,'" *Los Angeles Times*, Feb. 18, 2007.

12 Charlie Rose, interview with Barack Obama, Oct. 19, 2006 (http://www.charlie rose.com/shows/2006/10/19/1/an-hour-with-senator-barack-obama).

13 Dickerson, "Colorblind," *Salon*, Jan. 22, 2007.

14 Quoted in Obama, *Dreams from My Father*, 76, 104.

15 *New York Times*, March 18, 2008.

16 *Ibid.*

17 *Ibid.*

Index

Abbott, Robert, 151, 158–69
Abuza, Sophie, 47
Africa
  African Americans' ignorance of,
    218–19
  African Americans' journeys to, 30
  as cultural catchall, 29–30
  fluidity of nationalities of, 49–51, 74
  free blacks' migration to, 95–98, 134
  immigration from, late-twentieth-
    century. *See* fourth migration
  Loyal Blacks' return to, 95–98
  manumission in, 53
  Middle Passage from. *See* Middle
    Passage
  political unrest in, 207
  slavery in, 52–55
  slave-trading states in, 55–56
African American, shunning of name, 7
African Americans
  American born. *See* American-born
    blacks
  as closed population, 6, 202
  culture, creation and recreation of,
    18–19, 24, 31, 74, 78–98, 99, 123–
    29, 214–17
  as disproportionately at bottom of
    society, 202
  divisions among, 8–9, 11, 70–71,
    179, 183, 184, 189, 196, 212, 213,
    216, 217–29, 234–36
  elite. *See* elite blacks/Old Settlers
  foreign-born proportion, 6–7, 203,
    206
  free black. *See* free blacks
  history of. *See* history, African
    American

idioms of pluralism and, 42–43
migrations by. *See* migrations,
    African American
movement, importance to, 17–24
native born. *See* American-born
    blacks
Northern. *See* Northern blacks
other Americans and, 48
place, importance to, 17–21, 25–31,
    80–84, 136–39, 150, 239
politics of, 231
self-identity. *See* identity/self-identity
slavery-to-freedom narrative,
    relevance to, 10–11, 13
Southern. *See* Southerners, black
unification of, 111
unique experience of, 38, 42, 47
African descent, immigrants of, 5, 6, 7,
    11, 15, 23, 203. *See also* African
    immigrants; Caribbean immi-
    grants; *specific groups*
  age makeup of, 210
  American-born blacks, ignorance of,
    219
  American-born blacks and, relation-
    ship between, 8–9, 11, 212, 213,
    216, 217–29, 234–36
  Anglophone, 211
  children's' education, 223–24
  cities as destinations for, 213
  community formation by, 214–17
  diversity of, 210–11
  early, 202–3
  economic advancement of, 211–12
  educated professionals among, 211
  employment opportunities for,
    211–12

289

African descent, immigrants of *(cont.)*
 entrepreneurs, 214
 equality and, 220–21
 family sponsorship of, 204, 206,
  207–8
 homeland contact maintained by,
  208–9
 information sources for, 213
 institutions of, 214, 222
 majority status as familiar to, 218,
  220
 national concentrations of, 213–14
 nationalism of, 214–22, 228–29
 new identities of, 214–16, 219,
  228–29
 numbers of, 207–8
 Obama and, 232
 political awareness of, 232
 racism and, 217–20
 reluctant, 208
 sexual makeup of, 210
 transnationalism of, 215–16
 violence against, 217, 222–23
 visitors, 208, 209
 white America as seen by, 221
 work ethic of, 223
African immigrants, 204, 207–8
 destinations for, 213
 diversity of, 210
 educational attainment of, 211
 numbers of, 207–8
 poverty of, 211
 returns to homeland by, 209
African Methodist Episcopal Church,
 93
African National Congress, 13
African National Union, 216
Africans, as product of New World, 15,
 30, 49–50
African Union Society, 92
Afro-Christian church, 92–94, 147
 interior passage, effect on, 128–29
 Loyal Blacks and, 97–98
 Northern migrants and, 189
 spread of, 95
agricultural system, Southern, 68,
 81–82, 88, 105–6, 139–43, 157–58,
 159, 162–63. *See also*
 plantation(s); *specific crops*
 black landowners in, 145, 146, 162, 163

 reduced need for labor in, 162, 163
Alabama
 age and sex of slaves in, 108–9
 black depopulation of, 154
 black landowners in, 145
 movement of slaves from, 104
 movement of slaves to, 103
 slave laws in, 107
 slave population of, 105
 third migration, effect on, 167
 urban black population of, 159–60
Allen, Richard, 11, 93–94
American-born blacks
 African immigrants and, relationship between, 8–9, 11, 212, 213,
  216, 217–29, 234–36
 African immigrants' ignorance of,
  219
 racism as seen by, 220, 228
American Colonization Society, 134
American revolution
 migration following, 94–98
 weakening of slavery by, 89, 90
amnesty programs, 204, 205
Amsterdam News, 185, 222
Angelou, Maya, 27, 28, 29
Angola/Angolans, 42, 73, 215
animal sacrifice, 221
Antigua, 207
Appomattox Club, 178
Arkansas
 movement of blacks from, 155
 movement of slaves to, 16, 102
 slave population of, 105
armed forces, desegregation of, 185,
 190
Armstrong, Louis, 168
Asante, 51
Asian immigrants, 5, 43–44
Association des Sénégalais aux USA, 7
Atlanta Black Shirts, 163
Atlantic Creoles, 67, 68
Australasia, 206
auto industry, 186

Baline, Israel, 47
Ball, Charles, 85–86, 116, 117, 125
Bambaataa, Afrika, 225
Banneker, Benjamin, 3
Baraka, Amiri, 34

Barbados, 85, 96, 207
Baruch, Bernard, 137
Bennett, Lerone, 37
Berlin, Irving, 47
Bight of Biafra, 73
black belt, passage to. *See* interior,
    passage to
blackbirding, 102
Black Codes, 133, 143
blackness
    celebration of, 197, 226
    meaning of, 23, 32, 55, 218, 235, 236,
        239–40
    of Obama, 233–34, 236–37
Black Panther Party, 233
Black Power, 197
blacks. *See* African Americans
Blake, Blind, 199
blues, 148–49, 197–99
boll weevil, 157, 158
Boston, 156
Boudron, Joseph, 78
bozales, 85, 86
brain drain, 44
branding irons, 59, 60
Brand Nubian, 226
Break dancing, 224
Breedlove, Sarah, 173
British colonies, former, 207, 211
British West Indies, 94
Bronx, 224, 225
Bronzeville, 184
Brooklyn, 214
Broonzy, Bill, 149
Brotherhood of Sleeping Car Porters,
    185
Brown, William Wells, 114

Calabars, 42
California, movement of blacks to,
    155
call-and-response, 34–35, 67, 86, 200
Camden, 156
Cameroon/Cameroonians, 215
Campbell, Clive "DJ Kool Herc," 225
Canada, 95
Cape Verde Islands, 203
capitalism, labor requirements of, 12,
    44–45, 204
Caribbean, 95

Caribbean immigrants, 7, 203, 204–7.
    See also specific groups
    destinations for, 213
    diversity of, 210
    numbers of, 207
    women, 210
Carter, Lincoln, 83–84
Carter, Robert "King," 76–77
Caterers Club, 178
census, 208
Central America, 94
Century Club, 178
cereal cultivation, 88, 105, 106
change, 23, 32, 33–34
    catastrophic, anticipation of, 24
Charles, Ray, 198
Chesapeake, 70, 81, 88
    indigenous vs. saltwater slave
        population, 69, 71
    nationality of slaves entering, 73–74
    number of slaves in, 68–69
Chicago, 7, 178
    black percentage of population, 157
    black population of, 156
    Wright on, 175
Chicago Defender, 151, 159, 162, 185
Chicken Bone Special, 25, 174
Chude-Sokei, Louis, 235–36
cities
    black vs. white population in, 157
    as destination for African immi-
        grants, 213
    inner. *See* ghetto/inner city
    Northern. *See* Northern cities
citizenship
    denial of, 164, 165
    dual, 209
city dwellers, blacks as
    in North, 135, 154, 156–57, 196, 201.
        See also ghetto/inner city
    in South, 159–61
    in West, 156
civil rights acts, 142, 230
civil rights movement, 184–92
Civil War, U.S., 132
    end of, 130
    hope initiated by, 131
    outbreak of, 104
Clark, Laura, 119
Clarkson, Thomas, 67

Cleveland, 156, 172
  age composition of black population, 167
  employment opportunities in, 180
Clinton, Henry, 94
Colored Organization of New Jersey, 28
Committee of racial Equality, 186
Compton, 226
Congressional Black Caucus, 205
contrapuntal narrative, 18, 19, 31–36, 48, 154, 175, 229
  first sounds of, 67
  music and, 34–36
convict labor, 143
Cooke, Sam, 198
Coromatees, 49, 73
cotton, 68, 103–4, 111–12
  collapse of economy of, 157–58, 159
  demands of cultivation of, 122, 124
  insatiable demand for, 100
  mechanization of production of, 163
Courier, 185
credit, 196
Creole, 116
crime, 194
criollos, 85, 86
Crosby, Bing, 47
Crouch, Stanley, 234
Cuba/Cubans, 207, 213
Cuffe, Paul, 218
Cugoano, Ottobah, 64
cultural reformation, 18–48

Davis, Judy and Nelson, 116
debt, 141–42, 144, 153
decolonization, 204–5
deindustrialization, 192–94
Democratic Party, 131, 184, 185, 190, 231
Department of Labor, U.S., 158, 161
De Priest, Oscar, 185
Detroit, 186
  black percentage of population, 157
  black population of, 156
Diallo, Amadou, 217
diaspora. *See* migrations, African American
Dickerson, Debra, 235, 236
disembarkation points, 68–71

slaves' continued proximity to, 81–82
disenfranchisement, 152
Dr. Dre, 226
Dominican Day Parade, 7
Dominicans, 7, 213
Dorsey, Thomas, 197
Double V campaign, 186
Douglass, Frederick, 11, 17, 25–26, 238, 239
drugs, 194, 195
dual citizenship, 209
Dube, John Langalibalele, 13
Dubois, W. E. B., 13, 150, 151, 177
Dunbar, Paul, 17
Dunmore, Lord, 94
DuSable Museum of African American History, 7, 215

economy, U.S.
  cotton and sugar production, shift to, 100, 103–4
  decline of plantation agriculture, 106
  eighteenth-century changes in, 88
  slaves as marketable asset in, 106–7
  World War I, effect on, 158
  World War II, effect on, 163, 166, 187–88
education/schools
  African immigrants and, 211, 223–24
  of Northern migrants, 167–68
Egbe Omo Yoruba, 7, 216
Egypt, 203
elite blacks/Old Settlers, 178–79
  clubs of, 178
  ghettos and, 183
  Northern migrants and, relationship between, 179, 183, 184, 189
  Southern-born, 188–89
  vanishing of, 201
Ellison, Ralph, 17
El Salvador, 207
emancipation. *See* freedom/ emancipation
employment opportunities
  for African immigrants, 211–12
  "negro work," 177
  Northern, 158–59, 163, 165–66, 177–78, 180–81, 186, 187–88, 191–92

Southern, 138–43, 160, 162–63
for women, 181, 191
England, 95, 206
entrepreneurs, black, 177, 178, 188,
192, 208, 214, 225
equality
African immigrants and, 220–21
in the afterworld, 89
civil rights movement for, 184–92
free blacks and, 97
as goal of American-born blacks, 228
through freedom, 97
Equiano, Olaudah, 78, 116
escapes and revolts, 56, 57, 58, 62,
66–67, 77, 83, 116. *See also
specific escapes and revolts*
Ethiopia/Ethiopians, 207, 208, 213
ethnicity, 43, 215–16
Europe. *See also specific countries*
immigration from, 4, 5, 6, 15, 37–39,
42, 43–44, 46, 75–76, 157, 158
manumission in, 54
slavery in, 54
Ewes, 216

Fair Employment Practices Commission, 186–87
families/family life
immigration sponsorship by, 204,
206, 207–8
men's disappearance from, 194
post-Civil War reconstruction of,
130–31, 137–38
for slaves, 82–84, 100, 104, 109–10,
111, 125–27
during third migration, 169–71, 194,
195
Federal Housing Administration, 190
Fédération des Associations Régionales
Haïtiennes à l'Etranger, 7
female circumcision, 221
Ferguson, Mary, 119–20
first migration. *See* transatlantic
passage
Fish, Carl Russell, 37
Florida, 108–9
movement of free blacks to, 133
places of origin of slaves in, 110
food
Africans' preferences, 72

new, adjustment to, 20
of Northern migrants, 168
price of, 141
production of. *See* Agricultural
system, Southern
on slave ships, 19, 59, 65
fourth migration, 4, 5, 6, 7, 15, 23,
201–29, 231–32
decolonization's effect on, 204–5
destinations for, 212–14
music of, 224–27
national ties strengthened through,
214–22
numbers involved in, 206–7
origins of, 204–5
places of origin, 206. *See also specific
places*
rate of, 204–5
Franklin, Isaac, 113
Franklin, John Hope, 3, 9
Frazier, E. Franklin, 160–61
free blacks, 89–98
Africa as presence to, 90–91
attachment to place of, 27
church as center of life, 92–93, 147
conservativeness of, 147, 159
debt of, 141–42, 144, 153
economic independence sought by,
138–39
families reconstructed by, 130–31,
137–39
institutions of, 92–93, 131, 146–47,
150. *See also specific institutions*
labor extracted from, 138–42, 152
as landowners, 145, 146
Loyal Blacks. *See* Loyal Blacks
migration of, 94–98, 132–33, 152
names of, 90–91, 130
numbers of, 90
post-Civil War immobility of, 134–37,
143–46, 149
poverty of, 95, 139–43, 146, 152–53
rights of, 131, 133, 146–47
sense of ownership toward land,
136–37
separate world and institutions of,
146–47, 150
violence against, 147, 153
white domination of. *See* white
supremacy

Freedman's bank, 130
Freedmen's Bureau, 136, 138, 142, 143
freedom/emancipation
    arrival of, 130
    authorship of, 1–2
    changes following, 131–51
    equality through, 97
    false promises of, 65
    of movement, 133
    numbers of black enjoying, 90
    ownership of land as concomitant
        with, 136–37
    slaves' demand for, 89–90, 99
    for slaves in Africa, 54
    for slaves in Europe, 54
    through military service, 89, 94–95
freedpeople. *See* free blacks
From Slavery to Freedom (Franklin), 9
frontier. *See* interior, U.S.
Funky Four Plus One, 225

Gambians, 73
gangs, 195
Gary, 156
George, David, 97
Georgia
    immobility of black population in, 135
    movement from, 103, 129–30
    nationality of slaves entering, 73–74
    number of slaves in, 70
    third migration, effect on, 166, 167
Germany, 206
Ghana/Ghanaians, 208, 213, 215
ghetto/inner city, 181–84, 188, 190
    blacks' flight from, 195, 196
    blacks' ownership of, 197
    complexity of, 189–90
    decaying conditions in, 194–96
    elite blacks and, 183
    hip-hop and, 225–27
    poverty of, 202
GI Bill, 190
Gilroy, Paul, 18
Giovanni, Nikki, 27, 29
Glover, Kofi, 222
gospel, 197, 198
government, U.S.
    residential segregation, role in, 190
    third migration, role in, 158
Grandmaster Flash, 225

Great Migration, 153–55. *See also* third
    migration
Gullah, 78
Guyana, 207

hair, 32, 49, 84, 183, 214, 218
Haiti/Haitians, 207, 209, 211
Haley, Alex, 9
Handlin, Oscar, 37
Harlem, 28, 184, 200, 214, 222, 224,
    226
Harvard University, 222
hate strikes, 187
Hayden, Lewis, 24
Hicks, Otis, 175
hip-hop, 201, 224–27
    white teenagers and, 227
history
    African American. *See* history,
        African American
    migration as ubiquitous in, 43–45
    U.S. *See* history, U.S.
history, African American. *See also*
        past, the
    black Americans' attitude toward,
        2–3, 7–8, 9
    contrapuntal narrative of. *See*
        contrapuntal narrative
    cultural innovation in, 239
    migrations in. *See* migrations,
        African American
    narratives of. *See* narrative(s)
    Obama as exemplar of, 232–40
    as one piece, 13
    ownership of, 9
history, U.S. *See also specific topics*
    exclusion of blacks from, 37
    immigration as master narrative of,
        37
Horton, Willie, 231
Howard, Charles, 136
Howard, O. O., 136
Hudibras, 74
Hughes, Langston, 17, 18
Hunter-Gault, Charlayne, 27
Hurt, John, 149
Hymnal (Allen), 93–94

Ice-T, 226
identity/self-identity, 30–31, 45, 240

for African immigrants, 214–16, 219, 228–29
incorporation of past into, 33
language and, 78
markers of, 61
national, 15, 30, 45, 49–52, 253n
Obama and, 232–33, 236–38
stripping of slaves', 77
visible marks of, 84–85
imagined communities, 10
immigrants. *See* migrants/immigrants
immigration. *See* migration/ immigration
Immigration and Nationality Act, 3, 4–5, 6, 202, 230
as ignored by blacks, 5–6, 231
incarceration, 194
indigo, 81
industrial work/workers, 158–59, 163, 180–81, 186–87, 192–93
women as, 186
In My Place (Hunter-Gault), 27
inner city. *See* ghetto/inner city
interior, passage to, 100–149
age and sex balance distorted by, 108–9
bonds forged during, 116
conditions during, 112–16
effect on South, 101
escapes during, 116–17
families destroyed through, 100, 104, 111, 126
length of journey, 112
maintain ties, efforts to, 120–21
moment of departure, 119–20
mortality rate, 113, 114
numbers involved in, 100, 103, 104, 106
preparations for, 119
reasons for, 100, 101, 102, 104
revolts during, 116
scattering of black people through, 130
slaves' attempts to fight against, 116–19
slave traders' role in, 101–2. *See also* slave trade, U.S.
sudden termination of, 131–32
third migration compared with, 157, 171–73, 175
transatlantic passage and, comparison between, 100, 105, 109, 111, 114, 115–16, 121, 122, 126
transportation, means of, 101–2
trauma of, 16, 100, 104, 111, 112, 115
youth of deportees, 108
interior, U.S., 152
arrival in, 122
black depopulation of. *See* third migration
blacks' settlement and mastery of, 123–29, 142–43
passage to. *See* interior, passage to
internal slave trade. *See* slave trade, U.S.
Invisible Man (Ellison), 17

Jackson, Mahalia, 197
Jamaica/Jamaicans, 214, 215
Jamhuri Day, 215
jazz, 154, 199–200
Jazz (Morrison), 17
Jefferson, Thomas, 35–36, 82
Jim Crow, 10, 11, 164, 201
Johnson, Andrew, 131, 133
Johnson, Charles, 164
Johnson, Lyndon, 4, 230
Johnson, Robert, 18, 199
Johnson-Reed Act, 4
Jollas, 216
Jolson, Al, 47

Kallen, Horace, 42
Kamus, Abdulaziz, 8
Kansas, 133
Kennedy, Edward, 4
Kentucky
immobility of black population in, 135
movement of slaves from, 110
Kenya/Kenyans, 208, 215
Keyes, Alan, 8, 234
King, Martin Luther, Jr., 9, 10, 11, 13, 196, 238
birthday as national holiday, 2
King, Riley "B.B.," 17, 35
Kirkpatrick, Joe, 126
Kongo, 73–74
Korea, 206

labor shortages
World War I, 158
World War II, 163, 166, 187–88
labor/workers
capitalism's need for, 12, 44–45, 204
convict, 143
ladinos, 85, 86
land
blacks' as tied to, 125, 138, 144–45
free blacks' sense of ownership
toward, 136–37
reform, 138
in Southern interior, 123, 124
landowners, black, 145, 146, 162, 163
language(s)
African nationality and, 78
identity and, 78
new, 33, 66, 78
slaves' multiple, 49, 52, 66, 75, 78
transnational, 33, 66, 78
Latin American immigrants, 5
Lawrence, Jacob, 16–17, 27, 173
laws and legislation. *See also specific*
laws and legislation
immigration, 3, 4–5, 6, 204–5
immobilization of blacks by, 143–44
slave, 107
white supremacist, 142–44, 146, 164
legislatures, planter-controlled, 133, 138
Levine, Lawrence, 34
Lewis, Furry, 149
Liberia/Liberians, 134, 207, 208, 213,
214, 215
Liberian Independence Day Parade,
215
Liele, George, 95
Lillis, Harry, 47
Lincoln, Abraham, 1, 115–16
literacy, black, 146–47
literature, migrants in, 17
LL Cool J, 225
Locke, Alain, 184
London, 95, 96
Lorre, Ben, 199
Los Angeles, 156
Louisiana
movement of blacks from, 155
movement of slaves from, 119
movement of slaves to, 94, 102
slave laws in, 107

low country. *See* Georgia; South
Carolina
Loyal Blacks, 94–98
Afro-Christianity and, 97–98
descendants of, 206
rights as important to, 97
whites on, 96

McClennan, Tommy, 199
McCoy, Joe, 199
Mandela, Nelson, 13
manumission. *See also* freedom/
emancipation
in Africa, 53
in Europe, 54
March on Washington Movement, 185–
86
Marsalis, Wynton, 200
Martin, Roberta, 197
Maryland, 81
movement of slaves from, 103, 110
number of slaves in, 68–69
slave laws in, 107
slave population of, 105
masters. *See* slaveholders
MCing, 224
melting pot, 42–43
Memphis Minnie, 199
Miami, 213
middle class blacks, 178, 189, 191–92,
195, 196, 197, 202
Middle East, 206
Middle Passage
conditions during, 59–60, 62–67
fear as omnipresent during, 59–60
length of, 58
new languages of, 66
second. *See* interior, passage to
shipboard rebellions, 62
symbolism of, 14
variety of experience in, 57–58, 59
migrants/immigrants. *See also specific*
groups
black. *See* African descent, immigrants of
enslaved Africans as, 38–39
illegal, 204
in literature, 17
motivations of, 39–41, 44–45
in music, 17

names stripped from, 46–47
as nationals, 15, 30, 49–52
Northern. *See* Northern migrants
numbers of, 5, 6
past divested by, 33
migration/immigration
African American. *See* migrations,
   African American
Asian, 5, 43–44
effect on white America, 202
European, 4, 5, 6, 15, 42, 43–44, 46,
   75–76, 157, 158, 202
European and African American,
   relation between, 37–39, 42, 46,
   75–76
forced vs. free, 33, 37–41, 44–47,
   75–76
interrelatedness of, 46
Latin American, 5
laws, 3, 4–5, 6, 204–5
as master narrative of U.S. history,
   37
nativist policies, 4
quotas, 203
as ubiquitous in world history, 43–45
migrations, African American, 5, 9, 12,
   14–16, 19, 20, 21–24
to Africa, 95–98, 134
from Alabama, 104
to Alabama,103
to Arkansas, 16, 102
as backbone of black history, 24
bonds created by, 47
cultural reformation through, 18–48
differences among, 39–40
first. *See* transatlantic passage
to Florida, 133
forced vs. free, 38–42
fourth. *See* fourth migration
by free blacks, 132–33
of free blacks, 94–98, 132–33, 152
from Georgia, 129–30
idealization of past in, 22
interior, passage to. *See* interior,
   passage to
to Kansas, 133
from Kentucky, 110
from Louisiana, 110
to Louisiana, 94, 102
from Maryland, 103, 110

meaning of blackness affected by, 23
to Mississippi, 103, 133
new polarities following, 23–24
to the North, 133. *See also* third
   migration
from North Carolina, 110
places of origin of, 6
post-revolutionary, 94–98
rate of, 6
as refashioning of consciousness,
   22
reverse flows, 40–41, 155, 201
seamless incorporation of, 24, 31
second. *See* interior, passage to
significance to study of African
   American life, 95
from South Carolina, 103, 110
from Tennessee, 104
to Tennessee, 103
to Texas, 102, 104, 133
third. *See* third migration
from Virginia, 103, 110
to the West, 134
Miles, Lizzie, 199
military service
freedom through, 89, 94–95
in World War II, 165
Miller, Kelly, 183
Minas, 49
Mississippi
immobility of black population in,
   135
movement of free blacks to, 133
movement of slaves to, 103
slave laws in, 107
slave population of, 105
third migration, effect on, 167
"Mississippi Road Trip," 149
mixed farming, 105, 106
Montserrat, 207
Morocco, 203
Morrison, Toni, 17
Morton, Jelly Roll, 200
Motown, 199
movement. *See also* migration/
   immigration
as constant in slaves' and planters'
   lives, 129–30
importance to blacks, 17–24
in music, 129–30, 199, 225, 227

movement *(cont.)*
  place and, tension between. *See*
    contrapuntal narrative
  in U.S. history, 37
MTV, 201, 226
Murphy, Eddie, 219
music
  blues, 148–49, 197–99
  call-and-response, 34–35, 67, 86, 200
  commercial market for, 197–99, 225
  contrapuntal narrative and, 34–36
  of fourth migration, 224–27
  gospel, 197, 198
  hip-hop, 224–27
  interior passage, effect on, 128–29
  jazz, 154, 199–200
  migrants in, 17
  movement in, 129–30, 199, 225, 227
  place in, 148–51, 199, 225–27
  post-Civil War, 148–51
  religious, 93–94, 128–29, 197, 198
  rhythm and blues, 198
  rock and roll, 198, 199
  slaves', 35, 67, 86–87, 128–29
  on slave ships,35, 67
  spiritual, 128–29
  third migration and, 153–54,
    197–200
  urban blues, 198
  whites as audience for, 198, 227
Myrdal, Gunnar, 187

NAACP. *See* National Association for
    the Advancement of Colored
    People
names
  free blacks', 90–91
  slaves', 46–47
Narrative (Douglass), 17
narrative(s)
  contrapuntal, 18, 19, 31–36, 48, 67,
    154, 175, 229
  linear, 9–11
  master, 9, 11, 37
  slavery-to-freedom, 9–11, 13
National Association for the Advance-
    ment of Colored People, 7, 13,
    186, 229
Native Americans, as market for slaves'
    produce, 124

Native Son (Wright), 17
nativist policies, 4
Nat Turner rebellion, 107
Negro History Week, 2, 3
New Deal, 162, 185
New Negroes, 184
New Orleans, 114
newspapers, black, 185. *See also specific*
    papers
New York, 7, 156, 213
Nicaragua, 207
Nigerian Festival, 7, 215
Nigeria/Nigerians, 7, 208, 213, 215
Nixon, Richard, 231
nonslaveholders, 124, 125
North, the
  arrival in, 175–76
  black elite in. *See* elite blacks/Old
    Settlers
  employment opportunities in, 163,
    165–66, 177–78, 180–81, 187–88,
    191–82
  great migration to. *See* third
    migration
  movement of free blacks to, 133, 152
  professional class in, 177–78
  racism of, 150, 176–77, 180–81,
    187–88
  South and, connection between, 172,
    175
  South and, difference between, 176
North Carolina
  immobility of black population in,
    135
  movement of slaves from, 110
Northern blacks. *See also* Northern
    migrants
  black Southerners compared to,
    150–51
  church membership of, 189
  institutions of, 189
  numbers of, 152
Northern Cities. *See also* ghetto/inner
    city
  attachment to, 27–28
  black ownership of, 183–84
  black political power in, 184–86
  residential segregation in, 182, 190
  structural decay of, 194–95
  youthfulness of, 167

Northern migrants
  age of, 166–67
  character of, 167–68
  civil rights sought by, 184–92
  deindustrialization's effect on,
    192–94
  educational attainment of, 167–68
  elite blacks and, relationship
    between, 179, 183, 184, 189
  food of, 168
  information sources for, 170–71
  institutional aids to, 174
  locations of, 156
  neighborhoods of. *See* ghetto/inner
    city
  political affiliations of, 185
  poverty of, 193
  racial subordination of, 176–77,
    180–81
  sex of, 166
  uncertainties of, 165, 169
Northern migration. *See* third
  migration
Nova Scotia, 95, 96, 97
N.W.A., 226

Oak and Ivy Club, 178
Oakland, 172
Obama, Barack, 8, 230, 232–40
  African immigrants and, 232
  blackness of, 233–34, 236–37
  identity and, 232–33, 236–38
  speech on race, 237–38
occupations, 177–79, 189, 191, 192, 201
Odom, Helen, 16
Old Settlers. *See* elite blacks/Old
  Settlers
Olmsted, Frederick Law, 136–37
one-drop rule, 218, 236–37
Organization for the Advancement of
  Nigerians, 7

Panama Canal, 203
Panic of 1837, 103–4
Parks, Gordon, 17
past, the, 20
  as denied to blacks, 3
  idealization of, 22
  as impossible to recoup, 32–33
  weight of, 32

Perkins, Maria, 119
Peters, Thomas, 95, 97
Philadelphia, 156, 177
Pittsburgh, 156, 165
place. *See also* land
  diasporas as rooting people in, 25
  free blacks' attachment to, 136–39,
    150
  importance of, 17–21, 25–31, 80–84,
    136–39, 150, 239
  in music, 148–51, 199, 225–27
  segregation's effect on, 150
  sharecropping as tying blacks to,
    140
  slaves' attachment to, 80–84
  as social imperative, 19–20
  special meaning of, 19–20
plantation(s), 26. *See also specific crops*
  blacks' abandonment of, 135–36
  boundaries of, 81
  changing requirements of, 12, 101,
    105, 106, 109
  decline of, 106
  expansion of, 68
  mechanization of, 162, 163
  slavery, 54–55, 68, 100–109
  stability of, 81
planters, 26, 29. *See also* slaveholders
  black belt, 107, 109, 110
  legislatures controlled by, 133, 138
  postbellum, 139
  third migration fought by, 161–62
political asylum, 204, 205, 209
political office, blacks in, 3–4, 131, 178,
  185
political power, black, 184–86
Portugal, 54
poverty, 10, 38, 202
  of African immigrants, 11, 211
  of free blacks, 95, 139–43, 146,
    152–53, 157
  inner city, 193, 202
  of Northern migrants, 181
  of Southern blacks, 157–58, 160
Powell, Julie, 119
Powledge, Fred, 28
professional class, 177–78, 202
projects, the, 195
Providence, 214
Public Enemy, 225, 226

Quarles, Benjamin, 3
Queens, 224

race
American-born blacks' and immigrants' different views of, 220, 228
definitions of, 23, 32, 55, 206, 218, 220, 235, 236–37, 239–40
as force in understanding American life, 43
protocols and ideas of, 23
significance of, 202
two-caste system of, 218, 220
race riots, 183
racism. *See also* white supremacy
African immigrants and, 12–13, 217–20, 220
American-born blacks' view of, 220, 228
Northern, 150, 176–77, 180–81, 187–88
slave societies as root of, 13, 61
Southern, 3, 165
ubiquity of, 11
Radical Reconstruction, 131, 142, 152
Rainey, "Ma," 198
Randolph, A. Philip, 185
rap. *See* hip-hop
Reagan, Ronald, 231
Reconstruction, 133, 134
Redding, Otis, 17
Redeemers, 152
religion. *See also* Afro-Christian church
free blacks', 92–93, 128, 147
interior passage, effect on, 128–29
music of, 93–94, 128–29, 197, 198
slaves', 87, 88–89, 128–29
Republican Party, 131, 178, 185, 189, 231
reputations, 144–45
reunions, 29
revolts. *See* escapes and revolts
rhythm and blues, 198
rice, 68, 101
rock and roll, 198, 199
Rolfe, John, 50
Roosevelt, Franklin Delano, 185–86
Roots (Haley), 9
Rose, Charlie, 236

Run D.M.C., 226
Rush, Bobby, 233
Rwanda, 207

St. Louis, 156
St. Lucia, 207
San Francisco, 156
Sarah Bonadventure, 74
Screven, Arena, 119
second migration. *See* interior, passage to
segregation, 146–47, 150, 164
battles against, 185–86
overthrow of, 201
place, effect on, 150
residential, 182, 190. *See also* ghetto/ inner city
self-emancipation, 1
self-identity. *See* identity/self-identity
Senegal, 214
Senegambia, 73
sexual abuse, 64, 115
sharecropping, 139–43
collapse of, 162–63
shipmates, as kin, 19
Sierra Leone, 95, 96, 97, 207
slaveholders, 107, 109, 110
African, 52–53
black belt, 107, 109, 110
divisions among, 76
exploitation of divisions among slaves by, 85
holdings consolidated by, 104
Loyalist, 94
methods of control used by, 76–77, 82, 106–7
movement as a constant for, 129–30
numbers of slaves held by, 68, 76
preferences of, 71–73, 75, 110, 111
slavery, 10–11, 12
African, 52–55
codification of chattel bondage, 68
cracks in edifice of, 88–89
domestic, 52–54
in Europe, 54
expansion of, 100
Northern colonies' liquidation of, 89–90
plantation, 54–55, 68, 100–109
profitability of, 105

revolutionary warfare's effect on, 89
slavery-to-freedom narrative, 9–11, 13
slaves/enslaved Africans
    African as name for, 15, 30, 49–52
    Atlantic Creoles, 67, 68
    Atlantic seabord as initial location of,
        97
    attachment to place of, 25–27
    broad marriages of, 82, 126
    children of, 83–84, 109–10, 127
    as collaborators on interior passage,
        114
    as collaborators on slave ships,
        64–65
    control of, on ships, 60–61, 64–65
    economy of, 84, 124–25
    escapes and revolts, 56, 57, 58, 62,
        66–67, 77, 83. *See also specific
        revolts*
    family life of, 82–84, 100, 104,
        109–10, 111, 125–27
    first arrivals, 50, 67–68, 77
    former. *See* free blacks
    gatherings among, 79
    hired, 105
    identity, marks of, 84–85
    as immigrants, 38–39
    indigenous vs. saltwater population,
        69, 71, 85–86, 99
    inheritances of, 84
    interior passage of. *See* interior,
        passage to
    kinship networks of, 25, 78–79,
        82–83, 125–27
    labeling of, 49–52
    leadership structure, 128
    male as preferred sex of, 71, 108
    male mortality, higher rates of, 109
    as marketable assets, 106–7
    masters' control of, 76–77, 82, 106
    mobility of, 81–82
    mortality among, 59, 62, 63–64, 77,
        109, 113, 114
    names stripped from, 46–47
    nationalities of, 71, 73–74, 75
    new arrivals, treatment of, 76–77
    numbers of, 68–71, 99
    property of, 84, 124–25
    realization of destiny by, 61
    rebellious, sale of, 106

relations among, on slave ships,
        65–67
    religion of, 87, 88–89, 128–29
    rental and loaning of, 89
    rights and freedoms gained by,
        87–88, 124–25
    skilled, 87, 106
    suicide attempts of, 63–64, 113
    transatlantic passage of. *See*
        transatlantic passage
    wages earned by, 124
    women, 64, 115
    youth preferred in, 71, 108
slave ships
    collection of slaves by, 74–75
    conditions on, 59
    control of slaves on, 60–61, 64–65
    crews and captives of, relations
        between, 64, 65
    distribution of cargo, 71
    forced dance on, 63
    as funerary trains, 40
    hazards of ocean travel for, 58
    mortality rates on, 59, 62, 63–64
    music on, 35, 67
    rations on, 63
    rebellions on, 62
    suicide attempts on, 63–64
    violence of, 60
    white supremacy as originating on,
        61
    women on, 64
slave trade, African, 6, 15
    African resistance to, 72
    competitive nature of, 59, 72
    customer preferences in, 71–73, 75
    disembarkation points, 68–71
    end to, 70
    numbers of arrivals, 68–71
    post-Revolutionary reinvigoration of,
        99
    regional identity and, 72, 74–76
    systematic removals of, 38–39
slave trade, U.S., 101–2
    Georgia men, 102
    infrastructure of, 114
    language of, 102–3
    local, 105
    numbers involved in, 100, 103, 104,
        106

slave trade, U.S. *(cont.)*
post-Revolutionary reinvigoration of,
94
preferred places of origin in, 110
regularization of, 113–14
seasonality of, 103
Smith, Bessie, 17, 198, 199
Snoop Doggy Dogg, 226
Somalia/Somalis, 208, 212
soul, 184
South, the, 10, 13, 15, 16, 17, 19, 27. *See
also specific places*
agricultural system of, 162–63
black exodus from. *See* third
migration
black population as tied to, 134–37,
149
as cultural catchall, 29–30, 46
effect of interior passage on, 101
employment opportunities in,
138–43, 160, 162–63
migration from. *See* third migration
North and, connection between, 172,
175
North and, difference between, 176
proportion of black population
residing in, 132, 156
return to, 41, 155
sharecropping system of, 139–43
tenancy systems of, 139–43
South Africa, 203
South Carolina, 58
Gullah language, 78
indigenous and saltwater slaves,
relation between, 70–71
male vs. female slaves in, 71
movement of slaves entering, 103, 110
nationality of slaves entering, 73–74
number of slaves in, 70
South Central, 226
Southerners
black. *See* Southerners, black
black people as, 27, 28
Southerners, black
despair as endemic to, 163–64
employment opportunities for, 160
free. *See* free blacks
as landowners, 162, 163
Northerners compared to, 150–51
peculiar character of, 150

poverty of, 157–58, 160
rights denied to, 164, 165
as rural population, 135, 152
violence against, 163, 164
Southern interior. *See* interior, U.S.
Spain, 54
Sport of the Gods (Dunbar), 17
Stono Rebellion, 70
Strayhorn, Billy, 200
suburbs
blacks' move to, 195, 196
white flight to, 190, 196
Sudan/Sudanese, 207, 211, 212
suffrage, 184, 230–31
sugar, 68, 100, 103–4
demands of cultivation of, 122, 124
Sullivan's Island, 70
Sykes, Roosevelt, 199

Taulbert, Clifton, 22
tenancy, 140, 141, 142, 143, 144, 162
Tennessee
movement of slaves from, 104
movement of slaves to, 103
Texas
movement of blacks from, 155
movement of free blacks to, 133
movement of slaves to, 102, 104
slave population of, 105
third migration, 15, 153–200
age patterns of, 166–67
Alabama, effect on, 167
as chain migration, 172, 173
as city-to-city migration, 160–61, 167
as community endeavor, 171
destinations for, 156, 157, 165–66,
167, 172
duration of, 154–55
ebbs and flows of, 165–66
families in, 169–71
governmental role in, 158
interior passage compared with, 157,
171–73, 175
Mississippi, effect on, 167
music and, 153–54, 197–200
numbers involved in, 28, 154,
155–56, 157
original impetus for, 157–61
planters' efforts to stem, 161–62
reasons for, 157–65

regularization of, 174
reluctance of blacks to undertake, 159
reverse flow, 155, 201
routes of, 172–73
seasonal rhythm of, 174
selectiveness of, 166–67
sexual patterns, 166
timing of, 44
to-and-froing of, 171–72
transatlantic passage compared with, 157, 168, 169, 170, 171–73, 175
transportation methods, 168–69, 173–74
travel conditions, 168–69
two vectors of, 165–66
women during, 166
World War I, effect on, 165
World War II, effect on, 163, 165, 166
Thomas, Piri, 29
tobacco, 15, 68, 101
decline of, 88
tokenism, 191
Tombigbee, 103
towns, black, 146
Townsend, Henry, 199
transatlantic passage, 15
Africans' role in, 55–56
coastal factories, 56–57
interior passage and, comparison between, 100, 105, 109, 111, 114, 115–16, 121, 122, 126
march to the coast, 56
Middle Passage. *See* Middle Passage
third migration compared with, 157, 168, 169, 170, 171–73, 175
transportation, means of, 56. *See also* slave ships
transatlantic slave trade. *See* slave trade, African
transnationalism, 12
transportation
during interior passage, 101–2
during third migration, 168–69, 173–74
during transatlantic passage, 56
Tucker, Sophie, 47
Turner, Frederick Jackson, 37
Turner, Henry McNeal, 134

unemployment rate
black, 193–94
black vs. white, 180, 187
unions, 187, 193. *See also specific unions*
United States
African slave trade, end to, 70
foreign-born population, 4–5
history. *See* history, U.S.
as nation of immigrants, 4
Up from Slavery (Washington), 9
urban blues, 198
Urban League, 7

vagrancy laws, 143
Vessey, Denmark, 58, 114
Vietnam, 206
violence
against African immigrants, 217, 222–23
against free blacks, 147, 153
on slave ships, 60
against Southern blacks, 147, 153, 163, 164
Virginia
age and sex of slaves in, 108–9
movement of slaves from, 103, 110
number of slaves in, 68–69
U.S. slave population, proportion in, 104–5
vote, right to. *See* suffrage
Voting Rights Act, 3, 5–6

Walker, C. J., 173
Washington, Booker T., 9, 151, 238, 239
Washington, D.C., 8–9, 213
Washington, Harry, 95
Waters, Mary C., 214–15
Watson, John, 93–94
welfare rights movement, 195
Wells, Ida B., 173
West, the
movement of free blacks to, 134
as third migration destination, 155, 156
West Indian Carnival, 7
West Indies/West Indians, 215
Wheatley, Phyllis, 3
White, Graham, 36
White, Shane, 36
white-collar jobs, 191–92

whiteness, 43
white supremacy, 42, 152–53, 163–65
  black challenges to, 164
  legal apparatus of, 142–44, 146, 164
  musical response to, 148
  origins of, 61
  wavering of, 190–92
whites/white America
  African immigrants' opinion of, 221
  as audience for black music, 198, 227
  in black churches, 94
  immigration's effect on, 202
  on Loyal Blacks, 96
  slaves' first impressions of, 60
  unemployment rate, compared to
    blacks', 180
  urban population of, 157
white teenagers, hip-hop and, 227
Whydads, 49
wiggers, 227
Wilkerson, Moses, 95
Williams, George Washington, 3
Wilson, August, 17
women
  as Caribbean immigrants, 210
  employment opportunities for, 177,
    181, 186, 191
  as factory workers, 186

  during interior passage, 115
  occupations of, 177
  ratio of male slaves to, 71, 108–9
  on slave ships, 64
  during third migration, 166
Woodson, Carter G., 2
Woolman, John, 83
work and residence, spatial mismatch
    between, 195
workers. *See* labor/workers
Works Project Administration, 16
World War I, 154
  effect on U.S. economy, 158
  third migration, effect on, 165
World War II, 154, 155
  civil rights movement, effect on,
    185–86, 187–88
  labor shortages of, 187–88
  military service in, 165
  third migration, effect on, 163, 165,
    166
Wright, Richard, 17, 29, 169, 173, 175

Yoelson, Asa, 47
Yorubas, 215–16

Zangwill, Israel, 42